INTO THE WONDER

SHAWN SMALL

Copyright © 2023 by Shawn Small

All rights reserved. Except as permitted under the U.S. Copyright Act of 1976, no part of this publication may be reproduced, distributed, or transmitted in any form or by any means, or stored in a database or retrieval system, without the prior written permission of the publisher.

HIS Publishing Group is a division of Human Improvement Specialists, llc.
For information visit www.hispubg.com or contact publisher at info@hispubg.com

ISBN: 978-0-9971017-7-5 *paperback*
         978-0-9971017-9-9 *hardcover*
         978-0-9971017-8-2 *ebook*

Printed in Canada

10 9 8 7 6 5 4 3 2 1

Division of Human Improvement Specialists, llc.
www.hispubg.com | *info@hispubg.com*

We live life forward, but we understand it backward.
—Soren Kierkegaard

For

Mike Yengo
who set free an explorer longing
to wander to the edges of the earth,
and into the heart of humanity.

Stephen Lawhead
who saved me in my darkest days
with sublime storytelling, an anchor of
hope for one who felt abandoned.

Valeria Hawkins (Mama Val)
who proved to me, wonder can be
discovered in unexpected places,
deadly hurricanes, and spicy fried chicken.

Contents

Foreword 9
Preface.. 11

Chapter 1   Moonflower 13
Chapter 2   Monsters 23
Chapter 3   Epiphany of the Lost Ark............................ 31
Chapter 4   Exchange Day 37
Chapter 5   Bula 45
Chapter 6   Secret Passage 51
Chapter 7   Crayon God 55
Chapter 8   Dive 61
Chapter 9   Cliffs Edge 65
Chapter 10   Holy Curiosity 69
Chapter 11   Mona Lisa Smile 79
Chapter 12   Snake Charmer 93
Chapter 13   Pink Paper Heart 103
Chapter 14   Yengo... 111
Chapter 15   Wrecked 125
Chapter 16   The Caning 135
Chapter 17   Leap 143

Chapter 18	Mama Val	153
Chapter 19	Gone	167
Chapter 20	Wantok	189
Chapter 21	Otherworld	199
Chapter 22	Sublime	213
Chapter 23	Shadowlands	223
Chapter 24	Blessed Disillusionment	231
Chapter 25	Toss the Hat	241
Chapter 26	An Unconventional Pilgrimage	249
Chapter 27	Reluctant Pilgrim	261

Epilogue	Into the Wonder	273
Gratitude		277
About the Author		281

Foreword

March isn't the best month to visit Denmark. My wife, five-year-old daughter, and I flew to Copenhagen with the grand plan of taking in the sights before heading to Germany to visit friends. Our visit was just before the tourist season. Nothing was open, the weather was cold and bleak, and we were limited to inns and restaurants catering to locals. But the people were friendly, and the food was hearty.

In those pre-internet and mobile phone days, you planned your travel by reading guidebooks. As we drove through the barren Danish farmlands, I noted a marking on our map designating a ship. That was a little mysterious since we weren't near the coast, but it held promise as we traveled through the land where Vikings had lived.

We arrived at a small farmhouse in the middle of nowhere. There were no signs or even a parking lot. Things looked pretty closed up. Yet, I'd had enough travel experience to get out of the car and knock on what I hoped might be the front door. There was a long pause before I heard footsteps. The door opened, revealing the inquisitive and somewhat surprised face of a short, older woman looking up at me. She did not speak English. I pointed to the ship symbol on my map. She looked at me with a bemused, but not unfriendly, expression. Holding up a finger, she stepped back a few paces, took a key off the wall, and handed it to me before pointing to a place beyond the surrounding buildings. She somehow conveyed that I was to lock the door associated with this key and return it when I was done.

The three of us walked past the buildings into a field with a large mound in the center. Following a footpath around the back of the mound, we came to steps that led down to a modern glass door. This door was the way into the center of the mound. I turned the lock into an echoing, dark, spooky space. My hands fumbled around until I found a switch just inside the doorway. I flipped a switch that triggered a large air vent to turn on in the midst of the darkness. As the three of us stood in the doorway, lights slowly flickered on. We found ourselves before a beautifully restored Viking burial ship. Decades later, that remains one of my most profound moments of wonder.

> *Down in the ground, there is buried a ship,*
> *Wonderfully made to behold,*
> *Lost in my prayers, I have sailed it away,*
> *Out through this window I hold*
> *my heart's longings,*
> *And carry them into the clouds above,*
> *I fly away.* *

The book you hold tells the origin story of Wonder Voyage – the "heart's longings" of an extraordinary couple—Shawn and Cheryl Small. Their somewhat "Shakespearean" journey has been full of near-death accidents, broken promises, and dashed hopes. Yet wonder has saved them, and their moments of wonder have given them the audacity and gravitas to trust it and share it with others.

Shawn sees wonder in everything and, together with Cheryl, strives to live life as if he's on a pilgrimage. Traditionally, a pilgrimage is a journey to a place where something significant and sacred happened. Yet when people view their entire life as a pilgrimage, they know God's Kingdom on earth is present all around them. This kind of life takes the words of Jesus in the Beatitudes (see Matthew 5) and the Lord's Prayer (see Matthew 6) to heart. Wonder Voyage organizes pilgrimages with the hope that the experience leads the participants to deeper faith and eyes open to wonder.

You're about to read how it all began. For the moment, think of yourself standing at a mysterious portal in the middle of nowhere, and someone is about to hand you a key to a door that will lead you to something you didn't expect but just might change the way you look at your life and the way you live it. - Jeff Johnson/ArkMusic

*From the song "Prayer" by Jeff Johnson
©1994 Sola Scriptura Songs/arkmusic.com

Preface

I lay beneath the Milky Way, mesmerized by star clusters as thick as the sands of the Sahara tickling my bare toes. At Merzouga, we entered on camelback a desert as large as the continental United States. Growing accustomed to the rhythm of a dromedary saunter, I drank in perpetual hills of blond sand accentuated by the shadows of the sinking sun at our backs. From the top of a dune, we stopped to watch the sun dip beneath the horizon, its rays stretching hopelessly heavenward under the encroaching nightfall. Our hidden oasis, a precise rectangular camp illuminated by torchlight, was a lap of luxury in the middle of nowhere. After enjoying a Middle Eastern feast, we lounged on silk pillows around a blazing fire, sipping mint tea and listening to the melodic songs of our Berber hosts. The quarter-nail moon shine did little to dampen a billion stars. I was in a living dream that lodged in my brain long before the reality of Wonder Voyage's existence.

Wonder Voyage was an idea birthed out of an encounter with the Holy and a belief that wonder is abundant in our lives. The simple, focused, tenacious proposition to bring pilgrims on spiritual journeys was improbable at best, more likely, impossible in theory. Yet, 25 years later, we continued to create voyages, allowing seekers to experience sacred wonder in fascinating locations across the globe, allowing our travelers to give back to the communities they are visiting. Our trip to Morocco was another manifestation of a dream born out of wonder.

This book is the story of how the dream of Wonder Voyage came to pass.

Chapter 1

Moonflower

San Francisco - October 1989

A seasick sensation hit me. A tidal wave of car alarms erupted as I stood before the floor-to-ceiling window overlooking San Francisco Bay. My mind knotted. The four-and-a-half-mile-long Bay Bridge was billowing side to side. As I watched cars skip across the highway, my hotel, an impregnable steel, concrete, and glass structure, swayed like a mast.

I stumbled onto the bed, gripping the pulsating mattress to avoid what looked like a poltergeist free-for-all. The TV toppled to the ground, lamps flew through the air, chairs tipped, and dishes danced across the table. I nervously laughed as the king-size mattress slid to the floor. Alarm and elation wrestled for control of my brain. Though I had come to San Francisco for a youth ministers' convention, I was now part of something infinitely more interesting. I could only ride the seismic shockwaves and wait for them to end.

Once the earth stopped shaking, I rose from the floor, my body coursing with adrenaline. Looking out the window, I saw pillars of smoke rising throughout the city. I needed to evacuate the building, which no longer held any illusion of safety. As I stepped out of my room, the ground gave way. I picked up my foot, peering through a pencil-thin crack onto the hall beneath my eighth-floor room. Elation cowered to alarm.

Across the hall, the elevator groaned, re-engaging from a dead stop. Ten seconds later, the doors shuttered open. A lanky-limbed bellhop pushed his thin frame through the slowly opening gap. The young man fell to his hands and knees before letting loose a barrage of swear words. I was sad he didn't have a larger audience to witness his salty-tongued diatribe that lasted longer than the earthquake. When he finally stopped to breathe, I said, "We need to check the rooms and make sure everyone is all right."

Emotionless, he stared into nothingness before he said, "You're right." Then, with the reflexes of a rabbit escaping the jaws of a wolf, he exited the door to the stairs, erupting into another swearing soliloquy.

I knew that I needed to evacuate the building immediately. I worked my way down the hallways, knocking on doors through the eighth and seventh floors, before meeting a team of security officers. Taking the stairs, I passed thick cracks spiderwebbed across the walls on each floor. The dangerous descent divulged the gravity of the disaster. Reaching the ground floor, I slogged through a maze of strewn furniture and metal shelves now bent like melted wax. Eight-inch-thick concrete walls had disintegrated, revealing the rebar beneath. Caved-in ceilings created an obstacle course of cement, glass, and metal studs. Eerie dust clouds dancing in the setting sun's light hung in the abandoned front lobby.

Outside the hotel, hundreds of confused guests gathered. A dust cloud billowed out of the hotel across the street—the result of an elevator crashing down several floors. Miles away, smoke in the Marina District filled the skies. With no underlying bedrock, the ground near Fisherman's Wharf had liquefied, collapsing several structures. Gas mains had burst, sparking pillars of flame that shot a hundred feet into the air. The city sank into an apocalyptic aura.

I had unknowingly become a witness to one of the most cataclysmic natural disasters in U.S. history. Centered near the Santa Cruz Mountains, sixty miles southeast of San Francisco, the Loma Prieta earthquake hit at 5:04 pm on October 17, 1989, shortly before the Oakland Athletics and San Francisco Giants met at Candlestick Park for game three in the World Series. The earthquake lasted fifteen seconds at a magnitude of 6.9. The damage caused by the quake was widespread. Three thousand people were injured, and sixty-seven died, many trapped under a collapsed one-mile section of the Nimitz Freeway viaduct.

After a few hours, the hotel guests for the religious youth workers' conference were allowed back into the lobby. The quiet pious, led by a woman playing hymns on a piano in a darkened room, prayed in low whispers. A few hundred youth ministers huddled in a large ballroom, telling terrible jokes and playing games to pass the time. The long bar at the hotel restaurant was filled with beer-drinking philosophers delving into the metaphysical questions mass tragedy dredges to the surface. Regardless of where they settled, most people's response to the hundreds of aftershocks was consistent. As the ground began to rumble, their faces were plastered with the fear of being swallowed up by the earth. The Loma Prieta quake felt like a portend of the world's end to most people around me. For me, it was a moment of wonder. I wanted to feel the vibrations of the earth course through my body.

As long as I can remember, wonder has been the North Star guiding my steps and steadying my soul. Wonder is the lens that brings clarity and color to what might otherwise be a monochrome existence. I define wonder as those indescribable moments when I've experienced something joyful just beyond the veil of my physical reality. A glimpse of wonder causes potent longings to erupt in the deepest parts of my soul. Wonder makes me long for something beyond this earth, beyond my grasp, beyond my hopes, beyond my faith, beyond my reason, and beyond my imagination. Wonder reflects an indescribable Source I will one day meet face to face. Wonder is what fueled my soul during the Loma Prieta earthquake. Still, for most other participants, their sense of wonder dwindled under their anxieties and confusion. Whether literal or metaphorical, earthquakes tend to smother wonder.

Although the Loma Prieta quake had ignited my sense of wonder, there was a precise moment in time when, at the age of nine, my sense of wonder had been pulsating with life. In an instant, however, it was nearly obliterated by an earthquake that shook my family to pieces.

I was a shy child who made up for my lack of height and weight with a prolific imagination. From sunrise to sundown, I was lost in the adventures I designed in my head. My parents never asked why I was covered in mud, why I smelled like skunkweed, or what I was doing with the treasures I had picked out of the neighbor's trash or from the woods behind our home. My mom said my dogged curiosity was proof I was a born explorer. Every day, I entered a new realm rife with possibilities.

Everything changed one stormy October evening. My father gathered my two younger siblings and me into his car, driving us into the expanding darkness. The growing pitter-patter of rain on the car roof added weight to my father's silence. A hive of bees swirled inside my stomach. The last few months had been chaotic, but I had not connected the dots. My world was about to collapse.

My parents, from small Iowa farm towns, were looking for an escape when they met in college. Six months later, they married. Not long after, my mom was pregnant with me. After the devastating loss of their second child during birth complications, my mother had my brother, Shane, and sister, Audra. My parent's world progressed at a ruthless pace, giving them little time to process their grief of loss or their rapidly growing family.

When I was five, my father accepted a job on the East Coast, and we settled in a small town in northern New Jersey. My dad was a workhorse who, at the time, found solace in his job, while my mom pursued, through education, an independence that sat just out of her reach. I hardly remember them being together. By the time I was in grade school, their marriage had become an unspoken truce. Theirs were two separate lives hiding behind the thin façade of a marriage.

I first became aware of the tension in our household the summer before my fourth-grade year. Once hidden behind closed doors, their fights had flared into raised voices and slamming doors, a shaky armistice on the brink of war.

One day, I came home from school to find a moving truck in our driveway. Before I could process what was happening, the whole family was packed into our station wagon, leaving New Jersey in the dark. Two days later, we arrived in Paton, Iowa, to temporarily live with my grandparents.

During my elementary school years, my siblings and I had spent most of our summer breaks in Paton. I loved the farm town, and I adored my grandparents. I was thrilled to be living with them. While still in New Jersey, I'd overheard my parents talk about moving to the Midwest to buy a house in the country with a white picket fence. The sudden relocation to Paton convinced me that the house with the white picket fence was near, and it was the answer to our troubles.

After deliberating with my grandparents, my dad left the family in Iowa. He continued to Milwaukee, where he had a new job. I assumed he went to find the house with the white picket fence. In reality, my father was suffering from debilitating depression. Milwaukee was his self-imposed exile to sort out the boiling angst in his head.

While my father was away, my siblings and I attended the local elementary school, and my mom tried to keep us distracted. My grandparents doted on us more than usual, most likely because of our parents' disintegrating marriage. As autumn slipped toward winter, my mom's anxiety worsened. Left in limbo, she sank into depression. Dad was not communicating, and no one knew when he might return for us. My grandparents desperately worked to keep life normal, but an explosion was building, and the fuse was short.

Three awkward months as houseguests became too much for my mom. Once again, we were packed into the station wagon in the middle of the night and were driven to be with our father in Milwaukee. The surprise reunion did not go well. He helped us move into the house he was renting before he promptly moved out.

After a hasty registration into my third school of the year, my mom scrambled for a job. Her world was a nightmare. As hard as she tried, she could no longer hide her tears. I held onto a sliver of hope that my father would return home and our family would return to normal. He didn't. Over the next month, Dad's sporadic visits were punctuated with tense arguments and tearful accusations. I took it upon myself to keep my brother and sister distracted and out of earshot during these episodes.

We knew something was wrong when Dad showed up one evening and put us in the car. I watched Mom's face, illuminated by the porch light, as we backed out of the driveway. She looked as if she'd never see us again. Sitting in the front seat, I turned toward Dad and saw tears on his face. My father, whom I had barely seen in the last few months, was crying. To me, Dad was the bravest man in the world. Whatever brought him to tears must be dreadful. As the sky darkened, so did my thoughts. All I wanted to do was get out of the car.

We reached Lake Michigan as the rainstorm grew furious. Dad pulled into a parking space near an obscure wharf. The hair on my arms rose with the screeching of the wind. Shutting off the car, Dad turned toward the three of us. As the windows started to fog, blurring the growing murkiness, my heart throbbed in my eardrums. The prickly lull in the conversation caused me to flush. Continuing to face forward, away from my dad, I focused on the swirling waters of the lake, blurred by the downpour on the windshield.

"I want you to know I love you. What I am about to tell you is hard to say." There was an uncomfortable pause as he gathered his emotions. "Your mom and I are getting a divorce."

I stiffened to stone. His voice and my siblings' soft sobbing became a murmur in the background. My imagination, which had always been a sanctuary, turned into a gruesome monster. I concluded the divorce was our fault. My hand began to grip the handle, ready to open the door and run because I knew what was coming next. My dad would take me, my brother, and my sister and throw us into the angry waters of Lake Michigan. Once he got rid of us, his and Mom's life would be better. The wonder underpinning my world started to crumble in a singular earthquake of perceived blame.

San Francisco, October 2009

Twenty years after my first visit, I was back in San Francisco leading a group of students on a journey that focused on the challenges of homelessness in urban America. We worked with St. Boniface

Catholic Church in the Tenderloin District, serving the economically poor and marginalized.

While there, I attended the Franciscan Eucharist at St. Boniface Cathedral. Established in 1860, the sanctuary was built after the infamous 1906 San Francisco Earthquake wiped out its predecessor. The Gothic cathedral is open all hours, allowing anyone needing shelter a safe place to rest and sleep. Before religious services, guests resting on the pews are gently asked to sit up and participate.

Sitting with my brothers and sisters during the noon Eucharist, I eyed an enormous circular stained-glass window hanging directly over the altar. I had never seen a window directly over an altar. My curiosity was sparked. Light flooded the Lord's Table, illuminating the cup as the priest held it up and declared, "The Blood of Christ, shed for our sins." After the service, I introduced myself to the celebrant priest and asked him about the window. The elderly Franciscan beamed.

"That window," he said, "has an extraordinary tale attached to it. Not many people ask about it. Would you like to hear its story?"

When St. Boniface was built after the Great Earthquake, the architects added a rooftop window to illuminate the altar. For decades, the window lit up the sanctuary during the day. But after Japan bombed Pearl Harbor, cities on the West Coast of the United States went on red alert, believing they might be the next target. If there was an air raid at night and the church sanctuary was lit up for an evening service, the altar window would've been a potential bullseye for a bomber. The window had to be covered. After being boarded up and reroofed on the outside, a faux ceiling covered the once beautiful window.

After World War II ended, the busyness of the post-war church made the altar window restoration a low priority. For decades, the exceptional window was forgotten and shrouded.

The morning after the 1989 Loma Prieta earthquake devastated San Francisco, the parishioners of St. Boniface gathered in the sanctuary to pray. As people earnestly meditated, a few noticed an odd shaft of light piercing through the roof onto the altar. Looking for roof damage, an architectural crew

Into the Wonder

pulled away an unmatching patch of roof tiles. When the crew removed the roofing, they uncovered a multi-colored glint of stained glass. The altar window, invisible for 40-eight years, was once again exposed.

As I gazed up at the window, it began to rain. The pitter-patter of raindrops echoing through the silence of the sanctuary triggered the memory of my childhood earthquake: a terrified nine-year-old boy sitting behind a blurry car window on a stormy night. As his world shook, his sense of wonder, previously an inferno, died down to a barely visible flame until he finally snuffed it out.

For most people, a day comes when a quaking trauma causes their wonder to wither. When our sense of wonder is undermined, the aftermath is devastating. Once upon a time, most of us were full of playful imagination. While we lived under the shelter of wonder, we felt safe and protected, naïve to the inevitable pain in the world. As we grew older, life-altering events caused us to exchange the gift of wonder for the burdens of a broken world.

Even if we cannot remember the first tremor that caused us to doubt the gift of wonder, unexpected trauma changed how we viewed the world. As we experience emotional and spiritual earthquakes, we subtly substitute faith and hope with bleakness and despair. Possibilities are replaced with probabilities. Curiosity is smothered by complacency. Beauty can no longer compete with selfishness. Our joy drowns in a swirling pool of cynicism. Awe is replaced by the awful. A loss of faith, hope, or the will to live is, fundamentally, a loss of wonder. The death of wonder is a casualty we cannot endure.

Abraham Joshua Heschel, one of the great Jewish theologians of the twentieth century, wrote, "The beginning of our happiness lies in the understanding that life without wonder is not worth living."[1] Wonder covered over, locked away, and forgotten holds us back from living life's greatest joys.

---

1   Abraham Heschel, *God in Search of Man: A Philosophy of Judaism* (New York: Farrar, Straus and Giroux, 1955), 90.

My favorite plant in my yard is a moonflower. Its thick green vines wander freely outwards and upwards. In late spring, its large white flowers, miniature porcelain trumpets, bloom under the moon's light. They offer a delicious fragrance that lasts a few hours during their lifecycle. You've missed the miracle, however, if you don't see the moonflower the night it blooms. By late fall, the vines wither, curling in on themselves until the plant looks like a russet-colored tumbleweed. The first year I planted the moonflower, I cut away the dead plant, leaving no proof it existed. My assumption was I'd need to replant in the spring. What I did not realize was that the seeds of the moonflower remained dormant. To my delight, new moonflower shoots broke the surface the following April, growing larger and healthier than their predecessor. Where a single moonflower plant grew, a bouquet took its place.

Wonder is a moonflower. Those momentary miracles happen when we least expect them; their aroma stays lodged in our minds long after they are gone. Even in the coldest winters, the seeds remain, ready to bring new life. Wonder, like the moonflower seeds, can be buried but not obliterated.

Sitting in St. Boniface as I heard the rain end and saw sunlight illuminate the altar, I had an epiphany. The wonder I had buried as a child was now the center of my existence. Something or Someone extraordinary had transformed me. Even the tragedies I had faced throughout my life had been transfigured into moments of transcendent beauty. Heart-shattering earthquakes had morphed into moments of wonder. The wonder I had buried as a child was now the center of my existence.

As I departed St. Boniface, I asked myself, *If wonder is hidden in every human heart, how does it reemerge throughout our lives, even in the most desperate circumstances and grievous tragedies?*

To begin my wonder voyage, I had to go monster hunting.

Chapter 2

Monsters

In my twenties, I served as a youth minister at a sprawling megachurch in Dallas, Texas. My weekly routine of preparing sermons, counseling youth, and creating events, such as summer camps and all-night lock-ins, was a rich outlet for a budding storyteller. The church's youth group, comprised of ethnically and socially diverse city kids with little to no exposure to the delights of the outdoors, made camping trips my favorite activity.

I lived in a cabin thirty miles outside of Dallas that sat on the edge of hundreds of acres of woodland. It was the ideal setting for our annual camping trip for sixth-grade boys. I planned a weekend of hikes, capture the flag, fishing, and hot dog roasts—the perfect environment to invoke the boys' inner Lewis and Clark. But the *coup de grâce* of the yearly campout was a monster story they would never forget.

During the last campout of my youth minister tenure at this church, we roasted s'mores over the fire as the boys bragged about their outdoor survival skills. This group was a surly bunch, and they had given me a run for my money all year. The dancing flames of the fire had the boys feeling brazen.

"These woods aren't scary at all!" Marcus, a big teddy bear of a teen, started the fireside banter.

Travis pulled out a pocket knife that looked like a cereal box prize and said, "With this blade, I could easily survive in the woods as long as I'd have to."

Landon upped the ante with his step-by-step plan to handle a bear attack.

I assured them there was nothing in the woods hunting them, especially since their cackling had scared away every living creature within a mile.

Around 11:00 pm, I told them it was time for bed.

Into the Wonder

"I trust you boys will stay out of trouble. Go to the tent and try to get some sleep."

Shomari asked what they all were thinking. "Shawn, why aren't you staying with us?"

I explained I would be within earshot at my cabin. This was their chance to be woodsmen. "After all your bragging, I'm sure you'll be fine, especially if a bear attacks the tent."

All the boys wanted me to stay, but no one dared ask in front of the others. Even though they could see the lights of my porch a hundred yards away, each boy shuddered as they moved toward the sprawling tent. I smiled. Everything was going according to plan.

While preparing for this monster tale, I had found a stuffed dinosaur with an odd internal noisemaker in my daughter's toy box. When squeezed, the noisemaker made the awful bawling sound of a baby cow with a nasal infection. Back at the cabin, I retrieved the noisemaker and stealthily crept behind a tree a dozen yards from the tent.

Within the safety of the tent, bragging wars erupted to mask the boys' anxiety. After waiting for a momentary lull in the laughter, I squeezed the dinosaur.

MMMMMMMMMM… WWWWWWWWW… AAAAAAAAAAAA.

The rambunctious gaggle of boys became mute.

One of the boys whispered, "What was that sound?"

A hushed debate arose about what type of animal made such an odd noise. I waited patiently for the slow, predictable denial of danger. When the clamor revved up, I squeezed the dinosaur toy again.

MMMMMMMMMM… WWWWWWWWW… AAAAAAAAAAAA.

The only sound was of staggered breath as the single tent window filled with anxious faces.

"That thing is close," Marcus said.

Travis spoke. "Guys, I have to go to the bathroom."

I had to bite the inside of my cheek not to laugh out loud. Brandon, the wielder of an enormous flashlight, was deputized by the group as the window sentry. He kept his eyes peeled for movement in the woods while the boys huddled into the tent's center.

MMMMMMMMMM… WWWWWWWWW… AAAAAAAAAAAA.

The imaginary monster cried out. Two headlights of a car driving a quarter of a mile away on the road through the woods came into view.

Brandon yelled, "I saw its eyes, and they were glowing!"

Full-scale panic overtook the tent. Rattled voices were raised in helplessness. Travis' agonized voice was unmistakable.

"Guys, I really have to go to the bathroom!"

Unexpectedly, Brandon's floodlight landed on me, like a prison tower light searching for an escaped convict. I knew I was done for. The tree trunk I hid behind was not wide enough to hide my body. I dropped to the ground and froze.

Brandon's flashlight escaped his grip.

"That thing is HUGE, and it just dropped out of the tree! It's right there, in the shadows."

The tent was a tornado of pandemonium.

"I'm about to pee my pants. Why didn't I go to the bathroom before I came into the tent?" Michael scolded himself.

Panicked faces filled the window and blocked the light from shining into the woods, giving me enough time to crawl out of view.

Over the next hour, I circled closer, squeezing the noisemaker every few minutes. There was talk amongst the boys of trying to outrun what they now believed was a monster. They unanimously decided against an escape plan, but they all agreed I was a lousy youth minister for abandoning them.

By midnight, I had crawled within an arm's length of the tent.

Renald was sitting inside the tent, inches from where I was laying. He had the heart of a saint and the mouth of a sailor. He had decided to make a last-ditch effort to save the group by calling on divine help. He turned to the boys, and with the faith of a fiery Southern Baptist preacher at a tent revival, Renald made his spiritual pitch.

Into the Wonder

"Guys, God has not given us a spirit of fear but of power, love, and a sound mind. We need to stop being afraid and pray. Bow your heads and close your eyes. Let's ask God to save us." His prayer came out like a machine gun. "Dear God in Heaven You got to save us from the Monster that is hunting us because we dont want to die and a lot of us really have to pee…"

I would have fainted from laughter if I hadn't made my final move. I grabbed Renald's leg through the nylon fabric. Throughout the entire history of religion, there has never been a swifter transition from supplication to swearing.

"AHHHHHHHHHHHHH MOTHER F*$%ING SO NO FAB @#CH MONSTER GRAB BED MY F*&$ING LEG!"

The boys screamed like a pile of six-year-olds getting thrown into a pit of snakes. As they lurched to the other side of the tent, the whole shelter tipped over, sending tent pegs flying like little rockets.

My roar of laughter brought order to the pandemonium. The boys scurried out of the tent, their pubescent brains trying to connect the dots. The monster was only a figment of their imaginations. The minute they understood I was behind the elaborate hoax, every one of the emotionally spent boys ran behind a tree and began to pee.

We've all been hunted by a monster. Monsters emerge when we experience extreme trauma in our lives. Whether it happens as adults or when we are children, if there's no one to help lead us through our maze of questions about bad things in life and the pain we are experiencing, or if we find the answers they give unsatisfying, we begin to surmise that wonder is a fantasy. As our wonder fades, we squint in the gathering darkness and conjure shapes in the shadows. Our logical brains tell us that avoiding the monsters that are trying to consume us will keep us safe.

Our monsters become insatiable, hijacking our thoughts until we are trapped in a flimsy tent created from our anxieties. As we sit fretting behind the thin nylon walls, we convince ourselves that we'll never be hurt again if we don't venture out too far. We replace curiosity with security in a desperate attempt to make ourselves invulnerable.

But the trade-off is calamitous. Our worlds shrink as our curiosity and sense of wonder dries and cracks like arid farmland. We lose sight of beauty in the world. The shadows of "what might happen" become self-imposed prisons holding us from discovering the gifts the Creator longs to present.

Maasai Mara, Kenya - October 2010

While on safari in the Maasai Mara, I sat in the back of a dusty truck and watched a mother lion stalk and capture a baby warthog with surprising stealth and speed. Picking up the flailing, screeching piglet in her jaws, she violently shook it until it lay limp. I thought she had shaken it dead. The lioness carried the sagging carcass to a patch of tall, yellowed grass where three camouflaged cubs emerged in roly-poly playfulness. She dropped the piglet with a thump.

I stared as it worked out of a stupor. The juvenile warthog was running for its life in the blink of an eye. The cubs followed in pursuit. When they could not catch the terrified piglet, their mother swooped in, grabbed it, and carried it back to the grass. The catch, shake, carry, and release process continued for half an hour until the cubs, bored with their hunting lessons, refused to give chase. To my surprise, the lioness allowed the young warthog to leave, limping, broken, and bruised but alive.

Like the lioness, our monster stalks us when we are vulnerable. It waits to pounce until we are helpless. When that monster shakes us, our childlike view of the world is skewed and blurred, causing us to wander in apprehension rather than amazement. When bored, the beast lets us go until its next hunt. As we limp away, our perspective of the world is soundly altered.

Into the Wonder

After my parents' divorce, I became the self-appointed man of the house. I wanted to protect my mom and my siblings. Dad's visits were sporadic, and Mom began working long hours in a valiant attempt to pay the bills while finishing nursing school. On nights when she did not come home until after 10:00 pm, I hauled my sleepy brother and sister into a closet filled with pillows and blankets and barricaded the door with my body. There I was, a toothpick of a boy, gripping a baseball bat to my ribcage just in case a burglar broke into our house.

I was a ball of anxiety during those first few months after the divorce. Attending the largest elementary school that I had attended thus far made being friendless painful. Everything we owned had come in our station wagon. The house was cavernous. Furniture was sparse, and we had nothing in the way of decorations. Our dietary staples were Pop-Tarts, TV dinners, and peanut butter and jelly sandwiches. All these factors were the raw materials, giving bones and flesh to my monster. Worst of all, I constantly worried about my brother and sister. I wanted to be a protector, but I was terrified.

It whispered into my ear, *You are alone in the world. You are alone in your pain, alone in your fear, alone in your thoughts, and alone in your struggles.* Though I kept a good face and acted brave, I kept my eye on the stalking beast. It is impossible to hold onto anxiety and wonder at the same time.

But wonder is resilient. Though we might stuff it down, pack it up, and hide it away in the deepest recesses of our souls, wonder remains a tinder box ready for a spark to ignite it back to life.

As children, our deepest emotional, physical, and spiritual needs are met by our parents. They are, by default, our heroes. They put food on the table and teach us to become a part of the world. They pick us up when we scrape our knees and erect boundaries to keep us safe. When those relationships become dysfunctional, and no one fills the emotional and spiritual gaps created by abandonment, death, distraction, disinterest, or divorce, the child will suffer the consequences. After my parents' divorce, I had no one to train me to courageously face my monster of aloneness and reignite the smothered wonder in my soul. I wanted a hero to emulate.

Like all great stories, heroes show up in the most unlikely places. Mine happened to carry a whip.

Chapter 3

Epiphany of the Lost Ark

In the chaotic year following my parents' divorce, my mom moved us from the middle-class suburb of Mequon to the urban sprawl of Shorewood. We lived in a blue-collar neighborhood that served as a landing place for immigrant families. Shortly before my sixth-grade year, a schoolmate of my brother's was stabbed a few blocks away. Within a month, my mom moved us to the quaint, safer town of Cedarburg, twenty miles north of Milwaukee.

By the time I entered Webster Middle School, I had been in five schools in three years. Although the turmoil of those foundational childhood years was not ideal for my educational development, I became adept at making friends and acclimating to any place I landed.

You might say I tamed the monster and settled into my internal aloneness. Fiercely independent, I used my hyper-speed wit and quiet observations to navigate social situations. Friends were risky. Likable but introverted, I engrossed myself in adventure books, feeding my hunger for exotic locations and grand adventures.

Traveling to those places, however, was a childish fantasy quenched by poorness. Growing up meant living in the real world working a blue-collar job to earn a paycheck so that I could live in a home and pay bills. But the more I suppressed my longing for adventure and exploration, a subversive yearning pounded at the bars of my self-imposed beliefs. I longed for a hero to rescue me from my emotional solitary confinement.

After months of waiting and with minutes to spare, I secured the movie ticket, clutching it to my heaving chest—a priceless artifact obtained against the odds. I slipped into a front-row seat, the last in the theatre. As the lights began to dim, I sunk into the sticky velvet chair. Craning my neck, I looked straight up as the screen flickered with projected light and as the music of John Williams filled the darkness. I gazed, wide-eyed, at a film about to profoundly change my life.

When *Raiders of the Lost Ark* premiered in June of 1981, moviegoers were thrilled. Tapping into our collective consciousness, George Lucas and Steven Spielberg resurrected the archetypical hero of the 1930s serials and gave him to the masses. An old hero was reborn. I could not understand why my mom refused to take me to see it. She said it was the snakes.

As a little girl growing up on a farm in eastern Iowa, she had a handful of traumatic encounters with long ebony whip snakes. These harmless brushes with faux-cobras had solidified her opinion of any slithering reptile. Just hearing Indiana Jones say, "Snakes! Why did it have to be snakes?" on the television commercials had been enough to convince her the film was traumatizing. When *Raiders* came to Cedarburg's one-screen theater, no amount of debate, whining, or begging budged her resolve. She was not going to the movie, which meant I was not going.

Every kid, teacher, janitor, gym coach, and cafeteria lady in Webster Middle School had seen Indiana Jones in action. I grew frantic whenever I overheard anyone talking about it. In the days before DVRs and digital media, when cable television was a luxury, missing a film during its theatrical run meant you missed it forever. I could feel my chances slipping away as days passed into months. A bottomless pit stood between me and destiny, and I didn't have a whip to cross it.

Raiders called to me like the voice of God. "*You must see this film. You have no choice.*" My frustration grew into desperation.

Getting to *Raiders of the Lost Ark* was my quest. On Thursday, October 15, the last night the film was showing after its five-month run, I told my mom I wasn't feeling well and was going to bed early. As a pillow dummy lay under my covers, I tiptoed down the hall and climbed onto the second-story fire escape. Jumping to our garage roof, I shimmied down the drainpipe and made the two-mile run downtown. I stood in a long line, bouncing with tension, as ticket after ticket was sold. As I approached the counter, I asked for one ticket. Holding my breath, the man took my money and

Epiphany of the Lost Ark

handed me the precious slip of paper. He then lifted a sign into the ticket window: SOLD OUT.

For the next two hours, I was mesmerized by adventure, excitement, danger, and romance. I entered a different dimension as I watched Indiana Jones face every challenge, adversity, and impossibility in his path (even snakes). The film did not feel like an escape from reality but the promise of a new reality. I sat through the credits and refused to leave until the lights came up. I ran home, spurred on by possibility and imagination. Once I snuck back into my bed, I stared at the ceiling until the morning sun peeked through the shades. My sense of wonder that had been a pile of ashes before the film had become a phoenix on fire.

I had tasted a reviving elixir that had emboldened my belief that my travel fantasies could become a reality. Indiana Jones was the hero I needed. I wanted to be part of the adventures waiting for me in the vast, ever-unfolding universe. The prison door had been ripped off its hinges, opening a way into a new story. My cynicism toward becoming an adult in a world filled with pain and disappointment crumbled under a fresh sense of imagination.

Wonder shows up in curious places. Indiana Jones had become an epiphany. It was time to face my monster, seek wonder no matter the cost, and join the adventures that awaited me.

The Amazon River, Peru - April 2007

As I disembarked into the jungle-walled town of Iquitos, Peru, I wrote in my journal: *This is insanity. I've finally tipped over the edge. I'm about to vanish into the Amazon jungle for two weeks, exposed to God knows what and out of range of any modern communication. If I disappear, or worse yet, die, my family may never retrieve my body.*

Even though I had been to dozens of countries, the Amazon had remained out of reach. When I was invited to join a few of my traveling buddies on an impromptu Amazon River voyage from Iquitos to the Tres Fronteras, where Columbia, Peru, and Brazil meet, I didn't hesitate. I would fulfill a childhood dream that dropped into my heart when I saw *Raiders of the Lost Ark*. Although we knew where we wanted to go, we were unsure about how to get there. We departed on instinct. Wonder led us on an unknown and unplanned route.

The day we landed, we scoured the town, searching for a local crew to take us downriver. Iquitos is a town on the edge of the world. It draws the ultra-adventurous, isolationists, and fugitives. As crickets serenaded the setting sun, we sauntered through the humming streets into the town square, where a bluish hue from the Cathedral Tower set a melancholy tone. We hadn't researched the various guide companies available for our river adventure but felt assured all would be fine. At a local bar called the Yellow Rose, we met a big-hearted Texan ex-pat who owned the tavern. Our crazy idea didn't phase him. Within ten minutes, he had arranged a meeting with our future captain.

Percy, the owner of Amazon Explorers, had received a degree in eco-tourism in the United States. His sole purpose was establishing a small Peruvian outfit to meet the growing need for indigenous guides. As a Kampa Indian, he was deeply connected to the Amazon, her people, their stories, and nature. It only took five minutes of negotiations before we asked him to guide us.

Percy took us to our home on the river the following day: a baby blue, 40-foot-long, eight-foot-wide canoe named the *Valiente*. Designed to cut the water, the *Valiente's* tin roof, crowned with braided banana leaves, repelled the brutal midday sun and the inevitable afternoon downpours. Under benches running the length of her narrow sides were food and water stores. Our luggage was placed in the middle of the boat, along with other equipment, to act as ballast. The stern held fuel, tools, and a makeshift kitchen where nightly Peruvian delicacies like juane, macambo beans, inga fruit, and roasted palm grubs were prepared.

Launching from Iquitos, we sailed northeast on the Amazon. In the cool of the day, I sat on the boat's bow with my legs hanging over the port and starboard sides. My feet cut the black water while I surveyed the constantly changing downstream vistas. The bow of the *Valiente* was the exact spot I had dreamed of sitting as a thirteen-year-old watching my favorite movie.

Our adventures were as numerous as the bug bites covering every inch of my exposed skin. We landed on Monkey Island, a sanctuary for hundreds of simians that had been tamed as pets and then abandoned. There was the thrill of confronting an angry, sixteen-foot anaconda with a head the size of a football. We shared an emotional breakfast with a chieftain who told us the heartbreaking story of his tribe's long walk to freedom from European slavers. But the incredible memories we were cataloging were not without a price.

To protect our bodies from mosquito abuse, we slept in thick, windowless canvas tents with zero air flow. As a precaution against malaria and dengue fever, we slathered ourselves with an oily Crisco-thick bug repellent. As I lay there on our first broiling night, one of my buddies, growing more miserable by the hour, began grumbling from his tent.

"I feel like I'm trying to sleep in a stomach."

Our laughter ruined any chance we might have had for a few hours of rest. Laying in a pool of greasy perspiration, I couldn't picture anyone I knew who might enjoy this experience as much as I was. Here I was, abandoning all creature comforts and all assurances of what the next hour might unleash and embracing physical discomfort as a gift from the heavens.

When you throw yourself into unpredictable, risky, beyond-your-control exploration, wonder is at its peak. I'll trade creature comforts for unknown possibilities every time. Each evening, as I laid in my tent willing myself to sleep, I whispered a thank you to the Creator for fulfilling the outlandish longings of a thirteen-year-old boy whose epiphany of the *Lost Ark* sparked his wonder voyage.

Chapter 4

Exchange Day

My parents' divorce had become increasingly toxic. As I entered junior high, they tried to get me to choose sides. Instead, I decided to isolate myself emotionally. Though my Indiana Jones epiphany had reawakened dormant seeds of wonder, I grew comfortable in my aloneness. When my mom became determined to help us fit into our Cedarburg community, I reluctantly followed her.

One Sunday morning, Mom had us dress in our best clothes (that were well-worn and too small) and brought us to a local church. I had never attended church. The church world was foreign. Walking toward the towering spire, we followed a crowd of people wearing reverence like it was armor. We were mutts in a pack of thoroughbreds.

Sitting in wooden pews shined by the backsides of a century of parishioners, I stared at the impossibly high gabled ceiling. I listened to the tower bells' majestic ring announcing the beginning of the service. My mouth hung open as I watched the robed procession singing imposing songs. When the singing ended, people greeted each other and then sat down.

A man in a collar climbed up to the podium and spoke, quieting the low hum of the sanctuary. Barely a breath was heard when the man started a sermon filled with big words and philosophical musings. I let my mind wander while I cataloged the sanctuary: melting candles and well-worn hymnals, thick curtains and bright stained glass, velvet and brass, cups and crosses; it was all so theatrical and regal. The rich and the refined who sat all around us were remarkably posh. I felt as if I were sitting in the hall of a king. I was with royalty—and for a brief second, I believed that if this was where God lived, I might like to meet Him.

We returned the following week, but this time, we were monitored. This church was known for its religious snobbery, although we were ignorant of its reputation. Trying to fit in, we engaged in the rituals, unaware of the meaning of it all. With the same skills one adopts when eating in someone's home for the first time, we parroted everyone else's actions. We stood when everyone stood, knelt when everyone knelt, shut our eyes, and mouthed the unfamiliar songs—but no matter how hard we tried to blend in, we did not fit the unspoken standards set by the congregation.

When we walked to the altar for communion, we crossed an invisible line, sending a red alert to those aware of our presence. As I ate the communion wafer like a cookie, I noticed people looking at us like a person side-eyeing a homeless man on the corner begging for money. Walking back to our pew after communion, I looked into the cold eyes of those we passed. Realizing you are the "other" in the crowd is unsettling.

After the service, we descended into the basement hall for refreshments. My divorcée mom, with three kids in tow, stood by herself. No one approached or even looked in our direction. She walked us to the table with stacks of little cups filled with orange juice and a pile of fancy donuts. Mom couldn't afford such delights, so this was a special treat. Each of us grabbed our sugary prizes and tore into them like velociraptors. As mom poured herself a cup of coffee, three church elders surrounded her. Each mouth was as tight as a needle. I moved closer to my mom. The posse leader spoke with the polite stiffness of a security guard shooing away an annoying teenager.

"First of all, thank you for visiting. We've noticed your family in the last couple of weeks. Unfortunately, this church is probably not the best fit for you. We can't do anything to help you financially, and we're afraid you would be uncomfortable trying to find a place in our congregation. As a single mother, we think the church down the street might better meet your needs."

Mom got the point. Without saying a word, she collected us, and we rode home in silence. She fought to keep an emotionless face, but I knew the truth. We were alone even in the religious world where wonder should have thrived. Monsters also lurked in the halls of churches.

Exchange Day

A few months after my parents divorced, my Dad remarried, and started to find peace. My stepmom, Mariette, enthusiastically accepted us, making the new marriage easier for us kids.

Together, they found faith. For the first time, my father genuinely believed there was a God in the universe who loved him and longed to engage with him. This changed everything about the way he lived his life. He was still rough around the edges, especially concerning his ex-wife, but he had become a new man.

I found it hard to take his conversion seriously. The divorce left deep scars, creating an emotional barrier between us. My pain, born the night he told us he was divorcing Mom, was his fault. I blamed him for my confusion. I blamed him for our poverty. I blamed him for abandoning us. I blamed him for my loneliness. Though I loved him, he was the one who had released my monster. I was unable to forgive him.

My mom graduated from nursing school. Nursing jobs in Wisconsin were hard to find, so she relocated us to Dallas, Texas, where there was an abundance of well-paying jobs in the medical field. For the first time, she would provide for her family.

There was one huge flaw in her plan. Mom did not tell my father, who was 4,000 miles away in England on a consulting job, that we were leaving Wisconsin.

For me, the move to Texas was thrilling. Even though our circumstances were less than ideal in Wisconsin, they were predictable and safe. Texas, however, was a mythic place bigger than life. The move felt risky but also an exciting chance for a new life.

Shortly after my eighth-grade year ended, my mom lightened our move by selling most of our possessions. As my toys sold, I watched my childhood evaporate. I sorted through my stuff and found a silver-painted, fourteen-inch Eiffel Tower candle. Exposure to several summer suns had caused it to lean over like a tired question mark. I smiled as I remembered why the wilted candle was so significant.

Into the Wonder

If Mrs. Simmons was your third-grade teacher, you had won the lottery. She had a plump figure, and her graying hair was styled in a neatly fashioned bun. Her perpetual smile radiated a grandmotherly love. Mrs. Simmons was a storyteller and a generous treat-giver. Still, there was another reason she was revered amongst the children of Roberge Elementary. As early as kindergarten, we heard whispers of a secret ceremony in Mrs. Simmons' class: Exchange Day. I was eager to experience this magical event when I was placed in her class. But to our disappointment, there was no mention of Exchange Day. By Christmas vacation, our class had forgotten all about it.

A day before Spring Break, Mrs. Simmons stood at her desk and asked us to pack our knapsacks. Once the class settled, she announced, "Tomorrow, we will celebrate Exchange Day. I am sending you home tonight with one assignment. You should choose your worst toy and bring it to class tomorrow. It will be a toy you will not get back, so choose wisely."

As the bell rang, we were off, whispering excitedly in the hall. Kids in the other third-grade classes cursed us with their jealousy. Mrs. Simmons' previous students were excited. The anticipation of Spring Break paled in comparison to the mystery of Exchange Day.

On Friday morning, we placed our trade-in items on our desks. The collection of gnarly toys was straight out of Santa's nightmares—melted lumps of Legos, headless Barbies, Tonka trucks with no tires, and coverless books. An impossibly tangled Slinky, a mashed Mr. Potato Head, a stringless yo-yo, and armless GI Joes were scattered about the room. My toy, chosen from the carnage in my toy box, was a grimy, one-eyed teddy bear.

We went about the day following our regular routine and wondering when the event might begin. Mrs. Simmons led us through math, science, and writing lessons while we stared distractedly at everyone else's junk toys. By lunch, we were going bonkers.

During recess, Mrs. Simmons arranged our desks in a circular formation around a table in the center of the classroom. A black silk

Exchange Day

cloth covered hidden delights. She continued to teach for the next two hours as if the concealed surprises were non-existent. Building tension to a breaking point, she told us to put away our books.

"Exchange Day will now begin!"

Pulling the cloth away with a flick of Mrs. Simmons' chubby wrist and a dramatic swoosh, she revealed the treasures. For months, our teacher had perused garage sales and antique stores in search of riches only a third grader could genuinely appreciate. Porcelain dolls with carefully sewn dresses, an ivory-cased pocket knife, and a raccoon-skin cap were just the beginning. There was a small silver compact, a colossal skeleton key, foreign coins in a leather bag, a collection of cat-eye marbles, and a giant conch shell. The plunder was abundant. Even if everyone in the class took three things off the table, items would still be left.

We all drew numbers out of a purple velvet bag and were told to approach the table when our number was called. Each child was allowed to take as long as they needed to walk around the table, pick up items, test them, and ultimately make their choice. Once you picked your treasure, you took your old toy and set it where your prize had sat.

Sheila was the first to the Exchange Day table. She took an eternity to swap her broken Easy Bake Oven for a string of fake pearls. Ronald approached next, quickly assessing, and traded his dog-chewed baseball for the pocketknife. Several boys eyeing the knife looked defeated. Over the next hour, with Vivaldi's *Four Seasons* quietly playing in the background, the ritual proceeded. For those who had higher numbers, it was painfully slow. No one talked—we just watched as second-hand rubbish was exchanged for treasures.

I kept my eye on an Eiffel Tower candle standing atop the great horde in the center of the table. Black with shining silver paint carefully etched on the candle, there was something inexplicably foreign about it. Every time one of my classmates came near the candle, sometimes touching it, I held my breath. When my name was called, the candle was still waiting. I feigned interest in other goods to give a few other kids a scare, but I had made

Into the Wonder

my decision. Putting the stinky bear in its place, I returned triumphantly to my chair with the candle in my hands.

As Exchange Day ended, Mrs. Simmons walked around the table assessing the discarded junk. Picking up my teddy bear, she faced the class.

"Today, you have learned the most important lesson I will ever teach. As you get older, life will get harder. Things will happen that will make it seem as if the world is against you. But take heart—if your world becomes filled with broken things, you can choose to exchange broken things for treasures. The gift of choice allows you to decide the path you walk. Marvels and miracles are just under your nose. Wonder is waiting around every corner for you."

I heard these heady words, and they stuck somewhere in the back of my mind.

For several years, the candle sat on the bedroom windowsill of whatever house I was living in, reminding me a world of wonder awaited. Holding the twisted candle before our move to Dallas, I remembered Mrs. Simmons' lesson. I would follow her invitation into the unknown and embrace the journey ahead.

I've grown to understand that despair and hope cannot dwell in each other's presence for any sustained period. A battle for the preeminence of one or the other was brewing. Those seeds of hope, planted by a caring teacher, were another step toward wonder as a way of living.

Westminster Abbey, London 2010

I sat surrounded by damp limestone walls carrying the scent of centuries of incense. If prayer has an aroma, that's how it would smell. Years of hallowed supplication were palpable. If you listened long enough, you might hear the whispered prayers of Benedictine monks of eons past. After absorbing a hush that stilled my heart, I knew entering this room was no accident.

Exchange Day

When visiting London, I make a point of wandering through the majesty of Westminster Abbey. There are endless discoveries to be found in the thousand-year-old Gothic spectacle. To look upon the Coronation Chair, where the crowning of every British monarch since 1308 has occurred, or to come upon the graves of Charles Darwin, Isaac Newton, Oliver Cromwell, David Livingstone, and numerous kings and queens, is gluttony for history nerds. Sublime architecture, divine art, and the angelic voices of evensong will carry the staunchest agnostic dangerously close to a religious experience.

My favorite section of Westminster Abbey is Poets' Corner. I put my hands upon the graves of Charles Dickens and Alfred Tennyson or hunt for the memorials to William Shakespeare, C.S. Lewis, Jane Austen, and William Blake. Finding the names of writers who have shaped my life is an inspirational scavenger hunt. But there was one mystery in Poets' Corner I had not uncovered: what was behind the heavy oak door on the south wall? The door was blocked off with a purple velvet cord and an old "Quiet Please" sign. My curiosity prevailed. With crowds of memorial gawkers filling the Corner, I confidently moved aside the rope and stepped inside the door.

I had entered St. Faith's Chapel. Squinting in the dimly lit room, my senses came alive. The thick oak door muffled all the tourist traffic of Westminster Abbey. The dichotomy of moving from the shuffling and murmur of the daytime throng to abrupt silence was astounding.

A holy hush shielded the sanctuary. My eyes caught two small candles flickering on a raised table at the room's far end. They illuminated the green-clothed altar sitting in front of a red-marble arch. Small windows to the right of the altar dimly shone sunlight onto the stone-tiled floor. I moved close to see the ancient frescoes painted on the front wall, surrounded by a canopy of light blue and edged in yellow. The room magnified a sacred presence.

St. Faith's Chapel sits in the oldest section of the Abbey. Hundreds of years prior, this nook had been a private prayer space for the residing monks. But the chapel fell out of fashion in the early nineteenth century and was relegated to a storage closet. In 1849, Westminster's surveyor, Sir Gilbert Scott, saw potential in the room when he noticed the buried vestige of the old chapel under a pile of wooden beams. He cleared the space, designed and placed the heavy oak door, installed a tile floor, and moved the small altar to the eastern wall. There is an arresting piece of art behind the altar under the plain, pointed arch that had been lost under dust and dirt until it was discovered during the renovation.

A life-size oil painting of the chapel's namesake, St. Faith, stands on a deep red pedestal formed by two pillars. St. Faith, a teenage girl, wears a scarlet mantle thrown over an emerald robe. Her long hair flows in ringlets, and she is wearing a tiara. Her right hand clutches the Word of God, which she holds like a shield over her heart. Her left hand hangs to her side, grasping a small gridiron, the ancient torture device by which she was martyred.

I sat for an hour staring at the fresco of the young French martyr, wondering how she felt on the day of her death. There is a peace illuminating her face that says, "I am alone in my martyrdom, yet I was never alone." It gave me pause. I had often felt alone in the universe when I had been a young teenager. My existential quandary was terrifying. One day, I would die and cease to exist. And if I was alone in the universe, did anything matter? As I sat in the silence of St. Faith's Chapel, I knew I was not alone even when I was alone, and it made all the difference.

The morning we were asked to stay away from the church in Cedarburg became a replayed memory. I had constructed a wall around my heart regarding the Christian Church. Yet, I sat in an ancient chapel built to honor a martyred young girl. Healing had occurred between my first painful church visit and my time in St. Faith's Chapel. Faith had become the foundation of my life.

The monster was dead. My life had undergone several exchanges of unfathomable proportions. I had exchanged the safe and ordinary for the uncertain and extraordinary.

My transition to living a way of wonder started in Texas.

Chapter 5

Bula

Loading the bed of my grandparents' pickup truck to the brim with our meager possessions, we were again starting over from scratch—but I didn't care. The move to the Lone Star State was a chance for a new life. An RV became our home for the next couple of weeks as we meandered south, stopping at my mom's childhood farm in Iowa, camping in state parks, and visiting Dollywood. Crossing the Red River into Texas was a bridge to a new world.

Our new home was in a suburb of Dallas called The Colony. The town, founded by a Texas builder in 1974, was generic. The population was a mix of big-hearted Texans and migrating Yankees. I spent the summer inside, unaccustomed to the blistering fry-an-egg-on-the-sidewalk heat. As mom started her nursing job, we accumulated the necessities for our new home at garage sales. The transition was a happy time for our family. But as high school became a looming reality, my growing nervousness wrecked me.

The Colony did not have a high school, so I had to take a thirty-minute bus ride to Lewisville. I was a freshman who was entering high school, friendless. The thought of a bus ride filled me with anxiety, and on the first day of school, as I walked three blocks to catch the bus, my stomach tightened. Turning the last corner, I spotted a gaggle of misfits screwing around at the bus stop.

Walt, a gangly kid with tousled strawberry-blond hair and eyes containing deep wells of mischief, noticed me first. Scott, short in stature but as tough as nails, stood with an ease born out of struggle. Darin looked as nervous as I was, even though he knew the two other guys. At fourteen, his six-foot frame carried the weight of anxious responsibility. The guys introduced themselves, and within five minutes, I was invited into their zany antics. Don, who lived near the high school, became another addition to our group. Handsome, intelligent, well-liked, and (eventually) a swim team letterman, Don had the potential and pedigree to become a part of the high school elite. Yet Don had the mind of a poet, a rock drummer's rhythm, and a romantic's heart. His love for Dungeons & Dragons, comic books, and classic rock gave him an instant spot in our off-kilter group.

After years of moving from school to school, cautious about befriending anyone because of the inevitability of losing the friendship, all my fears and anxieties were wiped away. I'd found an unhindered, laughter-filled, open invitation to a brotherhood of nerds.

Throughout my teenage years, those guys were my family. On weekends, we squatted from home to home. Our parents all found they were raising five boys instead of one. Spurred on by hours of D&D and our love for movies, we created worlds to prospect our wild ideas. Taking our nerdish fantasies as close to reality as we could, we explored miles of sewers under our town, made a raft to float on Lake Lewisville, and attended the Scarborough Renaissance Faire fully costumed every May. Searching for lost treasure or finding mischief was our common pursuit. If we were not engaged in an outlandish escapade, this inseparable brotherhood was planning its next adventure.

When I look back upon the Colony Crew, as Don anointed us, we rescued each other from the trappings of the average high school student. We were outcasts who believed in and loved each other. Amongst this brotherhood, there were no masks and no need to harbor unspoken thoughts or hopes, no matter how ridiculous they might be. When you battle orcs and trolls together or shoot BB guns at each other in the woods, hearts are bonded (and bruises are created). We spurred each other's crazy dreams, spending hours exploring the mysteries of our small universe. Friendship helped us escape our daily mediocrity, lifting us above the anxieties and peer pressure our contemporaries slogged through.

A year before we graduated, we all went to see *The Goonies*. This light-hearted, chaotic adventure about a group of misfits searching for a pirate's hoard struck a deep chord. We were Goonies. Watching the film forty years later, I am captured by the wonder it continues to evoke within me. It's not the adventure, danger, or secret passages that keep *The Goonies* a beloved classic.

We love the film because of the friendships for which the Goonies fight. They are not searching for treasure. They are looking for a way to keep their misfit family together. In that bond of love, wonder is abundant. Deep, meaningful friendships invite wonder into our lives in small and significant ways.

The Colony Crew has remained united over several decades and through marriages, children, moves across the country, car accidents, tragedy, prosperity and near poverty, pain and joy, and the death of parents. Four times a year, we gather to play Castle Risk©, an obscure board game defined by strategy, luck, and lots of yelling. Our game day gatherings are our flimsy excuse to continue to connect friendships now forged in the fire of time.

Walt and I continue to launch on ever-expanding quests out of the Colony Crew. We've road-tripped through Europe, climbed waterfalls in Austria, raided castles in Liechtenstein, and hiked Germany's Black Forest. We have sailed through the Galapagos, swimming with sea lions and sea turtles, fellowshipping closer to nature than we could have dreamed. One autumn, we became pilgrims on the Camino de Santiago in Spain, and to celebrate our 50th birthdays, we boarded an exploration vessel bound for Antarctica. The treasured dreams of two boys who unwittingly met at a bus stop on their first day of high school live on. There is beauty and truth in the words of Shakespeare, "Those friends thou hast, and their adoption tried, grapple them unto thy soul with hoops of steel."[2]

I meet kind and open-hearted people in every country I visit. I've enjoyed Bedouin hospitality in the Israeli desert while devouring warm bread and sipping delicious Arabic tea over a crackling fire. Filipinos are renowned for showering their guests with culinary delights and quick smiles. When I trapesed through Manila, I marked my stops not by street signs but by the food handed to

---

[2] William Shakespeare, *Hamlet* (New York: Simon and Schuster, 1603), 7.

me. And I can't forget the Irish whose laughter falls off the tongue freely. A familial warmth emanates from all who visit the Emerald Isle. But far and away, Fiji is the place with the friendliest people on the planet.

Fiji - March 2006

I took in a 10,000-foot view of the big island of Fiji, an emerald outlined in jagged silver, and I speculated about what I might encounter on my first journey across the "Crossroads of Oceania." I was on a voyage with my friend Keith. When you travel with Keith, there is no set agenda. Each day is open to discovery.

Fijians are handsome people. Long-haired women look like bronzed South Sea goddesses, while the men, with their superhero bodies and sun-bleached teeth, make me think I might have arrived on the lost continent of Atlantis. While in Fiji, we were ceaselessly greeted with beautiful broad smiles given without reserve.

The most revered of all Fijians, as is true in many South Sea islands, are the big boys, and when I say big, I mean generously corpulent. The cultural belief passed down through generations is the stouter the man, the stronger his sex appeal. My friend Keith, who sports the athletic body of a man twenty years younger, is disgustingly handsome. I've traveled with him across the globe and seen the longing gazes people give him. While he is refreshingly naïve to the attention, I am painfully aware that my big body and bald head are the equivalents of an optical cold shower.

As we sauntered along the road, a car slowed down. Several young women hung out of the car windows, cat-calling and blowing kisses our way. Keith waved, assuming they were calling to him, but they scrunched their noses and pointed at me with a renewed round of whistling. Overcome by the fantasy-fulfilling moment, I turned to Keith.

"In your face! Now you know what it's like." In Fiji, I was sexy.

Though I enjoyed the unsolicited shouts, a different Fijian greeting took hold of me. I first heard it when disembarking from the airplane. The Fijians who greeted us used a word I've heard nowhere else: *BULA* (boo-LA). This greeting, native to these islands, is the equivalent of a verbal bear hug. It means life. To speak *bula* is to pronounce a blessing of joy and health onto the one you greet. Throughout the hundreds of times I was met with *bula* throughout Fiji, I knew I was unequivocally embraced by a people whose infectious acceptance was an invitation to partake of their community on a deeper level. Something so persuasive and contagious about the *bula* greeting made it impossible for me to feel like a foreigner. The summons to wonder in that simple word was profound.

Meeting the Colony Crew was my first *bula* experience. I moved from a world of loneliness into a life overflowing with best friends. They took me in as a brother, no judgment passed, no expectations other than mutual respect and the ability to laugh freely and dream exuberantly. They may not have used *bula*, but they invited me into their family with their clunky, nerdy ways. Decades later, we remain Goonies. Wonder is a feast to be enjoyed at a table full of friends, and to this day, our table always has room for another.

Chapter 6

Secret Passage

North Wales - July 2001

We drove along the wind-swept coast of Pembrokeshire before entering the heart of Wales. After passing the Titan, Mount Snowdonia, we reached the rural towns along the northern English borderlands. Pulling under massive sandstone gates onto royal grounds, I watched my children's faces as they spotted the castle.

In the booming voice of an English herald, I announced, "Tonight, me lords and ladies, we will be guests at the Tower Castle." They shouted huzzahs as we unloaded our bag at Rheinallt ap Gruffydd's Tower.

The five-hundred-year-old Tower House was the last of a few dozen fortified mansions built to remind the Welsh of Britain's English overlords. Wendy Wynne-Eaton, the caretaker and a direct descendant of the family who had cared for the tower for generations, opened the massive wooden medieval front door and led us into the regal establishment. We followed Lady Wendy into a library of floor-to-ceiling shelves housing hundreds of leather-bound books, a handful dating back to the 1600s. After her brief introduction, she crowned the children as Lords and Ladies of the Manor for the rest of their stay. They bowed in respect before letting out enthusiastic screams.

Lady Wendy placed Cheryl and me in the Lord's Chamber, one of thirteen echoing bedrooms. The children stayed in the nursery, larger than our Texas living and dining room. Each room was a masterpiece of 17th-century architecture: four-poster beds draped in silk curtains, wooden chests, fireplaces you could stand upright in, wardrobes made for kings and queens, arched windows overlooking acres of formal gardens, plush rugs on the floors, and tapestries with minstrels, knights, and unicorns woven into the fabric.

While exploring the grounds, the children found a small island in the middle of a pond connected to the main lawn by a wooden bridge. As I joined, they pointed out the gargoyles guarding every corner of the roof and the stone carvings of Henry VII and his queen that decorated the front of the castle.

After dinner, we surveyed the barrel-vaulted ceiling of the Great Hall. The walls were adorned with swords, battle axes, spears, and historical paintings of bloody battles. A table set for forty people was decorated with the formal trappings of fine dining, including candelabras and crystal. Suits of armor stationed around the Great Hall stood ready to spring to life if an enemy attacked.

Naturally lit, the Great Hall was darkening with the setting sun when Lady Wendy walked around the corner and froze in front of my backlit body, a hulking shadow-man. She let out an awful scream. After a few deep breaths, Lady Wendy sputtered an embarrassing apology. She explained that the tower had an unusual resident, the ghost of the Mayor of Chester, who was hanged in 1465 from the ceiling close to where I was standing. After Wendy scurried off to settle her nerves, the kids and I stared at each other with bugging eyes until we laughed at Lady Wendy's scare.

Walking the room, we followed the wood-paneled walls until we felt a wisp of air flowing out of a crack. Our curiosity was piqued, and we searched around the panel until Coeli, my eldest child, discovered a hidden slot. Reaching in, I found a handle and pulled. A concealed door clicked open. The dark corridor behind the wall led to a damp staircase, a secret passage behind the walls of the tower. What was back there? It might be dangerous or wondrous. There was only one way to find out. Hand in hand, we entered the dark passageway and started up the steps. What we found will remain between us.

As children, wonder calls out to us, wakes us from our slumber, and inspires us to open doors and search in dark and dangerous places. It does not let go of us until we let go of it. Wonder is animating and alluring. Our longing for wonder is the hallmark of our humanity and the foundation for art, science, architecture, writing, and a thousand other pursuits. We are *Homo admirans*, the wondering human. No matter who you are and what life has thrown at you, wonder pulls at you like a magnet.

My grandmother fostered my love for books when I was a toddler. She read to me as we swayed in her rocking chair. I loved the cadence of her voice. By elementary school, I had a well-used library card.

When I read *Tom Sawyer* in the fifth grade, I moved from simple storybooks into a frothing, surging sea of words. Books became secret passages into other worlds. When I wasn't doing homework or messing around with my friends, I was diving into a book where the realms I read about became as authentic as my world. The more I read, the more I longed for something I could not find.

The more I engaged in imaginary worlds, my tangible world drained of color. A gnawing dissatisfaction with my day-to-day life made every book a bittersweet journey. The pinnacle of these experiences came while reading *The Lord of the Rings*. The deeper I journeyed through Tolkien's Middle-Earth, the higher my soul flew. I cried the night I finished *The Return of the King*. Leaving Middle-Earth was soul-crushing, and I ached with the desperation of it all. I was consumed with *Sehnsucht*.

Sehnsucht is a German word defined as "the inconsolable longing in the heart for we know not what."[3] *Sehnsucht* is a universal longing triggered by reading your favorite book or by the first rain of the spring. It might be brought on by the cry of a newborn baby, a photo, or watching the sunset over the Grand Canyon. These moments of unexplainable longing remain dormant until a profound experience awakens your slumbering soul. The waves of the ocean, the movement of the planets, your grandmother's pumpkin pie; *Sehnsucht* is a moment of undefined nostalgia that yells, "There is something grander in the universe. There is more to life than what you are living. Come, seek, find."

My *Sehnsucht* moments became a fleeting aroma of joy that heightened an unfulfilled emptiness. My ever-increasing longing for another world was like the whisper of someone teasingly invit-

---

[3] Elizabeth Camden, "C.S.Lewis and Sehnsucht," *ElizabethCamden.com*, May 16, 2011

ing me to join a fantastic adventure but refusing to give me a map to get there. It was a secret passage I was unable to locate. Every human longing had an answer. I concluded that my longing for another world was proof of an invisible universe beyond my beckoning heart. C.S. Lewis wrote, "If I find in myself a desire which no experience in this world can satisfy, the most probable explanation is that I was made for another world."[4] By my junior year of high school, I was ready to find this secret passage.

I read numerous religious works, but my intellectual pursuit was like slogging through quicksand with concrete shoes. I researched how the basic tenets of different religions connected with a world beyond our reality. After months of reading, none of these sacred texts brought me closer to the inconsolable longing in my heart. There were endless strategies to connect with the divine, yet they contradicted each other. Who was right? Or were they all wrong?

After months of wrestling, I gave up. The only rational philosophy was agnosticism. I believed there was something behind the curtain of the physical universe, but I could do nothing to bring me to the divine. If God wanted to meet me, He or She or It had to instigate the encounter. If spiritual longing was the state of humanity, *Sehnsucht* was a divine gag.

One night, I lay in bed and did a little thought experiment. I thought back to my childhood: my dad's conversion, the unwelcoming church, farther and farther back to my grandmother's Bible, *A Charlie Brown Christmas*. Then it hit me. What was my earliest memory of God?

I jumped out of bed, opened my closet, and pulled out a weathered hat box filled with childhood photos and memorabilia. Near the bottom of the box, placed in a manila envelope, was the drawing I had made in preschool. There were words written in green Crayons across the top of the picture: "I think God looks like this." Had God put a love-soaked clue in the deepest recesses of my memories? I was standing at the entrance of a divine secret passage beckoning me to move into mystery toward God.

---

[4] C.S. Lewis, *Mere Christianity* (New York: Harper Collins, 1952),147.

Chapter 7
Crayon God

I sat still, hoping my parents had forgotten about me. I had wanted to spit up my Cheerios at breakfast when they said "preschool." Working up the courage, I squeaked out my petition from the station wagon's backseat.

"I don't want to go."

My quiet protest hung in the air, unheard above Sonny and Cher's "I've Got You, Babe." I stared at the small shiny spot in the middle of my daddy's thick black hair, thinking about his aftershave when he hugged me. His smell usually made me feel safe, but not today.

"I don't want to go."

Mommy's blonde ponytail swept to the front as she lowered the radio volume and turned around. Daddy's eyes looked in the rearview mirror. "What is it, honey?"

My upper lip quivered. "I don't want to go."

My mom, seeing my anxious eyes, reached back. My tiny fingers held hers with desperation. "Honey, it's only for a few hours. Preschool will be fun. There are toys and lots of kids your age to play with. You'll even get snacks." She smiled, trying to appease my welling tears.

I barely mumbled a final "I don't want to go" as we pulled into the gravel parking lot. I loved the sound of the crunching rock under the tires, but this morning it sounded harsh. The preschool was in an old church building converted into a daycare. My family members were not churchgoers, but they believed the highly recommended religious preschool might be a good start for me, a quiet and shy child.

Walking up the steps of the wood-framed building, I gripped both my parents with no intention of letting go. Hearing children laughing and squealing inside made me want to sob. My parents exchanged confusing adult words with a grandmotherly woman.

Softly cupping my face, the woman said, "Shawn will be fine." But I did not feel fine. I hugged my parents, whispering in both their ears.

"I don't want to stay. Please don't leave me."

My dad whispered back, "It will be okay. We'll be back soon. Try to have fun."

The grandmotherly woman showed me toys and the art center. Little boys ran over, asking me to join their shenanigans. The girls giggled. Overwhelmed with the noise, I refused to look at them. I sat at a table full of drying Play-Doh, watching a whirlwind of movement. I gradually grew comfortable with my surroundings but remained glued to my chair, preferring to study the enormous room. I liked the tall ceiling and the corner with the overstuffed pillows where kids read.

The morning sun backlit a stained-glass window on the far end of the building. This colorful window was my favorite thing in the room. I didn't know who the man in the picture was, but I liked his bearded face. He had a kind smile and long hair. The big white bathrobe he was wearing was silly. The smiling man, made of colored glass, held his arms open wide like he wanted to hug the world. Several children were also in the glass picture. Maybe the man was happy because the children were running to him. Perhaps he was about to take them to the park or out for ice cream. The more I stared at the picture, the more I thought he had to be their daddy.

"Okay, children, time to go to your tables."

A young assistant teacher looked like she was chasing butterflies as she directed the rambunctious tots into chairs. Laying piles of construction paper in front of us, the teacher gave instructions.

"Now, children, I am going to ask you to draw something special. You're going to have to think hard."

Each child grabbed their crayons of choice. The room quieted as we waited for her directions.

"Take your paper and draw me a picture of what God looks like."

If given to adults, this assignment would be confusing. But for a group of children armed with crayons and uninhibited imaginations, the challenge was exciting.

"When you finish, bring me your pictures, and I'll give you cookies and milk."

Crayons sped across papers. The hasty drawings looked like tornadoes or tumbleweeds, while others drew pictures of creatures flying through the sky. Thinking about cookies and milk, one little girl forgot the assignment and drew a picture of her cat.

I sat still for several minutes. I wanted to draw a picture of God. But what did God look like? I looked up at the man of colored glass and smiled at his joy-filled face. Seeing his picture gave me an idea. Rubbing my hands on my corduroys, I grabbed a magenta crayon and drew, as meticulously as a four-year-old is able, the man in the white bathrobe. His arms were so wide that it looked like he had wings. His eyes, two tiny lines on the paper, shined. He was running to his children with a smile covering half his face.

I didn't think the picture was good. Once I finished coloring, I sheepishly handed it to the grandmotherly woman.

"This is beautiful, Shawn." She laughed at the man's smile.

Hearing her laugh gave me courage. "Can I have my cookies now?"

I spent a few weeks at my dad's place in northern New Jersey the summer before my senior year. Dad and Mariette's outward dedication to Jesus sometimes made me uncomfortable. Jesus came up in casual conversation with strangers at the supermarket, with passionate prayers before meals, and in their weekly church attendance. To their credit, they never pushed their faith on me. Whether they sensed my discomfort or gave me space, I was under no obligation to discuss or participate in their religion. The one thing they did ask every Saturday afternoon was if I wanted to go to church. My answer was always a polite, "No thanks."

During my last week with them, I reluctantly agreed to visit their church. My decision was one of respect. I attended Hamburg Assembly of God Church on Sunday, June 23, 1985.

Into the Wonder

As we gathered in long pews neatly centered around a raised stage, a music leader led the congregation into a spirited time of singing. People raised their hands, danced in the aisles, and let their hallelujahs fly. The guy behind me shouted, "Praise the Lord!" so loud I wondered if he had a hearing impairment. I was sweating when the singing and praying ended, and my nerves were shot. The sermon was agonizing. So long. So boring. I was ready to leave. My church experiment was a bust.

After an hour, the minister closed his Bible. *Finally*, I thought, *it's over!* He had everyone close their eyes. Something in his closing words caught my attention.

"Since the dawn of time, people have been hunting for God. Let's pretend God lives on the top of a mountain. There are an uncountable number of trails at the bottom. Do they all lead to God? We could spend a lifetime trying each, but what if they don't lead to God? What if some trails are dangerous or deadly? What if some circle around the mountain or take us near but not to the top? How do we know which path to take? This is the conundrum of religion.

"What pride-filled beings we are when we believe we can reach a transcendent God with our rituals and religious ways. We must look for a path that God makes to us—not us to God.

"This is the wonder of Christ. Jesus tells us, 'You can't reach God. It is impossible. Let Him come to you.' It's His bold claim that He came down from the mountain in search of us. He said, 'I am the Way, the Truth, and the Life. No one comes to the Father except through me.'"

In hearing this explanation of Christ's proclamation, I was undone. I had searched for the proverbial needle (God) in the proverbial haystack (world religions). I had read the rules and ways different religions claimed to ascend to God. I had tried to climb the mountain of religion and had come up short. How did I ever think I would reach God? The story of Jesus made sense. God, in the person of Christ, came down into the dirt and dust of mankind to grab our hands, pull us up, and lead us to God.

As the minister invited people to walk down to the altar to be prayed for, I loosened my fingers gripping the pew. Amid these peculiar people, I hesitantly walked down the aisle for prayer, asking God to come down from the mountaintop to meet me. I was not a willing seeker nor a desperate sinner looking for forgiveness. I was not performing an act of contrition. I simply wanted to give God a chance. I decided to do the thing I wanted to do the least.

The minister went from person to person for the next few minutes, praying long, fervent prayers. Many people started to cry or fall to their knees, overwhelmed. What had I got myself into? The minister eventually stood in front of me and looked into my eyes.

"Son, may I pray for you?"

"Sure," was all I could muster.

He gently held my hands in his as he whispered, "Jesus, may he know You face to face."

That was it. Nothing profound. A seemingly unremarkable moment shook my entire existence. As he had whispered the phrase, "know you face to face," in my ear, I, who felt alone in the universe, experienced a Presence impossible to describe. I did not shake nor shout amen. In my stillness, the "inconsolable longing in my heart for I knew not what" had engulfed me with His Fiery Presence.

The words of Flannery O'Conner captured that moment of Presence. "Whatever you do anyway, remember that these things are mysteries and that if they were such that we could understand them, they wouldn't be worth understanding. A God you understood would be less than yourself."[5]

The God who had tugged at my four-year-old heart when I drew with a magenta Crayon a picture of Jesus was now embracing me. My aloneness was swallowed in a tsunami of invisible wonder. God's arms wrapped around me. I began to sob, unable to process the spiritual atmosphere swirling around me. I was free. A Holy, Loving, Grace-filled, Mysterious, Divine, All-Encompassing Presence had replaced my aloneness.

The God who clothed Himself in humanity met me face to face, and a whirlwind Presence was about to let loose into my life. Nothing would ever be the same.

---

[5] Flannery O'Conner, *The Habit of Being* (New York: Farrar, Straus, and Giroux, 1979), 523.

Chapter 8

Dive

One of the highlights of my childhood was my dad's company picnic. In 1970s fashion, the opening ceremony was a series of competitions, such as three-legged races and an egg toss. At noon, we ate from checkered-clothed tables stocked with burgers, hot dogs, potato salad, chips, pies, cookies, and soda. When the adults had adequately gorged on picnic fare, they settled under the pavilion, drinking and chatting about politics and sports, while the kids ran to the creek to swim. There was one big problem. At eleven years old, I didn't know how to swim.

The slow-moving creek was six feet deep in the middle, with a bridge connecting the banks. I sat on the shore brooding, watching kid after kid jump into the water from the top of the bridge. A couple of seconds after going under, they'd pop up like a bobber, laughing and flailing their arms in relief from the warm summer day. Their happiness caused my aggravation to flare. One of the older kids yelled at me.

"What's wrong, kid? Can't you swim?"

"I can swim," I yelled, annoyed at becoming a target.

"Then jump in," he replied.

Other kids echoed his sentiments. Without clearly thinking, I decided to prove them wrong.

Walking to the top of the bridge, I formulated a plan. Determination superseded fear. With all the naysayers watching, I leaped into the stream. Sinking like I had bricks tied to my legs, my feet hit the gravelly bottom of the creek. I pushed hard enough to break the surface, breathe, and turn my body toward the bank. Down again. A steady push upwards. Another breath. I was now closer to the bank. By four pushes, the water was only chest deep. I waded out, alive without having had to tread water. I repeated my rhythm for hours: off the bridge, into the creek, and a slow jump to the shore. Though I was bouncing rather than swimming, no one

Into the Wonder

knew the difference. I had joined the ranks of the water svelte by cheating the system.

After a while, I grew tired. My "bouncing" technique was more physically taxing than actually swimming. I watched others kick and flail their arms with ease. There didn't seem much to it, but when I hit the water, my brain refused to let me try. I had a system that kept me from drowning and looking like a loser.

Worn out, I decided I'd go for one last daring jump. I knew it was stupid to try a forward flip, but I also reasoned, "How hard can it be?" I'd been watching the older kids do flips all afternoon. Standing on top of the bridge, I declared my intention. The older kids started a countdown. 3…2…1, hurrah! I flopped.

Sucking in a mouthful of water on impact, I wriggled my body below the bridge where the lakeweed grew. Feeling the slimy hair entangling my feet, I pushed hard but did not break the surface. Panicking, I sucked in water as I moved again, this time into one of the wooden piers supporting the bridge. Holding on tight, I shimmied up enough to get my head out of the water and cough up the creek flow. I was in real trouble. Although kids surrounded me, I hung alone, clinging to a moss-covered pier, in the deepest part of the creek, with no momentum to help push me back to the bank. If I asked for help, everyone would know I couldn't swim, leaving no doubt I was a fraud.

Seeing me hanging on the pier, one of the older boys yelled, "Hey, kid. There are leeches all over that pole."

Terror launched me like a water cannon. I shot off the pier, flailing my arms and legs, swimming to the shore. Reaching the bank, I was overcome with marvel: I was a swimmer. All it took was the will to jump, letting go of the safe place, and enough fear to get me flailing. I had flung myself into the jaws of danger and won the day. I spent the next hour in the river, diving into a world that only minutes before had been unreachable.

I spent the ride back home trying to wrap my mind around what had happened to me. My encounter with a Holy Presence had come unexpectedly. A fog was evaporating. My black-and-white world was starting to bleed colors. A padlocked universe, where I thought I was alone, was alive with Someone who loved me.

I had come face to face with *wonder*, not a sense of wonder but the Source of all Wonder. I had reluctantly walked into a church with no expectation of meeting God. Now I was undone by a Presence, both terrifying ecstasy and dreadful joy.

The hammer of God had smashed my minuscule fishbowl world and cracked open the whole cosmos. I needed understanding. In a week, I'd be back in Dallas with no clue how this discovery would work back home. Seeing my distress, Mariette set up a meeting for me the following day with the youth minister at the church.

On Monday morning, I sat on a couch in the dimly lit office of Budd Smith. Budd was seated behind his desk, his 300-pound backlit frame a massive shadow. For several minutes, I nervously recalled the pull on my heart triggered by the minister's words and my experience at the front of the church when I was prayed for. Years later, Budd told me he had sensed an urgency to be simple and speak plainly when talking to me that morning.

"Shawn, you've experienced God's presence in a special way. You've met the Creator of the universe face to face. Your heart is beginning to beat with the message of Christ: God is near. It is what you were created for. He is your hunger, sustenance, answer, and longing."

For the next hour, Budd gave me thoughts on my spiritual journey. He encouraged me to read the Bible daily, asking the Holy Spirit to guide me into truth. "Read it for what it is. Ask tough questions. Wrestle with its words. Soak in its poetry. Hear God's voice within its narrative. Let it be your love letter before someone else tries to give you their version of what it means."

Budd said following Jesus was a daily pilgrimage, not a one-time decision. "Either join Him every step of the way or get out now and go back to enjoying your old life. There is no middle way. We have enough pretenders in church. We don't need another."

Into the Wonder

I either dove into the river and learned to swim or stayed landbound. The decision was mine to make.

That night, I paced the floor with the decision before me. One moment I was alone in the universe, and the next, I was immersed in what I could only comprehend as Ultimate Love. And in Love, I was no longer alone. My moment of wonder was undeniable.

At 2:00 am Tuesday morning, roughly 32 hours after my divine encounter, my unexplainable, unexpected, uninhibited moment of wonder was as real to me as anything I had ever experienced. My view of the universe had been upturned, and who I was before was a crumbling husk. I got on my knees by the bed, the way I saw people in the movies pray, and spoke to an invisible God.

"I don't know if You're alive, but it feels like You are. I give You my whole life, everything I am, everything I will be. Show Yourself to me. Let me remain in Your love, let me not be alone, let me know Your wonder. I will call You mine if You call me Yours."

Philosopher Juan DePasquale says, "The experience of wonder brings the world into relief and makes a person take life serinity to swim through the river of life rather than just float on it, to own your own life rather than be owned by it."

I embraced my fear, released my inhibitions, and let go of where I was standing so that I might dive into the arms of God—the arms of Wonder.

Chapter 9
Cliffs Edge

As I packed for my return to Texas, I unpacked my spiritual journey. My unexpected encounter with Jesus gave me a fresh perspective, allowing me to recall a path of divine love hidden beneath the surface of my life. Though I had stumbled through the dark maze of aloneness, I had never been alone. There was a reason I was alive, and discovering my purpose was now a collaboration with God.

Spiritual revelation is tame when it stays in your head, but speaking about your journey to others is risky. I deliberated how I would explain to the Colony Crew my encounter with God, of all places, in New Jersey.

Cliffs of Moher, Ireland - February 2001

I was in the Emerald Isle on business, but a few days of wandering are necessary when traveling to a place you adore. My rental car cut through the fog along the Clare coast like a plane piercing the clouds. On the edge of Ireland's western wilds, the magnificent seven-hundred-foot precipices of the Cliffs of Moher hang over the Atlantic. This region, known as the Burren, is characterized by land formations more akin to moonscape than anything on this planet. One hundred square miles of fantastical landscapes are dotted with caves, portal dolmens, burial chambers, fossils, and unearthly rock formations. These strange geological marvels abruptly end at the cliffs.

Irish monks came to this spot for ages and looked out toward the invisible Island of the Blessed. One of these, Saint Brendan the Navigator, journeyed by boat for years in search of the mythical lands beyond Ireland, where the Swift Sure Hand, the early Irish

Christians' colorful description of God's Spirit, led him to bring the light of Christ.

Visit the cliffs today and you will enter through an award-winning information center where tourists spend most of their time rather than walking along the cliffs. When I arrived in 2001, modern construction was a decade away. As I pulled my car into the gravel parking lot, no one else was around.

I insulated myself in rain gear and headed up the stairstep rocks toward the steady boom of the ocean waves, ambling my way through a forest of fog to a flat area of sand-colored shale, a porch stretching over several hundred square feet. Tip-toeing my way forward, I caught sight of a drop-off into nothingness.

I knew the cliff face went on for miles. In front of me, the Aran Islands were cloaked by fog in the middle of Galway Bay. And O'Brien's Tower sat a few hundred yards higher. I couldn't see anything but the death drop into clouds. The thundering voice of Manannan mac Lir, the Celtic god of the sea, invited me to join him below, an invitation I readily declined. Finding a comfortable observation point, I gazed into the nothingness pondering how the cliffs reminded me of the Creator: majestic, terrifying, glorious, dangerous, sublime.

Staring into an all-enveloping cloud, a sudden warm updraft began to intensify. The fog fled upwards in defeat as sunlight cut through the blurry atmosphere, creating an ever-growing window into the stunning views up and down the coast.

In a few minutes, I was looking west across the rumbling sea. Any description of my view is profane compared to the wonder I experienced in that moment. As poet Wallace Stevens wrote, "They go to the cliffs of Moher rising out of the mist, above the real, rising out of present time and place, above the wet, green grass."[6]

I have never been one for heights, but I had to look over the limestone shelf with my own eyes. Army-crawling tentatively forward, my stomach knotting up, I willed my head over the edge and looked into the breathtaking blue-green seafoam abyss. My body,

---

[6] Wallace Stevens, *The Rock* (New York: Penguin Random House, 1982).

slightly slanted toward the sea, felt as if it was gradually slipping over the edge.

Observing the seas below, I was gifted with a deeper understanding of God. Looking over those cliffs was like staring into the eyes of God—beholding His beauty, majesty, and wonder in a tangible, soul-altering moment. When you experience magnificent wonder, it is impossible not to share that moment with the ones you love.

When I returned home at the end of the summer, I gathered the Colony Crew. Pacing back in forth in my living room, the four guys stared at me with dumb grins. In a machine gun spray of words, I told them the story of my spiritual encounter and how I was now a follower of Christ. There was no turning back. They were unfazed. As always, they accepted my story for what it was. If anything, they were curious about my spiritual journey.

My introduction to the Bible came with no preconceived ideas. From the first page, I was hooked. Throughout my senior year of high school, I worked through all of the Bible: the godly and grotesque; the divine and the diabolical; acts of grace and head-scratching contradictions; a God who longed for love but sometimes commanded destruction. The stories about His followers did not mask their doubts or anger toward the Almighty. Struggles such as fear, confusion, pain, and bitterness were human emotions and not frowned upon. The Old and New Testaments were filled with drama, history, poetry, philosophy, mythology, prophecy, horror, and hope. The Bible was a beacon of what it was to be human.

After a particularly tough day, a barrage of uncertainty overcame me as I tried to pray. What if all this Jesus stuff was in my head? Maybe I was so desperate I couldn't bear the thought of a godless universe. I sat in the whirlpool of my doubts. The old monster of aloneness emerged. The fear of being utterly alone in the universe took me to the ground. My prayers felt like words bouncing off the ceiling. In desperation, I lay on my bedroom floor and cried myself to sleep.

In my fitful state, I had a strange dream. I stood, bound in heavy chains, on the edge of a precarious cliff. A fog below kept me from seeing how far the drop was, but I was sure I'd die if I stumbled forward. It took all my concentration to keep from losing my balance. Something crept up behind me. I began to sweat and sway. Hot breath moved up the back of my body and stopped on my neck. Sharp fingernails pressed my backbone. Slowly, the nails pushed me forward. I fought to counterbalance, but the pushing became more forceful.

Unable to stop myself, I fell forward in slow motion. The tips of my toes remained on the edge of the cliff face as I dropped toward my death. When my toes left the rim, mammoth muscular arms caught me. I was rolled over, and my bindings disintegrated. I was a baby in the arms of someone whose face I could not make out. Like the first thunder of creation, a voice echoed through my chest.

"Shawn, I will never leave you, and I will never forsake you."

As I awoke, I was bathed in the peaceful presence I had embraced in June.

I longed to spend time with that presence. Often, I took long walks during which I let my mind wander and my heart soar. I spoke to the Creator and listened to the still, small voice in my heart. My walks with God were an exercise of remembrance and hope: the world had not changed. I had changed. There was a God who longed to draw me out of my stumbling darkness and unveil abundant wonders if I was willing to fall into His embrace.

Chapter 10

Holy Curiosity

I am amazed at how seemingly minor events led me down lifelong paths. I had matured from an aimlessly wandering teenager to a man who was part of a bigger story. My future, once a dark and brooding forest full of monsters, had transformed into a compelling tale. I had entered a path promising adventure and challenge, mystery and magnificence, possibility and providence.

I needed an elective for high school graduation, so I signed up for Theater 101. During my first class, I performed a simple improv exercise. When twenty classmates laughed hysterically at my antics, I was hooked. Theater laid the foundation for my pursuit of live storytelling, the arts, and creative freedom. But Neely was the true gift of the class.

Barely five-foot tall, she had a smile that added inches to her. I wanted to be her friend. Seeing me reading the Bible, Neely asked where I went to church. I told her I was learning to follow Jesus and that the church scene was not my bag. Her boisterous laugh at my comment intrigued me. She invited me to her Wednesday home fellowship gathering.

"Like the Fellowship of the Ring?" I asked.

"I'm not sure what that is, but home fellowship will be fun. Do you want to come and try it out?"

I forgave her ignorance of nerd lore and agreed to come. I learned on my first visit that I was her spiritual guinea pig.

The home fellowship started in the fall of 1985 with Neely, her friend Liz, and me. The group steadily grew in enthusiasm and participants. By the spring, forty students from several area high schools filled Neely's living room. As the Bible study developed, the food improved, the prayer became more intense, and

Into the Wonder

the afterparty was louder. This was a safe place where all were welcomed and were free to ask questions or discuss any topic without judgment. It didn't matter your religious or non-religious background, your race, your sexual orientation, or your social standing in the school. The home fellowship always ended with comforting prayers, hugs, and new friends. Everyone was made in the image of God. Everyone had a voice. This was my first taste of what the Church was supposed to be.

One April evening, we had a guest. Joe, the tall, mustached Italian, was a youth pastor at the church sponsoring the Wednesday gatherings. He watched me as I led the evening study, carefully weighing my words. Afterward, while I hung out in the backyard, Joe introduced himself. He affirmed I was good at leading the group before asking me a few questions about myself. Then he surprised me.

"You might want to visit the church that is hosting this home fellowship that you are apparently leading."

As May approached, I had no post-graduation plan. Spring is when seniors are giddy with the prospect of leaving the nest. I was aimlessly wandering. As a mid-level student, scholarships were unrealistic. I had no money for school and did not want outrageous loans.

My love for the Bible sparked a wishful thought. What if I could study the Bible in college? One night, at the home fellowship, I heard about a school in Dallas that focused on the Bible, theology, and spiritual development. I decided to check it out.

I registered for Christ for the Nations Institute an hour after visiting the campus. I had no idea how to pay for school, but I was willing to do what was necessary. My choice was made on a holy hunch and the lack of a better alternative. This path of mystery is at the center of God's story for my life.

Evangelists Gordon and Freda Lindsay founded Christ for the Nations (CFN) in the 1970s to train future revivalists and missionaries. In its heyday, CFN was a bastion for charismatic renewal. We danced, sang, and prayed loudly before the Lord and each other. During weekly chapel service, the overtly demonstrative worship style made most evangelicals blush in embarrassment.

Our dome of serenity, created by manicured lawns, acres of city blocks scattered with sensible, white-washed academic buildings, and a vaulted auditorium graced with a flowing fountain out front, was designed to be an island of hope to the gang violence, drug abuse, and abject poverty encircling our campus.

Although I imagine this was a spot in which Jesus might hang out, the realities of the area were shocking for new students. Tensions were high as police sirens screamed in protest at all hours of the day and night. On the first day of classes, as I headed toward the auditorium from the men's dorms, I, along with hundreds of other students, passed a taped-off crime scene where someone had been stabbed hours before. A few days later, when I witnessed my first mugging a couple of blocks from campus, I knew Bible school would be different than I had imagined.

My dorm room was a big closet for three males who had never lived away from home. Smelly, tight quarters with two strangers made me realize I had never appreciated privacy. Between fulltime classes, homework, and two jobs barely covering my tuition, I was exhausted but happy.

While many of my other high school friends scattered to colleges, went to parties, dated, and drank, I tried to score free food at church gatherings. An internship at the Word of Faith youth group, which I adopted as my home church after I met Joe at the home fellowship, filled in any extra free time. The church became my bi-weekly reprieve.

One skill I perfected during my years at CFN was begging for rides. My lack of transportation meant I had a twenty-mile gap to overcome twice weekly to meet my church internship requirements. Unreliable lifts often led to late-night returns to the dorm. And late check-ins were a no-no at CFN

Like many evangelical Bible schools, CFN had a strict code of conduct. No dating without approval. No secular music. No alcohol or drugs. Chapels were required. No missing classes without permission. The boys wore long pants and collared shirts. According to the school's founder, facial hair was an affront. No smoking. No clubbing, though you could stand outside a nightclub and hand out Christian tracts. No gambling. No cursing. The curfew was at 10:30 pm because everybody knows sin blooms by 11:00.

Only weeks into my first semester, my ride dilemma had caused too many tardy nightly check-ins, leaving a mark on my record. I was called to face my charges. My lack of a vehicle and church attendance did not move the Dean of Men. He promptly said, "Tough luck," and doled out my penance: late-night campus security.

This is how I found myself outside the CFN library at 2:30 am on a crisp, moonlit night in early October. Every noise was heightened by the stillness of the evening. I heard dog fights, cat fights, human fights, and angry screams while watching vehicles with darkly tinted windows roll by. My only protection was an AA battery-sized can of mace the head of security handed me just in case I was attacked on the far end of campus.

My mind was in overdrive. What if a local gang wanted to break into the campus library to steal religious texts or outdated computers? During the witching hour, I paced back and forth in front of the pebbledash pillars of the CFN library façade. The punishment for my crime convinced me of one thing: I had to find more reliable rides or quit church altogether.

The crack of a pistol came from blocks away. I pulled out the capsule of mace and looked upon it with incredulity. I needed to know its range. Removing the lid, I carefully aimed at one of the pillars a few paces away. Unnerved and out of my element, I squeezed the trigger without realizing the spray was pointed toward the palm of my hand, which filled with pepper spray. A bee's teardrop worth of liquid shot between my fingers and into the corner of my eye. The burning, minor at first, intensified when I dropped the little bottle and inadvertently tried to protect my eyes by covering them with a palm of spray.

Holy Curiosity

I sat on the steps for the next hour, crying and whooping out catch-my-breath coughs. If I had not been in agony, I might have wondered what the passengers of the Plymouth with tinted windows thought as they slowly passed me while I writhed on the ground in circles like Curly from the Three Stooges. I am sure they heard me howling. I was the worst security guard in the history of CFN.

Oddly enough, the library, where I temporarily lost my sight, became a jumping-off point for my transformation at CFN. It is where I learned that words could bring sight to the blind.

In high school, I did the least amount of work while still getting passing grades. When a class struck an intellectual chord, like English or History, I put in the effort and usually scored an A. I was lucky to pass the hard-edged math and science subjects. Outside of Mrs. Simpkins, my 4th-year English teacher who scolded me for having a brilliant, imaginative mind and doing nothing with it, I had no teachers or adults encouraging mental pursuits. Though I read prodigiously, my intellectual curiosity remained an unworked muscle. Considering my education beyond high school, I didn't believe I had the academic chops to handle real college work.

In one of my classes at CFN, I was assigned to read *Mere Christianity*, written by the world's most beloved Christian thinker, C.S. Lewis. I picked up my copy in the CFN library.

My first exposure to the writings of Lewis happened as a young teen when I watched the BBC-produced mini-series, *The Lion, the Witch, and the Wardrobe*. The program so took hold of me that I bought the seven-book series and moved through the fantastic world of Narnia in a few weeks. As a kid, I had no recognition of the allegorical overtones filling the pages of *The Chronicles of Narnia*. Something about the world of Narnia was more real to me than my everyday life.

As a young atheist, C.S. Lewis had a similar experience when he read George MacDonald's *Phantastes*. "That night my imagination was, in a certain sense, baptised; the rest of me, not unnaturally, took longer. I had not the faintest notion of what I had let myself in for by buying *Phantastes*."[7] Though I was years away from becoming a follower of Christ, *The Chronicles of Narnia* sparked a spiritual delight in me, of which I've never let go.

Reading what many consider Lewis' theological opus, *Mere Christianity*, did for my mind what Narnia had done for my imagination. I experienced intellectual delight. Lewis wrote in a profoundly philosophical yet accessible style, inspiring my mind to wonder and wander. Within a few chapters, Lewis had morphed beyond a children's mythmaker. He was a theologian, a philosopher, an academic, an apologist, and a professor. By the time I finished *Mere Christianity* (which I read three times in a row), I had moved from being a fan of C.S. Lewis to something more. Even though he died five years before I was born, I became one of his disciples.

There is an active connection between wonder and curiosity. The intellectually curious is, in essence, seeking wonder. There is a sacredness to curiosity when a person allows his or her mind to be open to truth and is willing to go wherever that truth may lead that person. Albert Einstein spoke of this sacredness. "The important thing is not to stop questioning. Curiosity has its own reason for existence. One cannot help but be in awe when he contemplates the mysteries of eternity, life, and the marvelous structure of reality. It is enough if one tries merely to comprehend a little of this mystery every day. Never lose a holy curiosity."

While most of my fellow students at CFN were seeking spiritual stimulation, I was experiencing a baptism of the intellect. Learning to study the Bible in the original languages of Greek and Hebrew, I plunged into the poetry, the passion, and the humanness of these sacred books.

The writings of Peter Kreeft, Alvin Plantinga, William Lane Craig, and Richard Swinburne introduced me to philosophy. Pastoral writings from Eugene Peterson, Brennan Manning, and Brother Lawrence challenged me to consider what a life following Jesus looks like in the real world. I probed the broad scope of man's pursuit of God through the Jewish mystic Abraham Joshua

---

7   C.S. Lewis, *Surprised by Joy* (New York: HarperOne, 1955), 177.

Holy Curiosity

Heschel and Bede Griffiths, a monk who moved to India to start a Christian monastery in a Hindu world. My favorite writers were those who painted faith with imaginative broad strokes, such as poet Calvin Miller and Gene Edwards, whose book, *The Divine Romance,* grounded me in the love of God more than any other.

Christ for the Nations became a place where my untapped intellect bloomed. Jesus implored His followers to love God with all their heart, soul, mind, and strength. The mind was something I had not, up to that point, thought about as a part of my faith journey. C.S. Lewis and many other writers taught me to love the Lord with *all* my mind. I became free to think, question, explore, and wonder.

Oxford, England - July 2011

I sat against the wall of the Rabbit Room. The wood paneling, mahogany bar, and framed fireplace mainly had stayed the same since the Inklings gathered here for Tuesday lunch. The smell of burning coal clung to the ageless walls like paint. As I sipped my black tea, the present faded into the past. I sat in this chamber in a circle of high-backed, long-armed, overstuffed chairs. A group of men, filling the ring like a wizard's counsel, warmed themselves around a fire while they smoked, talked, joked, debated, and drank. After twenty-five years of waiting, I was finally in Oxford, drinking tea in the Eagle & Child on St. Giles Street.

Between 1939 and 1962, this pub was a gathering place that fostered some of the 20th century's most influential authors. Hugo Dyson, Nevill Coghill, Charles Williams, J.R.R. Tolkien, and C.S. Lewis formed a nucleus of friends who spurred on each other's intellects, spirituality, and creativity; a holy curiosity. Lewis wrote, "My happiest hours are spent with three or four old friends in old clothes tramping together and gathering in small pubs."[8]

---

8   Alan Jacobs, *The Narnian: The Life and Imagination of C. S. Lewis* (New York: Harper Collins, 2005), 21.

Into the Wonder

My path to Oxford was as magical as entering Narnia through the wardrobe. Fantasy novelist Stephen Lawhead, my living literary hero, invited me to stay in his Oxford home, The Cairn, and explore the haunts of my favorite deceased author, C.S. Lewis.

I walked through The Kilns, Lewis' Oxford home, and visualized the professor drinking evening tea by the fire. For 33 years of his life, he viewed the enchanting woodland from his upstairs writing desk or smoked his pipe in the garden. I half expected Lewis to walk around a corner and extend his hand in a warm greeting.

A powerful sense of Lewis' presence continued alongside me as I strolled into the woodlands to sit on his favorite brick bench overlooking a small pond. When it was warm enough, he used to swim here. Might this woodland hold the original doorway to Narnia?

Lewis died in The Kilns on November 22, 1963, the same day President John F. Kennedy was assassinated and Adolphus Huxley died.

Headington Quarry, the location of Holy Trinity Church, Lewis' house of worship, is a 20-minute stroll from The Kilns. The day I visited, an excitable and silver-haired church warden in his 70s, who remembered the middle-aged Lewis when he was a young man, giggled as he told me how Lewis came up with the idea of *The Screwtape Letters*. Lewis had been daydreaming during a particularly dull sermon when the story hit. He rushed out of the church before the service ended, the hefty church door slamming loudly behind him, to capture his thoughts on paper. Jack, as he was known to his friends, and Warnie, his brother, always sat in the same pew next to the pillar. The epitaph on Lewis' white gravestone is etched with the final line from King Lear, "Men must endure their going hence."[9]

Back in Oxford, I looked from St. Mary's Hightower, observing a bookish city frozen in time through its architecture, tradition, and attitude. Her thoroughfares were jammed with tourists while her patch-like college cloisters sat empty. When the Augustinian brothers opened a training house for clergy in the

---

9 William Shakespeare, *King Lear* (New York: Simon and Schuster, 1606), 251.

late 1100s, settling in one of Alfred the Great's fortified villages, they never imagined that there would be more writers per square foot in Oxford than in any other place on the planet.

From the top of the tower, I eyed the primary spot on my Oxford agenda, the exquisite Magdalen College. Lewis, who held an academic position there for 29 years, called Magdalen beautiful beyond compare. As I entered the gates, into the grand cloister Lewis looked upon while teaching his students, I was instructed by a local that the school is appropriately pronounced "MAHD-lin."

Bordered by the Cherwell River and home to a herd of roe deer, Magdalen was enchanting. From the Fellows' Garden to the medieval cloister, the college was an easy setting to stir the imagination of the beloved writer. Magdalen was not just Lewis' place of employment; it was his little Eden.

Lewis' teaching chambers were where The Inklings met for decades on Thursday nights to read aloud their poems, essays, and various writings. The routine was always the same: Warren brewed a pot of stout tea, the smokers lit their pipes, and Lewis would say, "Well, has nobody got anything to read to us?"

I finished my tea in The Eagle and The Child after reading a letter Lewis wrote to an American in 1953. I felt like he was writing to me. "Poor boob!- he thought his mind was his own! Never his own until he makes it Christ's: up till then merely a result of heredity, environment, and the state of his digestion. I become my own only when I give myself to Another."[10]

I bowed my head and prayed a prayer of thanksgiving for the life of C.S. Lewis, the man who spurred me to enter into a holy curiosity.

---

10 Walter Hooper, *The Collected Letters of C. S. Lewis, Volume III, Narnia, Cambridge and Joy* (New York: Harper Collins, 2007), 348.

Chapter 11

Mona Lisa Smile

One evening, while leading the home fellowship, I was called outside to help with a peculiar situation. Karla and Tina, two sisters who attended the gathering, had brought a nineteen-year-old with them who lived in their apartments. When I walked out to the street, I saw a red-haired Amazon woman in a white sweat suit making an awful racket as she jumped up and down on the roof of a car. She was a bit intoxicated and a lot angry. Karla had revealed to Cheryl at the last minute that she had arrived at a Bible study. Cheryl had barely survived a physically abusive home and a spiritually abusive church. That did not go over well.

I laughed when I saw her.

"What the heck am I supposed to do?" I asked the sisters. I walked over to her and smiled. "Hey, you. There's a trampoline in the backyard. You'll get a lot more air on that than on the roof of that Toyota."

She gave me a Mona Lisa smile, crawled off the car, and followed me into the house. By the end of the evening, Cheryl had twenty people surrounding her, showering her with compassion and prayer. The home fellowship showed her more love in one hour than she'd experienced most of her life. When I hugged her before she left, I thought I had found someone to rescue. In the end, she saved me.

Our art teacher set a canvas reproduction of the Mona Lisa in front of the class. The students in Webster Middle School yawned in unison. "Who is the artist behind this painting?" she asked. After a few guesses, one young lady shouted Leonardo da Vinci. Our teacher told us the story behind Mona Lisa's popularity; however, if you stared at that tiny smile on Mona Lisa's face, you could almost hear her whisper, "I'll never tell."

She has been beloved throughout history, with most of her enthusiasts unaware of her humble beginnings. Art historians debate her origin. Leonardo da Vinci started his artistic masterpiece in the fall of 1503. Though she was an amalgamation of several women in da Vinci's life, the subject of his painting was modeled after Lisa del Giocondo, the wife of his next-door neighbor in Florence. One story tells of a wealthy couple who, seeing the genesis of the work in his studio, commissioned da Vinci to finish the painting for their collection.

Over the next four years, da Vinci became obsessive. He reworked and layered the wood she was painted upon weekly, month after month, year after year. The artist recorded laboring over ten thousand hours into the Mona Lisa. And the more he gave to her, the more he fell in love.

As her unveiling approached, da Vinci was muddled in his emotions. He was obligated to hand her over, but his heart longed to keep and continue to perfect his painting. When the couple stood before her, after staring intently at the Mona Lisa, they shook their heads, dissatisfied with what they had waited years to attain. She was nothing like what they had imagined. Refusing to pay, they departed da Vinci's studio discontented and empty-handed. In their ignorance and bloated with their preconceived ideas of beauty, they were blinded to the masterpiece staring back at them. Leonardo da Vinci was disappointed by the loss of income but relieved that the Mona Lisa was his. She stayed in his studio for the next ten years as he continued almost imperceptible improvements on the piece.

In 1516, Francis I, monarch of France, invited Leonardo da Vinci to visit his court. He brought his beloved painting and several other pieces to showcase before the king. When the Mona Lisa was uncovered, King Francis stood smitten. He recognized he was face to face with artistic genius, and his heart was captive to the wonder of da Vinci's masterpiece. Leonardo da Vinci was given the highest honors possible. The king invited him to come to France under his generous patronage. He was given a castle, a lifetime pension, and four thousand pieces of gold. The only catch was that the Mona Lisa became the king's property upon da Vinci's death.

Leonardo da Vinci stopped working on his beloved portrait in 1517, a paralyzed hand preventing him from further artistic improvements. He never considered her a finished work. Today the Mona Lisa is owned by the citizens of France, viewed worldwide as a priceless masterpiece. She is the most famous painting in the history of mankind.

I was now her newest admirer. I was taken with a facsimile, a reflection of her beauty. What I wanted was to see her face to face.

Cheryl was unlike anyone I had ever met. Our purely platonic friendship skyrocketed. We talked whenever we could steal away for a phone call or for a few minutes when we met after church. We chatted about everything: our families, our struggles, our faith, our doubts, our friends, and our dreams for the future.

As our friendship matured, dating Cheryl did not enter my thoughts. She was a 6-foot tall, fair-skinned, brown-eyed, red-headed force of nature. Cheryl commanded the room when she entered, booed my good jokes, laughed like a drunken sailor at my bad jokes, challenged me often, and had a short fuse. This made her safe. She was not the girl I wanted to marry. I did not need the distraction of a girlfriend.

During Christmas of 1986, I visited my dad and Mariette in New Jersey. Cheryl and I did not talk for two weeks. I shook as though I had seen Marley's ghost when I realized, on Christmas evening, that I wanted her sitting near me drinking hot chocolate and watching *It's a Wonderful Life*. She had penetrated my guarded heart. I shooed the thoughts out of my mind and went back to the consternation of George Bailey.

I succumbed to my love for Cheryl in the middle of a fight.

Spring semester was in full bloom. Borrowing a car from a classmate, I created an excuse to visit her on Valentine's Day.

After her bad day at work, my surprise visit was the last thing she wanted, so she asked me to leave. I was on edge. Filled with angst about college, my family, and mounting financial pressures, I picked a fight. Cheryl was impenetrable. She called me out for the drama I was stirring. My emotional boiler exploded. Never losing her cool, she listened to my ranting until I was worn out. Once I was out of words, she gently spoke into my pain. We talked for hours. Late into the evening, I apologized. I was determined to be a better man, a better friend, and a better Christ-follower.

As I drove back to my dorm, I was gut punched. Cheryl loved me authentically enough not to take my crap. She was willing to shipwreck our friendship to speak honestly with me. A wrestling match with my self-imposed emotional boundaries was in full swing. I was not looking for love, but it felt as if love was looking for me.

There was a facet of wonder that, up to that point, I had not experienced. Longing to be face to face with Jesus, I wanted to know Him. The word in Hebrew for that type of intimacy is *yada*. "Be still and know (*yada*) that I am God" (Psalms 46:10 NIV). The word *yada* is used for the most profound sense of relationship one being can have with another when two worlds come together, opening up the possibility for a whole new world. The wonder of knowing God face to face flows through a deep intimacy with a life partner. As you journey with a partner, you develop a profound sense of who they are and, in turn, who God is.

After a week and a half of wrestling, I no longer denied my heart. Cheryl was nothing I was looking for, but she was everything I longed for and everything I needed. The question remained; did she feel the same about me?

Cheryl picked me up from work the following Wednesday to bring me to church. I asked her to drive to a park where I blurted out my love for her as smoothly as a Mac truck smashing into a brick wall. She looked at me briefly, started the car, and drove. Her silence said it all. I had freaked out my best friend. Why had I opened my big mouth?

As we approached the church, she turned and said, "I love you, too." It took another week, but as we said goodnight on the stoop outside her apartment, she lost patience with my shyness and kissed me. I wish I could say I floated down the stairs. I stumbled down, barely catching myself, drunk with love. She was my first love, and I wanted her to be my only love. Three weeks later, I asked Cheryl to be my bride.

On June 23, 1988, a few weeks after I graduated, we stood at the altar of a small church for our no-frills wedding. Cheryl Garver became Cheryl Small, and I became the happiest man on the planet as I was united with God's most precious gift.

The Louvre, Paris - June 2010

I hired Pierre to take Cheryl and me to the world's most famous art museum, the Louvre. Pierre and I met at a picture-perfect café on the Seine overlooking the majestic Notre Dame Cathedral. At 72, Pierre, a Paris guide for fifty years, sipped a cappuccino, radiating an unflappable coolness. A neatly trimmed goatee framed a visage chiseled out of curiosity and grit. His eyes were lit with an intensity of one carrying the majesty of two millennia of French history. I hung on to his words, jealous of his smart tweed jacket and boundless enthusiasm, wondering if I would be leading groups with the same smoldering intensity when I was Pierre's age.

Pierre was no ordinary guide. He spent our first hour educating us about art composition, the use of light and darkness, the purposefulness of style, stroke techniques, and a hundred other artistic details. Through his eyes, we started to appreciate art in a different light. We learned the subtle nuances of marble in Michelangelo's *Twin Slaves*. We were riveted by the world's finest paintings, some of which span thirty feet long. *Liberty*, *The Raft of Medusa* by Gericault, and the *Emmaus Pilgrims* by Tintoret are all works of intricate exquisiteness. *Winged Victory*, a sculpture from 190 B.C., hushed all who passed beneath. Her majesty, aura, and ascendancy made me dizzy. Circumventing the *Venus de Milo*,

I breathed in unpolluted sensuality. But as lovely as all of these works of art, I desired only "her" eyes.

I worked my way through a human labyrinth to reach her. The crowd delicately shoved one another, moving near the little red velvet ropes, magically holding back the tidal wave of tourists. Most who had come to see her wanted a quick click of their cameras to prove, on social media, they had come as close to her as possible.

A strange phenomenon occurred when I moved to the ropes, looking intently at the Mona Lisa. We often think of a painting as immobile and static, but as I gazed, the background vibrated. The winding path on her left tugged at my senses like a doorway into her world. The stream on her right flowed like the passage of time. The petrified mountains in the background crumbled as the weight of time patiently wore them away. Yet she remained frozen, a three-dimensional figure, epochs unbroken on her brow. I was no longer observing a painting. Somehow, Mona Lisa was watching me. The observer became the observed. Time was interrupted. She was full of motion, even as the world around me screeched to a halt.

Suppose you gathered the elements used for creating the Mona Lisa—the wood, brushes, oils, and paints—and break them down into today's prices. In that case, you'd have $70 dollars of raw material. Yet, the Mona Lisa is priceless. What makes her invaluable? Her fame? The style of art? Her age? The time it took for her creation? All those things are the fruit of the finished product. The one element separating the Mona Lisa from all other art is the touch of the master, Leonardo da Vinci.

My face-to-face relationship with Cheryl reflected my connection with the Creator. As I began to know Cheryl, first as my best friend, then as my fiancé, and finally as my bride, I saw the double edge of humanity: the blatant inadequacies of creatures formed from mud and the masterpieces we are because of the breath of God residing within us. We are a jumbled mixture of dirt and dust, yet we can reach the heavens. Is it any wonder Christ-followers are called the Bride of Christ?

Cheryl and I bring out the worst and the best in each other. There is no hiding our faults, scars, blood, or tears. She is my

Mona Lisa, with her soft smile and radiant eyes. When I look at her, the world around me swirls to life. Sometimes we both feel of little value, yet we remind each other we are touched by the hand of God, the Master of All, and we are priceless no matter what our minds or the world may tell us. We were in His heart and a part of His canvas before we were conceived. Paul's correspondence to the Ephesians contains my favorite verse of his letters: "For we are God's masterpiece, created in Christ Jesus for great adventures, which God prepared for us before the creation of the universe" (Ephesians 2:10). We are His masterpiece, and He is in love. He has made us both seekers of wonder and wonders in ourselves.

"Reaching the ground floor, I slogged through a maze of strewn furniture and metal shelves now bent like melted wax." (San Francisco October 17, 1989)

"In late spring, its large white flowers, miniature porcelain trumpets, bloom under the moon's light." (Corinth, Texas 2021)

"I sat in the back of a dusty truck and watched a mother lion."
(Maasai Mara, Kenya October 2010 by Jason Wendel)

"We shared an emotional breakfast with a chieftain." (Peru 2007)

"Percy took us to our home on the river the following day: a baby blue, forty-foot-long, eight-foot-wide canoe named the Valiente." (Peru 2007)

"I had entered St. Faith's Chapel." (Westminster Abbey London 2010)

"A people whose infectious acceptance was an invitation to partake of their community on a deeper level." (Fiji 2006)

"Tonight, me lords and ladies, we will be guests at the Tower Castle." (Wales 2002)

"I grabbed a magenta crayon and drew." (1972)

"Looking over those cliffs was like staring into the eyes of God." (May 2019)

"I walked through The Kilns, Lewis' Oxford home." (Oxford, England July 2011)

"I became the happiest man on the planet." (June 23, 1988)

"I tapped the top of the cobra's hooded head with my lips." (Jaipur, India September 2014)

"I saw a pink heart hanging off my neck by a balloon ribbon." (2003)

Chapter 12

Snake Charmer

Jaipur, India - September 2014

Jaipur, which is India's commanding trading center, is known as the Pink City. Founded in the 17th century, the rulers of Jaipur commissioned exceptionally advanced architecture, creating a city that was the darling of British-ruled India. To accentuate the renowned hospitality of Jaipur, Maharaja Ram Singh had the entire city painted pink in 1876 to welcome the Prince of Wales and Queen Victoria for their royal visit. On the horizon, Jaipur appeared as a dreamland fading in and out of the rising sun.

My day in Jaipur started on the back of a massive elephant that lumbered up the steep, flat-stoned road leading to the impregnable gates of Jaigarh Fort built atop the Chal Ka Teela, the Mound of Eagles. The fort, never overtaken in battle, holds 6,000 Indian soldiers and the ghosts of a 100,000 others. Jaigarh blazes military might, yet the pinkness of it all radiates a peaceful ambiance.

Entering the fortress, I meandered through ever-downward steps before approaching a broad set of stairs. Halfway down the staircase, on a generous terrace, a crowd gathered around a street performance. Though I could not see what was happening, I heard the crowd's gasps and sighs swaying with a whining whistle. Curious, I broke through the throng to three turbaned men sitting in a circle around several baskets.

The oldest, gray-bearded and wafer thin in his red silk shirt and blue *dhotis*, the billowing trousers one sees throughout India, was whaling on a *pungi*, a strange flute akin to an elementary school recorder with an onion-like bulge at the top. A jet-black hooded cobra materialized out of a basket and stood erect, its eyes aimed at the old man's face. Every so often, to the crowd's gasps, the snake struck out at the *pungi* when it came too close. I was transfixed as I watched snake handling, striking cobras, and the old man kissing the top of a standing snake. When it was over, the offering basket in front of the three men was ripe with rupees. Charming snakes was their show. Charming people was their real trick.

When the crowd dissolved, the three snake charmers took a teatime. I asked if I might join them. I told them I loved snake wrangling and had a million questions about their profession. Amused, the youngest, who spoke English, wagged his head yes, inviting me to sit on the throw rug containing three baskets, each holding a deadly cobra. For half an hour, I peppered them with questions, curious about an ancient practice that is, in many ways, a dying profession.

Snake charmers emerged from the ancient, semi-nomadic Hindu Sapera caste of North India. *Sap*, in the Punjabi language, means snake. Their semi-secret vocation has been passed down from father to son for centuries. The origin of the practice is obscured by time. Still, it is thought by many that the Sapera were worshipers of the sacred Nagas, half-serpent/half-human creatures residing in the Netherworld. These semi-divine Nagas controlled all serpents on the earth's surface, wielding them as both bearers of prosperity and harbingers of death.

Any Sapera with the gift of snake handling became a healer, especially of snake bites, a major cause of death throughout the Indian subcontinent. Safely removing snakes that had taken up residence in homes was a common practice for the charmers. In India, it is illegal to kill a cobra. The charmer is an expert at safely removing the unwanted spirit from a family's dwelling.

Today, although snake charming is outlawed, the fading community of Sapera continues to have a vital role in Indian society. A cobra remains show-worthy for about four days. Eventually, they grow numb to the threat, sluggish from hunger, and bored. Snake charmers release their snakes every few days and hunt for their next performers. A newly caught cobra is milked for its venom, which is sold to the medical industry for vital anti-venom production. Not only does the snake charmer make a living off the venom he collects, but he's also rendered the snake venom-less for 12 to 15 days.

After its brief few days in the basket, the snake will stay in the care of the snake charmer for two weeks until it can hunt and defend itself in the wild. For the snake charmer, there is always the danger of becoming too relaxed and getting bit by a venomous cobra. Still, over the years, those in the clan have injected themselves with the tiniest doses of venom, building up their natural immunity to the poison. They become conditioned to the toxin. It is a rare incident when a snake charmer dies from a snakebite.

My short time with the snake charmers was enlightening. As my interview ended, the young man said it was my turn to entertain them. Before I could protest, he placed his bright red turban on my head and a heavy basket in my hands. Holding up the *pungi*, he started to play the eerie snake-charming music. The top was lifted off the basket, allowing a cobra to dramatically emerge, thankfully facing opposite my face, which was only inches away, and toward the swaying *pungi*.

The oldest gentleman in the group signaled me. The cost of my interview was to kiss the cobra on the top of the head. He laughed as my eyes widened. With music playing intensely, the English speaker wagged his head, telling me it would be all right. Even though the cobra was freshly milked and venomless, it did not lessen my fear of being bitten in the face. Not wanting to disrespect these men who had been so generous with their secrets, I cautiously leaned down, and with baby-kiss gentleness, I tapped the top of the cobra's hooded head with my lips. The men cheered and laughed, happy with their foreign recruit.

I continued exploring the fort, thinking back to 25 years earlier when I was hired onto the church staff of one of America's most infamous snake charmers, the charismatic televangelist Robert Tilton. Suddenly, kissing a cobra seemed tame in comparison.

My first exposure to Word of Faith Family Church came through the home fellowship group my senior year. Youth with a Vision (YWAV), a weekly gathering of several hundred teenagers, was a combo rock concert, youth rally, game show, comedy club, and drama performance. Everything rotated around a healthy dose of Jesus and the encouragement to live daring and meaningful lives. This was the best show in town for Jesus-freak teens. YWAV was housed in an office complex a couple blocks from the popular Dallas megachurch. While YWAV was dynamic, diverse, and thriving as a youth faith community, Word of Faith had evolved into something different, even in the history of American Christianity. This is where I took up my college internship.

The personality driving WOF into the Christian stratosphere was Robert Tilton. Tilton had an intense, charismatic conversion experience in his early twenties. Sensing a call from God and exhibiting a flare for the dramatic, Tilton christened himself a healing evangelist overflowing with the gifts of the Holy Spirit. Convinced of his mission, he packed up his family and honed his preaching in small churches and tent revivals across Texas and Oklahoma for a couple of years.

In 1976, after shaping and refining his hybrid-Pentecostal/prosperity religious beliefs on the road, Tilton rented a warehouse in central Dallas that became the home base for his new Word of Faith Family Church. He started a local television program called *Daystar*. This expanded Tilton's spiritual influence, featuring his fiery and persuasive personality.

Over the next ten years, the church multiplied at an astounding rate, attracting seekers from every part of the Dallas-Fort Worth area, many spiritually fatigued from what they considered a dull, lifeless Christianity. Black, Caucasian, Hispanic, Asian, wealthy, poor, and middle-class; people from every conceivable background filled up the church. Tilton's evolving message of health, spiritual warfare against the devil, and abundant prosperity, along with a healthy dose of laying on of hands for healing and speaking in tongues, talked to the affluent who were spiritually hollow within their wealth and the disenfranchised who longed for financial freedom, physical healing, or emotional restoration.

With all its flaws, Word of Faith was one of America's most diverse churches. Both men and women had equal status with God and could share God's anointing. No matter your gender, you could preach, teach, lead, and be a part of God's Kingdom at every level.

The church bought prime Dallas property at the meeting point of two major highways. A 4,000-member sanctuary was constructed and instantly filled. Three miles up the road, a local grain tower along I-35 was painted with a rainbow background and the gargantuan words: VISIT WORD OF FAITH THIS SUNDAY. PASTOR ROBERT TILTON.

While WOF was becoming one of the first megachurches in America, Tilton's television ambitions faltered. His *Daystar* show hadn't moved beyond Dallas viewership. Pastor Bob was confident there was greatness within him beyond his current viewing audience. Tilton launched his *Success-N-Life* television show in 1981 with a $1 million loan from a local bank. *Success-N-Life* was the first of its kind, an hour-long religious infomercial for the prosperity gospel.

Here is an overly simplistic yet accurate definition of the prosperity gospel: Sickness, poverty, and tribulations in life are either (a) caused by sin or (b) caused by demonic attacks. The way a person finds the freedom, prosperity, peace, joy, and healing that Jesus died to give us is to make a vow to God's prophet (also known as buying your way out of your troubles). Your offerings, especially those beyond your means, prove that God sees your faith.

The prosperity gospel was a small set of biblical paradigms twisted to a particular interpretation, then contextualized and repackaged to modern tastes, distorted to meet fundamental philosophical or emotional needs, then warped into a foundational doctrinal belief. Robert Tilton perfected and propagated his message through *Success-N-Life*. He became an international spiritual snake charmer who wanted to help you rid your home and body of demons and bring healing to anyone willing to pay.

At its high point, *Success-N-Life* was broadcast daily in every major market in the U.S. Hundreds of hours of broadcast television brought in more than $80 million a year in donations. Tilton's on-air antics, like bursting into spontaneous tongues, speaking specific words of knowledge to his home audience, and wacky facial expressions that looked like euphoria-induced seizures, certainly got him noticed. "Put your hand on the TV and let me pray over you!" or "Begone, you devils of poverty and doubt!" were everyday occurrences on his show.

During a short stint in college, I became a *Success-N-Life* phone counselor. A phone bank staffed by dozens of minimum wage "prayer partners" answered those calling for prayer as they watched *Success-N-Life*. These phone counselors, many sincere church members, prayed for the callers, prompted them to speak in tongues, and asked what dollar amount they believed God had asked them to vow to the prophet. Once the caller told the monetary amount they "believed" God put upon their heart to set them free from whatever hardship they were facing, they were added to a mailing list, along with millions of others.

Tilton's mailings became his optimum tool for drawing in the big bucks. There were posters covered with his giant face in squinting prayer and outlined in Scripture verses proclaiming prosperity. You might receive holy oil from Jerusalem, a nickel to send back as a seed for faith, prayer cloths prayed over by Tilton, carefully marked envelopes for ever-increasing vows, and even a re-creation of the widow's mite from the Bible. These tacky items were created to draw viewers into the world of Robert Tilton. The titles of his self-help books, *The Power to Create Wealth, How to Pay Your Bills Supernaturally, How to Be Rich and Have Everything You Ever Wanted*, painted a clear picture of his core message: give to God until it hurts, and whatever you want or desire shall be given back to you pressed down, shaken together, and running over.

Southwest Guatemala - July 1993

I've traveled to every country in Central America. Guatemala is my favorite. There are mountain villages where Western influence remains subservient to indigenous tradition. In these villages, one can sense the essence of ancient people. The old stories remain a part of the daily fabric preventing the modern world from completely escaping the past. Though I find these fading sites charming, they sometimes hold on to superstition that, when manipulated, can hold the locals under a cloud of fear. One town I came across lived under a startling superstitious haze.

My curiosity was piqued while walking on the mud-splattered roads of a non-descript farming town in the mountains of western Guatemala. I came across a disturbing strawman on the porch of a home at the edge of town. The portico was adorned like a small chapel; burning candles, waterlogged icons of Catholic saints, and scrawled prayer requests tacked to the wall around the strawman.

Several years earlier, a lame man had sat at the gates of this village greeting all who entered. His name was Maximone. His physical condition kept him from manual labor in the surrounding fields, but his affliction helped him develop a keen ability to read faces and charm people. Maximone was known for his wisdom and spiritual musings, a shrewd judge of the cases people asked him to settle.

As the farmers left in the morning for the surrounding countryside, Maximone shouted words of blessings. During the day, the town's women went to him for advice, to share their sufferings, or to speak local gossip. He listened with an empathetic ear and a lecherous heart, entering into multiple affairs with the farmers' wives. Over time, the men discovered Maximone's trysts.

One festival night, a drunken gathering of farmers turned into a raging crowd of jealous husbands. A mob stormed Maximone's house, dragging him to the city square. The men hacked Maximone to pieces with machetes while the village women watched, screaming in horror. The village's adult population was paraded past his massacred remains as a warning of the folly of adultery.

As the townspeople passed Maximone's mutilated corpse, strange "miracles" began manifesting. Over the next few weeks, healings, the sense of a spiritual presence, and visions were recorded. Rumors started that those who murdered the man were cursed, and the spirits that aided Maximone were looking for ret-

Into the Wonder

ribution. A local witch doctor whose home rested by the front gates where Maximone used to sit was inspired by the tales of the miraculous. He said he had an answer to the curse.

A few weeks after the murder, the witch doctor created a disturbingly accurate strawman, using Maximone's clothes on a paper mâché figure, and sat him in a chair outside his home. Travelers couldn't enter or depart the village without seeing this ragged representation. The witch doctor proclaimed the only way to hold off any devilish payback or to obtain worldly blessings was to honor the strawman.

People still visit the ghoulish, makeshift chapel and place money into its jacket pockets as offerings. The highest offering one brought to Maximone was purchased from the witch doctor through a little window on the porch. I watched a man tremble as he reached through the window, buying a soda bottle filled with yellowish homemade moonshine. He took the bottle, held it to the mouth of the figure, and poured it until it was empty. A plastic tube inside the strawman's mouth directed the liquid into another bottle to be sold to a new anxious seeker.

A religion built on fear and superstition of a literal strawman, where people tried to pay their way out of the torment of demons or to buy the blessing of a spirit, hit a little too close to home.

Like the snake-charmers of India or the strawman of Guatemala, Robert Tilton not only produced a fascinating show that drew in millions, but he proclaimed himself a prophet who could drive away the demonic forces hounding God's children, stealing from their purses, corrupting their bodies, and clouding their minds. When the performance was over, he sold the venom of doubt and fear he collected from his audience, and his basket was filled with their offerings. For the right amount of money, God would drive those serpents from your home through the prayers of the charmer/prophet.

Robert Tilton was the man I was working for as a newly ordained minister. You may ask, along with other friends and family during those years, how people become entangled in a crazy religious system. In many ways, WOF was, separate from the growing insanity of *Success-N-Life,* a loving and accepting community. The members of WOF were sincere, caring, down-to-earth people looking for relief from the pains and trials of life.

For my first few years, it was easy to compartmentalize my calling and spiritual journey from where I was serving. But in reality, little doses of the prosperity teachings I was exposed to over several years inoculated me from the poison. Like everyone else, I made vows, some in the hundreds of dollars, desperate for God's favor. Eventually, the church and *Success-N-Life gap* were so wide they barely crossed paths. The pastoral office where I worked was like any megachurch office except for the 85% of the building housing hundreds of employees keeping the *Success-N-Life* money-making machine cranking.

I was employed at WOF from 1989 – 1993. Even though the events of those five years were bizarre, I don't regret my time there. It's where I learned to seek truth and grow in my humanity and spirituality. None of my growth had to do with the wacky musings of Robert Tilton.

Donald Miller, in his book *Blue Like Jazz* writes, "At the end of the day, when I am lying in bed and I know that the chances of any of our theology being exactly right are a million to one, I need to know that God has things figured out, that if my math is wrong, we are still going to be okay. And wonder is that feeling we get when we let go of our silly answers, our mapped-out rules that we want God to follow. I don't think there is any better worship than wonder."[11]

The foundation carrying me through my years at WOF, the anchor holding my ship from sinking when so many others' faith was shipwrecked, was a handful of moments of wonder I clung to when the ocean raged around me. Those moments were the miracles that healed me from a world of pain I would soon experience.

---

11   Donald Miller, *Blue Like Jazz* (Nashville: Thomas Nelson, 2003), 206.

Chapter 13

Pink Paper Heart

London, England - June 2009

Sitting inside the tent that was lit with twinkling lights buzzing around us like a million snowflake-sized fairies, Coeli (pronounced Chay-lee), my oldest child, was soaring toward Neverland.

We were fortuitously in London at the same time as a revival of the beloved play *Peter Pan* in Kensington Gardens, the same grounds on which J.M. Barrie created tales of a magical boy who never wanted to grow up.

Coeli is the world's biggest *Peter Pan* fan. Her love for all things J.M. Barrie began when she, at age fourteen, read the book *Peter and Wendy* and became fixed in her love for the story. After the success of his novel featuring the origin story *Peter Pan*, *The Little White Bird*, Barrie created the stage play, *Peter Pan, or the Boy Who Wouldn't Grow Up*. The play's overwhelming success propelled the story into the collective consciousness of children worldwide.

Peter Pan is the quintessential story of every child's battle with the dark realities of adulthood that tries to smother their imagination and wonder. Children can swoop in and out of their imaginations unhindered, unafraid, unaware that life is any different than what they are experiencing. Watching the Darling children learn to fly, I wondered if I had forgotten how to fly. As Barrie wrote, "The moment you doubt whether you can fly, you cease forever to be able to do it."[12]

In 1991, Steven Spielberg directed *Hook*. In his continuation of Barrie's story, Peter Pan eventually left Neverland to be raised by an aging Wendy. Falling in love with her granddaughter Moira, Peter decided to grow up, becoming Peter Banning, Attorney at Law.

---

12 J.M. Barrie, Daniel O'Connor, Oliver Herford, *The Complete Adventures of Peter Pan and His Friends* (Musaicum Publishing, 2017), 112.

When Peter's children are kidnapped by Captain Hook, seeking revenge against his mortal enemy, Peter must return to Neverland to see if it is possible, as an adult who has long abandoned his sense of wonder and his joy for life, to regain what was lost.

Is it possible to regain the innate sense of wonder we possessed as children?

Cheryl and I had a plan for the first five years of our marriage. Once we were emotionally and financially established, we'd begin our family. We used the *rhythm method,* also known as the surefire pregnancy method. When Cheryl conceived nine months into our marriage, our five-year plan went down the tubes. We took it in stride, celebrating the pregnancy and getting ready for a new plan.

Morning sickness hit like a tidal wave. Thirty-one days into the pregnancy, nausea paralyzed Cheryl. If she ate, she threw up. If she walked, she threw up. If she talked, she threw up. If she watched TV, she threw up. If she breathed, she threw up. Over the next three months, she lost thirty-five pounds, was hospitalized twice, and lived in our darkened bedroom. By summer, Cheryl had started to regain her appetite in small doses. The worst was over, or so I thought.

In her last trimester, Cheryl gained back her strength. We snuggled in bed in the evenings while I read and talked to the baby, waiting for little kicks under my hand. When Cheryl's contractions started, we loaded the car on a freezing December evening and drove to the hospital. For 31 hours, Cheryl labored while I tried to comfort her, even though my insides were jello. While breathing through a contraction with her, Cheryl crushed my hand like a bionic woman. When I screamed louder than her, she gave me the stink eye, and I read her thoughts. *"You have no idea, little man."* I understood at that moment if men had to labor, the human race would've died out with Adam.

When Cheryl was whisked away to the O.R., I stood in front of an attentive anesthesiologist monitoring her pain levels.

Looking over the dividing sheet between Cheryl and our OB/GYN, I observed him cut into Cheryl's abdomen with a laser. Our little olive-skinned angel was lifted carefully from Cheryl's womb a minute later. The baby took her first breath while I struggled to breathe. Her cry cracked open a doorway into the heavens, and for a nanosecond, I was overwhelmed by the universal life force consuming the room. Coeli Michelle was the wonder of eternity. Her name, Coeli, is Latin for "gift from heaven." All I could do was weep at the wonder of her first squall.

Then, unfortunately, I looked down.

My eyes caught the doctor, uterus in his hand outside the abdomen, in mid-stitch. Feeling all the blood rush out of my head, I stared at the fleshy mass and garbled a few words, "Is that a deformed twin?" before the anesthesiologist caught me mid-faint.

I came to, looking up at Cheryl's scoffing eyes.

"Really, Shawn? A deformed twin?"

An hour later, in a dimly lit hospital room, I stared into a bassinet, bewitched by Coeli's face framed by two-mittened hands over her marshmallow cheeks. She looked like a little bear, a nickname she carried throughout childhood. Through scrunched lips, Coeli let out the faintest whimpering yelp. I picked her up like she was made of butterfly wings and eggshells. Rocking her, an invisible covenant sprang up. Attempting to put words to what was happening in my heart, I whispered prayers and promises over Coeli that I would try to be a better man, a more compassionate man, a more loving man, and the best daddy I could be. Her presence pried open the rusty, stubborn, and stunted parts of my heart.

To enter the world of a child you love is like diving into a waterfall of wonder. As Coeli grew, I watched her delight in "why" things are. I watched her long to make the world right. When she was six, a concerned kindergarten teacher told us Coeli went to the messy pile of shoes by the classroom door and lined them on the wall in order of size when all the other children were released to play centers.

Coeli loved bringing order out of chaos. Her classic childhood questions, "Why do we have a sun? Where do the stars come from? Why are some people mean? How do we breathe? Why did you and mommy fall in love? What happens when we die? Where does God live? What is love?" are clear signs of curiosity. Children are thrilled to find out the why of things. If we stop asking questions, we stymie wonder. Coeli reminded me of the simple wonders of the world and threw gasoline on the fires of my curiosity. As more children blessed our world, curiosity gained momentum in the Small household.

Kayla, our second born, came into the world with an explosion of red hair that made her look like a beautiful flower in bloom. From a young age, she displayed her emotions fearlessly and ferociously. She was the first in line, the one who rushed to the front, and the fastest to raise her hand when someone asked for a volunteer. One of her most potent giftings was her contagious enthusiasm for the present. She reminds us that one must live in the now to experience all life has to give you. Kayla was so tiny that when she clung to us for comfort, she was as light as a bug; thus, she was known amongst the Smalls as the Snuggle-Bug.

Hunter was a miracle child who came after Cheryl was told she'd never be able to have children again. His size earned him an instant nickname: Little Bit. Hunter discovered wonder through simple trust. When he was three, I gave him a red superhero cape. He zipped through the house beating up bad guys, saving stuffed animals, and performing feats of strength. It was not long before he took a giant leap off the top of the couch and landed on his face, knocking out a front baby tooth at the roots. It took every bit of willpower not to faint when I saw the blood. I picked him up and was surprised he was not crying. I sat him on the kitchen counter and asked him what had happened. Those trusting brown eyes looked me in the face.

"I was trying to fly like Superman."

Like all of our children, Hunter existed in a world of possibility. Children help us recapture a sense of amazement in tiny miracles we take for granted when the distractions of adulthood blind us. Children don't cling *to* wonder; they live *in* wonder.

Pink Paper Heart

There is a passage author Brennan Manning wrote about having a child's heart in *Prophets and Lovers: In Search of the Holy Spirit.*

"To become a little child again (as Jesus enjoined we must) is to recapture a sense of surprise, wonder, and vast delight in all of reality. Look at a child's face on Christmas morning as he enters the living room transformed by the midnight passage of Santa Claus. Or when he discovers the coin under the pillow or sees his first rainbow or sniffs his first rose. Few of us catch our breath at these things as we once did. The walk down the corridor of time has made us bigger and everything else smaller, less impressive. --- A truly balanced man retains a capacity for wonder and the willingness to express it in the very expression of his creaturehood, the spontaneous acknowledgement that he is a man and not a god, a being with limitations, who far from having embraced infinity is happily and hopelessly engulfed by it."[13]

Jesus compels us to become little children if we want to live in His Kingdom. Our capacity for wonder is the barometer to test how close we are to Jesus' bidding.

Sitting at my office desk, I looked through large windows past the thick oaks to the bump of a hill at the top of our gravel driveway. My favorite time of the day was about to commence. At 3:53 pm on the dot, Monday through Friday, Coeli walked down the driveway. Her only weight was a backpack full of chunky academic books.

Although she was 15, she maintained an uncomplicated outlook on life. Coeli guarded her childlike imagination as she grew into a beautiful, poised woman. Though many of her girlfriends were going gaga for romance and dating, Coeli remained neutral. When I asked her why she was uninterested, she said, "Dating is a nuisance. I'm too young to get involved in a silly relationship destined to end in heartbreak. There's plenty of time in the future

---

[13] Brennan Manning, *Prophets and Lovers: In Search of the Holy Spirit* (Dimension Books, 1985).

for romantic pursuits." As a protective dad, I was thankful for her dating philosophy.

Until Valentine's Day.

I worried about her feelings as she watched her friends receive roses, cute cards, and chocolate enchantments. I did not want her to feel the pain of not receiving a gift from an interested young man. Let's face it, we all love romance.

When the beeping of the bus caught my attention, I crossed my fingers and purposefully watched Coeli walk down the driveway. Her face was crinkled in deep contemplation. The front door opened, and I heard the familiar echo of her backpack landing on the wood floor.

"Hey, Bear! How was your day?"

The silence from across the house made me groan. The only reply was some rummaging around in the kitchen. Tapping away at my computer as a distraction, I determined to stay out of her space until she was ready.

A few impossibly long minutes passed when I felt her behind me. I did not turn around but waited for Coeli to speak. Something light fell over my head and onto my shoulders. I saw a pink heart hanging off my neck by a balloon ribbon. She slipped it over my head and hugged me from behind.

"I love you, Dad."

She knew I was caught off guard as I held the heart to examine it.

"What's this about?"

Her high school had a Valentine's Day tradition. Everyone was handed a cutout heart necklace when the students entered the school on February 14. The students were not allowed to utter a word until they gave the pink-ribboned or red-ribboned heart to the person they chose as their Valentine. The classrooms begin blissfully quiet, with only the teachers talking. Students then scurry through the halls between classes or at lunch looking for that special someone. Many want to find their Valentine so they can reveal a silent crush. Most want to get back to their normal gabbing. This flurry of silence doesn't let up until the afternoon pep rally.

The boy and girl with the most hearts around his or her neck are crowned Valentine King and Queen, each winning a prize.

Seeing my confusion, Coeli got face to face with me. Grabbing my cheeks in her hands, she answered, "Dad, I've been silent all day until now when I put the heart around your neck. Until I give my heart to the man of my dreams, you'll have my heart."

After a quick peck on the cheek, she ran out of the room while I sat wrecked. My heart exploded in love, and tears filled my lap. In that moment, Coeli could have asked for a car, and I would have said, "What kind?" All she wanted was my love. All I wanted was her heart; now I had a pink paper heart on a string to prove it.

Sitting at my desk, I understood a wondrous truth—an insight into God's longing for my love and heart. The paper heart, which sat in my office until Coeli's wedding day, reminded me there is nothing more wondrous than a child's love for his or her parents. Nothing is more astonishing to the Creator when one of us whispers, "Abba, Father. I belong to You." All wonder in the universe flows out of God's love for us.

Wonder as big as the universe can rest upon a pink paper heart.

Chapter 14

Yengo

There are a handful of people we befriend who affect the trajectory of our lives. Looking back, we can testify that their presence profoundly altered our lives. Mike Yengo was one of those people in my life.

In 1990, I was introduced to a missionary unlike anyone I'd ever met. Mike stood five feet, seven inches, with the long muscular arms and the deep chest of a competitive gymnast. The first thing you noticed about Mike was the twinkle in his eyes. Mike, the son of a first-generation Eastern European immigrant, had a rough childhood. Mike's mother, who had been abandoned by her husband, did what she needed to do for herself and her son to survive. This meant Mike was often caring for himself while she worked long hours. As a kid, Mike's stubbornness, anger, and fearlessness were unhealthy. He spun out of control in his late teens. Outside of the pleasures of his high school theater program, Mike was unhappy.

During a drug bender shortly after graduating, with his life hanging in the balance, Mike experienced a supernatural vision. Jesus laid hands on Mike's head, freeing him from his addictions. He told Mike his freedom did not come without a price. In the vision, Christ commissioned him to take His message of love and hope to tough places and challenging people. Mike was not religious, so this vision was unprecedented. Mike and others who knew him well said his addictions ended after two weeks of fierce detox.

From that point forward, Mike threw his energy into following the commission he'd been given. After he raised funds, Mike hopped on a plane to Paris where he trained at the Marcel Marceau School of Mimodrama. He was determined to utilize the theatrical arts to present the Gospel.

Once Mike was back stateside, he volunteered with a mission organization performing a cheesy, yet effective, cross-cultural street play, *A Tale of Two Kingdoms*. The short production was a dramatized children's tale using mime and dance performed to a musical soundtrack. Once the good versus evil drama was finished, a team member shared an evangelical message, often through a translator.

Mike led teams to several countries, but he grew tired of the distinctly Americanized Christian message presented to what the mission organization called "poor third-world citizens." The teams walked away excited about all the "saved" people but ignored the extreme physical needs of those with whom they shared their message. Mike's pointed and passionate differences with his superiors about the issue of faith without work led to him launching out on his own.

Though he continued to perform *A Tale of Two Kingdoms*, he sought ways to meet the practical needs of those for whom they performed. Mike raised funds, trained teams, and led trips to more than thirty nations over the next six years. His teams joined medical campaigns in Eastern Europe, helped rice farmers harvest in Thailand, worked in underdeveloped schools in Central America, and served as relief workers after a hurricane in the Philippines.

I met Mike through one of my Word of Faith youth leaders. I liked him immediately. We bonded over *Star Trek, Les Misérables*, and youth ministry. Mike saw Jesus in everyone and knew how to reach a person in pain. This was tempered by his internal pains, from which he had found healing.

We had a rhythm to our friendship. We hung out whenever he was between trips as he decompressed by telling me the story of his latest excursion. His tales were riveting. I volunteered to author his monthly newsletter, my first official writing gig. Mike's adventures caused me to long for the lost ark I'd been seeking since I was 13. At 22, I hadn't traveled outside of the United States. I had buried my desire for foreign exploration under the responsibility of marriage, fatherhood, and the rigors of ministry.

Mike Yengo helped unbury those longings. I wanted to visit other countries, explore new cultures, and meet people different from me. During our late-night conversations, I asked Mike how he'd obtained the courage to travel to dangerous places. I wanted to understand his ability to dive into foreign cultures, potentially risking his own skin so that he might share the love of Christ. Staring at me with his bright eyes, he quoted Helen Keller.

"Security is mostly a superstition. It does not exist in nature, nor do the children of men as a whole experience it….Avoiding danger is no safer in the long run than outright exposure….Life is either a daring adventure or nothing."[14]

Less than a year later, I would find myself in the middle of a daring adventure with Mike leading the charge.

Israel - October 1991

I was invited to go to Israel for my first trip out of the United States. Reading about the places where Jesus, Moses, King David, and Abraham had walked left the biblical story settings to my imagination. I jumped at the opportunity to pilgrimage to the Holy Land, and I invited Mike to join me.

We entered the ancient city of Jerusalem side by side. When we passed under the shadow of the Lion's Gate, my head swirled as five thousand years of history converged in one place. Ironically, the oldest town I'd visited before Jerusalem had been 400-year-old Salem, Massachusetts. Foreign travel can be existential dynamite, obliterating preconceived ideas and allowing the traveler to reconstruct an expanded worldview. This was the case for me as I explored Israel.

I mimicked Mike, who absorbed every second and experience with zeal. He asked the locals a million questions. I gained inside information that cut through the tourist trappings and guided my inquiring spirit to hidden gems. Tourists tend to surround themselves with an invisible shield, staying just out of arm's-length from the infection of foreign ideas. They keep a death grip on their points of view, interpreting their surroundings by their ethics, philosophy, politics, or theology. In Israel, Mike taught me to

---

14 Helen Keller, *The Open Door* (New York: Doubleday Publishing, 1957), 17,

Into the Wonder

let go of my cultural agenda and travel like a pilgrim, with open eyes, a humble head, and a willing heart.

Within an hour of entering the City of David, we were at the Wailing Wall, the original foundation of Solomon's Temple, where pilgrims come from around the world to stand, sway, and pray to the God of Israel. Mike quietly spoke with an elderly Jewish couple who had survived Auschwitz. As they shared the story of their imprisonment, Mike gingerly touched the blue-gray numbered tattoos on their arms, scars of the horror they survived. Mike started to cry. The couple threw their arms around him and wept with him. I walked to the Wailing Wall, closed my eyes, and swayed in place. My lips moved in silent prayer.

"Lord of All, teach me to love like that; to feel like that; to be a pilgrim who travels the earth loving people with Your heart, seeing people with Your eyes, serving people with Your compassion."

I filled an entire journal with thoughts, sketches, descriptions, and history from my time in the Holy Land. There were moments of visceral delight, like entering the Dead Sea, the lowest spot of land on the planet. The waters, chock full of a massive concentration of salt, sulfur, magnesium, and minerals, produce buoyancy, allowing one to sit upright in the water. I laughed like a boy who abandoned his training wheels as I propelled my upright body around with my legs until I flipped over and floated on my stomach with my hands and legs sticking several inches out of the water behind me.

Eating was an adventure. Whether it was a fried falafel pita from an Arab street vendor, mouthwatering bread straight out of a Bedouin fire, or seafood in a Greek restaurant housed within an 800-year-old Crusader Castle with the sun sinking into the Mediterranean, every taste reminded me that my palate was ignorant of the heights taste can reach.

After my first night in Jerusalem, I wrote in my journal, "What an incredible experience; to be a pilgrim in the places where the Almighty clothed Himself in humanity—in His creation; where He carried out His quest for redemption. I'm walking in the places where a story of mythic proportions revealed the

Truth. The region where the finite and infinite worlds collided for an instantaneous moment in the void of time and space."

Israel was foundational to who I was as a Christ follower, and I experienced the historical authenticity of my faith. Sitting on the Mount of Beatitudes, overlooking the Sea of Galilee where Jesus spent quiet moments in contemplation and fed thousands with a handful of loaves and fishes, it was effortless to imagine His love for creation.

We visited the High Priest's home, Caiaphas, today, a church, where Jesus was imprisoned in a dark pit the night before His crucifixion. I read Psalm 88 as I stared into the dark pit. My stomach tightened when I contemplated what went through His mind that Good Friday evening. What fellowship did He have with the Father knowing a tragic separation was coming?

> *"You have put me in the lowest pit,*
> *   in dark places, in the depths.*
> *Your wrath has rested upon me*
> *   and You have afflicted me with all Your waves.*
> *You have moved my friends from me;*
> *   and you have made me an object of loathing*
> *   to them;*
> *I am shut up and cannot go out."*

The chance to connect with the Messiah's passion was overwhelming.

Even walking through the frenzied Arab market, a maze of awnings and dizzying cacophony of voices as vendors contended for the attention of passing doe-eyed tourists, was a reminder of a world, in some ways, unchanged from the time of Christ. Wandering through the streets of Jerusalem, one of the holiest places for the world's three largest religions, added to my belief that life is a journey. We can view ourselves as tourists looking for momentary thrills, or as pilgrims filled with longing for the wonder surrounding us.

My excitement in Israel was tempered by a gnawing tension I had not faced in my safe, stable American world. Israel is a Middle

East political time bomb; cut the wrong wire, and everything blows to pieces. When a Jewish State was declared in 1948 and 250,000 Palestinians were forcefully ejected from much of Israel's current land, the Muslim-majority nations surrounding Israel declared war. The military conflict eventually quieted with shaky borders mapped out, but the deadly tension has never ceased. A military career is mandatory when an Israeli citizen turns 18.

Walking throughout Jerusalem and witnessing young people in army fatigues with assault rifles or grenade launchers strapped to their backs was unnerving. The air hung heavy, a constant reminder war might break out at any time. I battled cultural vertigo in the shadowed streets and swarming markets, fearing being stabbed, beaten, or robbed if I let my guard down. The ebb and flow of joyous discovery, coupled with unsteady anxiety, wobbled me.

My time in Israel ran parallel with the 1991 Madrid Conference. The talks, co-sponsored by the U.S. and the Soviet Union, were developed to revive the Israeli-Palestinian peace process. One morning while meandering in the Jewish Quarter, I watched a frantic woman pushing her baby carriage through the empty streets. The sonic BOOM of jets flying toward the Lebanon border scared the mother out of her wits. The fear on her face worried me enough to ask why we weren't taking cover. Army personnel vehicles slowly scanned the streets, hunting for potential terrorist strikes.

Later in the evening, while we enjoyed a creamy hot chocolate at a sidewalk café on a lively Ben Yehuda Street, a pipe bomb exploded a couple of blocks away. My neat, unrealistic, western view of the world was shattered. The world was full of people living in trepidation that I did not comprehend.

After a few days of travel, I drew a tub and filled it with Dead Sea bath salts. My capacity to process cultural differences, political tensions, and spiritual experiences was tapped out. I needed a night to rest, read, and fall into an early undisturbed sleep. At

9 pm, as I settled in the steamy water for me-time, Mike Yengo came crashing through our hotel door.

"Shawn, it's time for an adventure. Get dressed and meet me in the lobby in ten minutes. You don't want to miss this!" The hotel door slammed shut.

Mike knew my curiosity always overpowered my comfort. Eight minutes later, still wet, I stood in the hotel lobby with Mike and an unfamiliar Palestinian man. Ibrahim was short and stocky, with a Carlos Santana mustache undergirded by a persistent week-old beard on his cherub cheeks. Mike had befriended Ibrahim, the owner of a tourist shop in the Arab Quarter of the Old City. During their conversation, he asked if we could visit his home, meet his family, eat a proper Palestinian meal, and learn about Israel from an Arab perspective. Visiting Israel, one is smothered by political rhetoric that tends to vilify Palestinians and focus on the plight of the Jews. Mike wanted us to hear the other side of the story.

I was nervous to be jumping into the car of a stranger when I had no idea what his intentions might be. My internal prejudices were yelling, "You'll end up with a slit throat." We careened down a maze of tight streets leading to darkened Arab neighborhoods closely watched by patrolling Israeli troops. The environment changed as we passed a checkpoint and entered a part of town no tourists visited. Ibrahim pulled the parking brake in front of a giant concrete building, one home divided into five separate apartments, one for each son, holding 32 family members.

We were greeted with the warm handshakes of an elderly couple in traditional embroidered robes that carried the aroma of delicious spices. The patriarch, Mohammed, clutched a heavy set of marble-sized wooden prayer beads that he rifled through, one by one, all evening.

"I am praying for the Madrid Conference. I want peace in my country. I want peace for my grandchildren."

Mohammed Senior walked us arm in arm to the main sitting room dominated by an adorned portrait of King Hussein of Jordan. Mohammed Junior, the eldest child, gave me a smile-less, vicelike handshake. The hard lines on his face made it clear he did

Into the Wonder

not favor our intrusion. We sat on the floor on chunky tasseled pillows and were served honey-sweetened Arabic tea. Once we were comfortable, Mohammed Jr. cleared his throat like a professor preparing his class for a lecture. He had one subject on his mind, politics, and he was ready to lob his P.L.O. dogmas in our direction. The hairs on my neck stood on end as he shared the origin of his anger against what he termed "murderous Jews."

He was eleven the year the Jewish army took occupation of their ancestral lands, the same lands the Palestinians had known as home for hundreds of years. Mohammed recalled his entire family snatching what they could carry in their arms and fleeing from the threat of Israeli soldiers, on foot, to Jordan. When they returned to Jerusalem years later, returning to where their family had lived for six generations, poverty was their only possession. Mohammed wept to recall the pain his father and mother endured as they lived off scraps to survive. His anger was real. His pain was palpable. His bitterness was understandable.

As Mohammed composed himself, Ali, the youngest brother of the clan, fired off questions about America. When he discovered we were Texans, he asked if we rode horses, wore cowboy hats, and carried six shooters. Matta, the grinning middle brother, offered us his hookah pipe and observed us with as few words as possible. Ibrahim's wife, Summer, the family member most excited by our presence, translated for those who only spoke Arabic.

Summer ended our conversation with a "tsk-tsk" and led us to an outdoor dining spot overlooking a thick olive grove in the back of the home. We dove into mouthwatering Palestinian fare, including my first taste of seasoned Lebanese stuffed grape leaves. Halfway through the meal, the electricity went off. I'm ashamed to have thought, "This is where everything goes down. We may not come out of this alive." Mohammed Jr., seeing my wide eyes, laughed and promised he "would not eat us alive." He explained the Israeli army would shut down the electricity in Palestinian neighborhoods a few times a week to remind Arabs that the Israeli military was in charge, a subtle way of bullying the Arab minority.

After twenty minutes, the lights came back on. The family continued for hours with questions about America, our Christian faith, and our thoughts on Israel. We learned about their pains and joys, frustrations and fears, and hopes for the future. Like parents everywhere, they longed for their children to live peaceful lives. Ibrahim was the philosophical one of the family. Toward the end of the evening, he asked Summer to bring out their baby, a chuckling eight-month-old named Ayan. As Ayan was passed around with his arms always outstretched, laughing and tugging on our ears and noses, it clicked why this evening, this experience, was so important. The evening caught me off guard. As C.S. Lewis wrote, "God sometimes seems to speak to us most intimately when He catches us, as it were, off our guard."[15]

One of the most important lessons of my life was rooted in my soul that night. People are unique and communal. We have distinct backgrounds, look different, and speak uncommon tongues. Still, we love our children, long for something bigger, and need to connect. Travel will kill prejudice and narrow-mindedness. Removing ourselves from our safe little worlds broadens our horizons. It paints a clearer picture of the abundant kindness and goodness everywhere.

There are ugly gashes in our world, broken places created by broken people who bring pain and suffering through their decisions, prejudices, greed, bitterness, and ignorance. Finding wonder in the suffering seems unlikely when I look hard at these gashes. What I learned in a Palestinian home was the knowledge that people on both sides of these devastating conflicts are praying for their children to live in peace. Behind the ugly gashes in the world, people are looking for peace and longing for wonder. Small moments of wonder in these places are bright shoots of eternity, reminding us that the God of Abraham, Isaac, and Jacob weeps for peace between His children. My time with Ibrahim's family tempered my worldview. Still, one more event in Israel left an indelible mark on my soul.

---

15 C.S. Lewis, *Letters to Malcolm, Chiefly on Prayer* (New York: HarperOne, 1964), 114.

Into the Wonder

The gregarious Mike Yengo was mute.

"Are you all right?"

Mike, ashen-faced, silently entered Israel's Holocaust Memorial, Yad-Vashem. The first room, the Children's Memorial, was designed for visitors to walk single file in the manner the Jews entered the concentration camps. Mike was transfixed as we passed photos of five young children representing all the children murdered in an unimaginable human atrocity. We were unprepared for what we were witnessing.

The next hall, humming with a sorrowful tune, contained six lit candles. The multi-mirrored walls of the room illuminated these six points of light into a 1.5-million star-pointed galaxy. Each point of light represented one child killed in the Holocaust. Mike remained morose.

We decided to sit in the next chamber, surrounded by grotesque reminders of the Holocaust: a transparent plastic box filled with shoes discarded by child victims of the Nazi war machine, the picture of German soldiers arranging Jews in a single file line, front to back, to save the bullets used for their mass extermination, and a picture of a mother tickling her smiling baby's chin to keep its attention while a soldier pointed a rifle at her, readying to pull the trigger. Everything I saw horrified me.

Mike Yengo, the man who entered every country he visited with fearless unfettered zeal, started shaking. Overcome, he fled the museum as if ghosts were pursuing him. I took my time to finish the Memorial before walking outside to find Mike. He was sobbing uncontrollably on a bench in the courtyard. I waited for a few minutes until he quieted.

"What's going on, Mike?"

"My Jewish grandparents lived in Krakow, Poland, when the Nazis invaded. My mother, a few weeks old, was their only child. There were whispered warnings throughout the Jewish community about what was happening. My grandparents were barely adults. They panicked in the way only parents of a newborn can panic. They must have had some sense of the horrors that were about to come down on their heads.

"They begged Christian neighbors to take their baby and hide her from the soldiers. I imagine the couple saw the terror in the eyes of my grandparents. They'd give the child back once things cooled down.

"Nazi soldiers ransacked the Jewish neighborhoods. That evening my grandparents were taken away to a concentration camp. They didn't survive. The couple realized the soldiers were sweeping all the homes in town looking for sympathizers hiding Jews or their children. As soldiers entered their neighborhood, they feared the baby would be discovered. Their neighbors knew the young couple had no children. If they were caught with a child, the baby would be taken, and they would be arrested.

"That evening, soldiers showed up and searched their home, but they didn't find anything. Once they were satisfied, they left to search other homes. As soon as the door slammed, the young couple ran to the closet and moved a pile of shoe boxes. Carefully opening the bottom box, they pulled out a terrified baby, rolled in a blanket like a mummy, with a rag stuffed in its tiny mouth to muffle any of her cries.

"Shawn, I heard that story many times growing up, but it wasn't until today that I grasped the weight of the decision my Jewish grandparents and the Christian couple who put their lives on the line performed. They moved to another town and raised that baby, my mother, as their own. Walking through the Holocaust Memorial, I understand how close I came to not *being*. If it weren't for the sacrifice and bravery of my mother's parents who died in a concentration camp, or of that couple, the grandparents I knew, I wouldn't be alive. And for that, I am grateful beyond words. These are tears of grief and tears of thanksgiving."

Mike finished, and we sat silently in that courtyard for several minutes. He finally turned to me.

"Want a falafel?"

We both left that day as different people with a deeper friendship.

Into the Wonder

Is it possible to find wonder and meaning in suffering? A Holocaust Memorial feels like a far cry from a place to discover wonder. Austrian psychiatrist and Auschwitz survivor Viktor Frankl developed *logotherapy*, or therapy through meaning, to heal his patients who suffered horrendous evils perpetrated by others. He developed logotherapy out of his personal experiences in German concentration camps. After years of existential wrestling with the problem of evil in the world and attempting to answer the question, "Can beauty be found in the worst circumstances?" Frankl wrote one of the most influential books in the Western Hemisphere, *Man's Search for Meaning*.

One of the passages in his book answers that question. "An active life serves the purpose of giving man the opportunity to realize values in creative work, while a passive life of enjoyment affords him the opportunity to obtain fulfillment in experiencing beauty, art, or nature. But there is also purpose in that life which is almost barren of both creation and enjoyment and which admits of but one possibility of high moral behavior: namely, in man's attitude to his existence, an existence restricted by external forces….But not only creativeness and enjoyment are meaningful….If there is a meaning in life at all, then there must be a meaning in suffering."[16] Viktor Frankl seems to shout, "Wonder can be found despite suffering!"

At Yad-Vashem, travel crystallized into a moment of transformative wonder. As Abraham Joshua Heschel writes, "The ultimate insight is the outcome of moments when we are stirred beyond words, of instants of wonder, awe, praise, fear, trembling and radical amazement; of awareness of grandeur, of perceptions we can grasp but are unable to convey, of discoveries of the unknown, of moments in which we abandon the pretense of being acquainted with the world, of knowledge by inacquaintance. It is at the climax of such moments that we attain the certainty that life has meaning,

---

16   Viktor Frankl, *Man's Search for Meaning* (New York: Pocket Books, 2006), 63.

that time is more than evanescence, that beyond all being there is someone who cares."[17]

Mike Yengo anointed me with a longing to travel with an open heart to meet people, learn their stories, and search for wonder that shaped me into the man I am today, open to wonder even under crushing suffering. Little did I realize a year after I returned from Israel, I'd face crushing despair and put all I had learned to the ultimate test.

---

[17] Abraham Joshua Heschel, *God in Search of Man* (New York: Farrar, Straus and Giroux, 1955), 235.

Chapter 15

Wrecked

A year after my Israel pilgrimage, I took my next trip: Thanksgiving to my grandparents in Iowa. We decided to save money and do an all-night drive. A twelve-hour road trip is not a big deal when you're young and ready to leave town for a few restful days.

My enthusiasm for visiting Iowa was fueled by the opportunity to introduce Cheryl to the ancestral center of my universe. I wanted her to spend time with Grandpa and Grandma Lindgren, my favorite people. Coeli, almost three, would play on the same playground equipment I climbed when I was her age. We were excited about watching the faces of my grandparents when Cheryl revealed she was two months pregnant with our second child.

The night drive would bring us to Grandma's doorstep by lunchtime on Thanksgiving Eve. Sitting in our driveway, we buckled in and went through the mental pre-travel checklist. I held Cheryl's hands asking God for protection, guidance, and a sign if we were not supposed to go. The last part was an odd request; I didn't know why I prayed for it. For a moment, I examined the naked woods illuminated by the rising moon. I thanked God for His goodness, and we started our trek.

Our drive north on Interstate 35 brought us near the Kansas border around midnight. The first few hours in the car had been easy as we traded off driving. The excitement of revisiting the place holding my treasured childhood memories kept me alert. I could almost taste the mouthwatering turkey, baked to perfection, creamy mashed potatoes oozing with butter and brown gravy, and green bean casserole topped with crispy fried onions. Cheery memories occupied my thoughts when the first snowflakes hit the windshield. As Texas residents, we rarely see snow, so this was a wonderful surprise. It did not take long, however, before the surprise became a threat.

We were unprepared as we drove into one of the most significant November snowstorms to hit the Midwest in a decade. Our lack of credit cards offered us limited options. Halfway through Kansas, we entered a dangerous and unnerving whiteout. We were forced to pull over and rest every couple of hours, usually under the mocking lights of motel parking lots, trying to wait out the storm. We stayed parked, turning the car off to conserve fuel, until the cold became unbearable. The temps had dropped fifty degrees. This allowed us a few minutes of shivering pseudo-rest while the brutal blizzard intensified. When we woke up from each short nap, the windshield was coated with a thick blanket, creating a sense of claustrophobia.

"God, please be with us through the storm," was the constant prayer in my head.

Breakfast at Shoney's across the Missouri border brought us a needed break. By the time we reached the Iowa border, we were tapped out. The rising sun illuminated a substantial snowfall. Transformed fields, barely emptied of their fall harvests, looked like the North Pole. One to two feet of snow had covered the state in the previous twelve hours. I shivered as I called my grandparents from a parking lot pay phone to tell them we were safe and arriving for lunch.

"You kids drive slowly and be careful. I can't wait to hug your necks."

Though we did not look forward to returning to the road, the coziness of my grandparents' home motivated me to move ahead. Feeling the onset of morning sickness, Cheryl climbed into the back seat to keep Coeli company. The unplowed I-35 toward Des Moines was a snowmobile track. There were no visible lanes. I stayed in the car tracks using half-buried guard rails as freeway path markers. We moved at sled dog speed.

A serious scare came ten minutes later as we passed through Des Moines. A semi-truck barreled past us creating wind shear. Our car slid slightly on the snow-packed road for a few seconds, and we braced for the worst. I recovered control but shuddered.

"We've got to get off this highway. That was too close. Let's take the back roads slowly and get there in one piece."

Cheryl was not comforted by the biting stress in my voice. Jumping off the highway might add a couple of hours to the drive, but it was better than becoming a big rig pancake.

We took the next exit, relieved to leave I-35 behind, and entered a farm road with light traffic. Heavy tractors had been driving along the road leaving a clear tire path to follow. Cautiously, I sped the car up to forty-five miles per hour. The sun glared off the hoary fields on both sides of the vehicle. I took a breath of deep relief. The whole world was bright and unspoiled.

A quarter mile ahead, a black Ford Mustang topped the rising road, a dark spot growing on the white horizon. My foot moved toward the brake pedal. With a single rutted track down the middle of the two-lane road, we needed to slow down and pass each other at a snail's pace. When I pushed on the brakes, my heart seized. The brakes activated, but the car didn't slow down. At that moment, the other vehicle's driver hit his brakes, which also froze. We raced at each other, both cars locked at a deadly 45 m.p.h.

Seven seconds is a long time to rush at another car. The sensation of time standing still was instantaneous. In the moments before impact, I had layers of thoughts running through my mind.

I yelled at Cheryl and Coeli in the backseat, "WE'RE GOING TO HIT!"

I saw hundreds of students at the Word of Faith youth group crying at my funeral.

I knew Cheryl and Coeli would survive.

But how would they cope with the loss of my life?

I prayed for God's grace, a husband for my widowed wife, and a father for my child.

I thought, "Why is this taking so long?"

"Will my death be painful or instantaneous?"

We were traveling too fast toward each other for disaster not to happen. In the early 90s, most cars didn't have airbags. But I experienced peace, the strangest emotion in this circumstance. I was not afraid. I was excited about experiencing the presence of God.

A millisecond before impact, I saw the face of the other driver. His mouth was agape, and his hands were raised as if to stop the crash. I probably would've laughed if I had had time. The next moment brought the grinding sound of metal gorging upon metal. I can recall the crunch of 4000 pounds of plastic, glass, and steel. Thinking about it still makes my jaw tighten.

On impact, the Mustang slid backward into the deep, snow-filled ditch. Our compact Geo Prizm rotated backward for a couple of spins and stopped at an angle facing the opposite way down the road. I lifted my bloody head from a steering wheel pressed into my chest, wiping a mask of blood out of my eyes. I raised my eyes to my driver's side window and gasped. A second vehicle traveling behind us slammed into our front left fender, sending us again sailing down the road in another mad spin.

Miraculously we did not veer off the narrow road, but we slid past the Mustang, its front headlights peeking over the snow-packed ditch. When our car stopped sliding for a second time, I panicked. My chest felt as if it had taken a cannonball, and I was nearly pinned to my seat. The steering wheel had been pushed forward by a car engine peeking through the dashboard. In a rush of adrenaline, I reached for my door handle. Hyper shock took over, and I felt no pain. Remembering all the car crashes I'd watched in the movies caused me to force the door open to escape an inevitable explosion. A Hulk strength kicked in as I pushed the driver's door flush with the engine, partially hanging out the side panels like a gutted deer.

I reached for the back door, ready to pull my family from a burning vehicle. Thankfully, flames never appeared. Cheryl's door was jammed shut. Looking into the back seat, I saw my wife, who had been sitting directly behind me, unconscious. Her face was planted on the front seat headrest. Two seconds before the crash, Coeli had unbuckled herself and crawled out of her car seat to pick up a book. My little girl lay still on the floorboards. I jumped back into the car and crawled into the back seat. Cheryl moaned. A crimson thread of blood was streaming out of her ear.

"What happened?" she softly mumbled but did not move or open her eyes.

I did not answer her. Panic exploded as I saw my baby girl face down on the car floor. She was motionless. I tenderly scooped her off the floorboards, with her body resting along my arm. She was not breathing. I started to cry and begged aloud.

"God, please don't let her die! She's too little. God, she needs to breathe!"

Cheryl remained in the same position.

"Shawn, what happened?"

As desperate prayers left my lips, I recalled my first aid training. Never move a victim if there is a possibility of a neck injury. I froze, continuing to beg God. We sat silently for several seconds, feeling the icy air creep into the car. As my hot tears fell on her back, Coeli screamed in pain. It was the most miraculous outburst I've ever heard.

"Don't move, baby. Daddy has you," I whispered in her ear.

The woman driving the second car that hit us ran to Cheryl's window, looked in, and screamed.

"OH MY GOD!"

Her shrieks were unnerving. We must have looked frightening. I wondered how long we had to live.

The hazardous road conditions delayed the ambulance for forty-five minutes, leaving us waiting in -10° weather. Thankfully, as severe shock set in, the frigid air numbed our physical pain and slowed the bleeding.

Cheryl swayed in and out of consciousness, asking, "What happened?" whenever she came around. Her jaw had smashed into the back of my headrest, and she couldn't move without significant pain.

Three ambulances arrived: one for the driver of the Mustang, one for Cheryl, and one for Coeli and me. Coeli was strapped onto a baby board on the upper right side of the ambulance. I lay on an adult board on the lower left side. Where I was positioned, I could see my baby clearly, but she couldn't see me. Coeli began to go unconscious as we slowly headed toward the Mercy One Des

Moines Medical Center. The medics tried to stir her. They told me I had to keep her awake when their attempts failed. Her life may depend on it.

"How?" I said with confusion.

"Any way you can, Mr. Small."

"Coeli. Baby girl. You need to stay awake."

"I'm so tired, Daddy. I want to sleep," came her weak reply.

She started to fade. I firmed my voice. "Coeli, listen to Daddy. You have to stay awake."

"No, Daddy. It hurts too much. I want to sleep."

If Coeli had been able to see me below, she would've witnessed her father strapped to a board, tears flowing out of his eyes because he knew the pain his daughter was experiencing was so intense that what he had to do sounded mercilessly cruel even though it might save her life.

"COELI MICHELLE SMALL. IF YOU SHUT YOUR EYES, I AM GOING TO SPANK YOU!"

She started to ball.

In a tiny tear-shattered voice, she said, "Why are you being so mean to me?"

Her sobbing kept her awake for the rest of the ride.

What should have been a ten-minute ride took forty minutes. All three of us were taken to different areas in the emergency room. Of the nine deadly accidents around Des Moines the morning of the blizzard, we were the only one without a fatality. The next few hours were a blur. I heard bodies wheeled into the same room as Cheryl, doctors feverishly trying to save lives, repeatedly saying, "We've lost her." I waited in agony for several minutes before a nurse passed close enough for me to fearfully ask if it had been my wife or child who had died. Though the answer was always no, repeating this event over the next six hours became my private hell.

Once new accident victims stopped arriving, I was assessed by the doctors as banged up and concussed but with no life-threatening injuries. The front of my body was covered with ugly blue and yellowing bruising, resulting from the dashboard being shoved into my chest. My head was sliced above my eye; a ragged gash emptied what felt like a gallon of blood over my face and upper torso. Coeli had a right arm fracture and multiple breaks in her left leg, needing to be pinned. Cheryl had suffered the worst with a broken jaw, which would be wired shut for months, and a shattered left hip.

I spoke to Cheryl before she and Coeli went into surgery, telling them I loved them and that everything would be okay. Then I waited, flat on my back, immobilized by pain, wondering if I'd see them again. That is when it hit me. Would our unborn baby survive the battering Cheryl's body had endured?

After several hours of post-surgery recovery in the ICU, Cheryl was placed in the orthopedics wing while Coeli was transferred to pediatrics. I planted myself next to my daughter, wanting her to see me when she woke. Cheryl was out for the night. The doctors believed our unborn baby was safe.

Coeli's screaming started around ten at night. She had been unconscious since the operation, where two surgeons worked in tandem to set the break in her right arm and place pins in her left leg. She lay on her back; her left arm and right leg were elevated above her by a series of cables, making her look like a broken marionette. Though they gave her meds to dull the tenderness, the doctor said Coeli would be in significant pain for several hours. Each little movement would feel like a shock of electricity.

"Daddy! Pray for me. It hurts so bad."

I jumped off the couch from a restless sleep feeling like I was going to pass out or puke. I moved beside Coeli, placing my hand on her chest and whispering prayers into her ears until she fell asleep. Once she was down, for a few quiet minutes, I shuffled back to the couch and lay down to cry myself back to a nightmare-filled sleep.

Fourteen hours had passed since the dreadful impact, and so had my world of wonder.

Thanksgiving morning arrived after a night filled with a dozen sudden screams from Coeli. By the morning, she settled. I, on the other

Into the Wonder

hand, was in physical and emotional agony. The cries of anguish from my baby girl had worn me down to bits. The word "thanksgiving" had become a punch to the gut. The nurse on call assured me Coeli was in good hands. She encouraged me to visit the shower down the hall to wash the caked blood off my body. I moved slowly, incrementally, like a man traveling through a wall of molasses. Doctors assured me there were no internal injuries, but drawing a full breath was difficult. The short walk took me twenty minutes.

I felt as if I was being flayed as I stripped off my clothes. The stranger staring at me in the mirror was a horror show. With as much strength as I could muster, I willed one leg, then the other, over the 15-inch tub wall and into the shower. When I turned the water on, I was hit in the chest with a cold blast. I flinched backward, and my chest buckled.

SNAP! Something cracked.

The MRI had not detected the hairline fracture in my sternum. I grabbed the sides of the shower, fighting to keep from fainting. My brewing anger welled up enough to keep me upright. Looking toward the heavens, I roared at the so-called Almighty.

"IF THIS IS WHAT YOU'RE ABOUT— IF THIS IS YOUR LOVE—I WANT NOTHING TO DO WITH YOU. STAY OUT OF MY LIFE."

We spent six weeks in the hospital. After two more surgeries, Coeli was encased in a full-body cast. Twice a day, I took the long walk to the other end of the hospital to spend time with Cheryl. She wanted me to be with Coeli, but the downside was her isolation. She had to learn to walk and to eat with a straw through a wired jaw. Her meals were whatever was palatable enough to combine in a blender. An egg and bacon puree for breakfast or meatloaf and mashed potato puree for dinner became part of her daily diet. A pair of emergency cutters for her wired jaw was on her person in case morning sickness hit. Thankfully, she never had to use them.

Our daily physical therapy regimen was not as challenging as the emotional wringer we all experienced. A cavernous reservoir of bitterness toward God was filling my heart. The unanswered prayers in my driveway before our road trip reminded me of the delusion I had lived with for the last seven years. We had faithfully served God the best we knew how. We had asked for His protection and guidance. How could He let this happen, especially to an innocent child?

Along with visits from my Iowa kin and my mom, I received calls from family and friends, especially our adult youth group leaders from the church. I mumbled through those conversations, unwilling to discuss what I was going through. If someone asked to pray for me, I asked them to do it after we hung up. Words of hope, prayers of faith, and even kind exchanges were wormwood. The slough of depression was my bunker. I wanted to brew in my disappointment. Hearing about God's goodness was a cruel cosmic joke. I could not process the logical leap of God's sovereignty, His love, with the evils rained down on innocents. One minute, I would start to relax, only to be interrupted by tormenting questions: Why did two sets of brakes lock simultaneously? Why did my decision to get off the dangerous highway almost cause our deaths? It made no sense for Coeli to be out of her car seat at that moment.

The long-forgotten monster, the overwhelming sense of abandonment that had tormented me when I was younger, swooped back into my world with the metallic crunch of a head-on collision. God was no longer my dwelling place; He was no longer safe. The monster was, once again, my reality. My world was absent of lasting joy.

Even with the abandonment and pain, there was one almost imperceptible connection to wonder I still clung to, even if not consciously.

The Ericksons served as adult leaders for the youth group. They became our coaches in ministry, marriage, and parenting. They loved us like they were our parents. Dan and I shared a fondness for fantasy novels, and we both wanted to become authors. About two weeks into my hospital confinement, after visiting

Cheryl, I found a large package wrapped in brown paper and tied with twine sitting on the couch in Coeli's room.

"A present came for you, Daddy." It was nice to see Coeli smile again.

The package was sent from the Ericksons. As I unwrapped it, three large hardcover books slipped out. Dan had sent me fantasy author Stephen Lawhead's Albion Trilogy. The book's burnished dust covers were filled with blue-daubed Celtic warriors, exquisite knot-work, and numinous landscapes.

For the next four weeks, cooped up in the hospital as fall transitioned into winter, I dove into the parallel universe of Albion. I paced myself as I read *The Paradise War*, *The Silver Hand*, and *The Endless Knot* in the quiet hours after Coeli fell asleep. When the series' hero, Lewis Gillies, entered a mystical portal and slid from our world to the Celtic world, I followed him. Albion was my place of escape. As I emerged into Albion for short periods, away from the horrors filling my real world, I was free.

Lawhead's books reminded me there were dimensions beyond my senses. Like an anchor, the Albion Trilogy kept me spiritually moored to beauty, to wonder. It was a sweet subliminal song reminding me that all was not lost even though I wanted to abandon my beliefs.

I cried for an hour after finishing the trilogy. I didn't want to exit the Celtic Otherworld. Leaving meant I had to reenter the real world, a terrifying prospect. We'd fly back to Dallas in a week and face life. I was returning to be a spiritual example to several hundred youths, and I didn't know if I believed in a loving God anymore. My heart-aching doubt was going to be a problem.

Chapter 16

The Caning

We were in a strange parade the night we arrived at the Dallas/Ft. Worth airport. Two wheelchairs met us at the jet bridge. I awkwardly held Coeli in my lap. She looked like a petrified elf in her whole-body cast. A hundred people with signs, balloons, and party hats were drawing attention in our direction. When we saw the large gathering at the gate, they cheered and whooped as though we were soldiers returning from war. It took all the emotional gusto I had to muster a smile. I did not want any of it.

During our weeks of recovery in Iowa, we missed Thanksgiving, Christmas, and New Year's Eve. The calendar had turned to 1993, but for the Smalls, time had frozen, perpetually stuck in 1992. It's hard to explain the level of detachment we experienced. No cell phones. No iPad. No internet. Limited stations on the hospital television. A lot of time to kill with little knowledge of what was happening in the outside world. No one wanted to burden us with their lives while we were in the hospital, so conversations were one way, always focused on how we were healing. Our hospital time had ended, but our recovery was just beginning.

I had sunk into an abysmal existential despair. The One I had lived for, had sought with all my heart, had given my life to, had abandoned my family. He had turned away, and we suffered for His lack of action. I believed in God, but the God I believed in was indifferent, if not cruel.

When we arrived home, we were led inside by our giddy youth group leaders. Our home was shining with actions of love. Anything in the house needing attention, from cracked light fixtures to doors unable to shut properly, had been repaired. Floors shined. Counters sparkled. Fresh paint covered the walls. Our pantry and refrigerator were bursting with our favorite foods. A huge Christmas tree, fully trimmed and decorated, was overflowing with gifts. A new bedroom set replaced the third-generation hand-me-downs in the master bedroom. Everyone was festive, especially Coeli, who wanted to dive into her presents. Our friends, a part of our church community, had left no good deed undone. They had created a safe and beautiful home for us to return to post-accident.

Yet, all I wanted was to be left alone. Depression is crafty, turning treasures into turds and sweetness into a biting poison. My dark inner battle, waged in a hospital room, had become an all-out war.

My most challenging times were at the church. Each morning I entered my office, closed the blinds, and turned on the tiny light on my desk, emitting a faint yellow glow. The playful, rambunctious character everyone knew was gone. I spent my days brooding. No one challenged my melancholy. Everyone assumed I'd get over this rough patch through faith and prayer.

I wrestled with how long I could remain a pastor before the hypocrisy did me in. I needed a paycheck and was in no shape to explore a different career path. Admittedly, a small part of me wanted to sink my spiritual ship. It was only a matter of time before they unmasked me. When they did, they would, no doubt, fire me for my lack of faith. At that point, I'd abandon all the silliness. I was a hypocritical, spiritual bastard who had been abandoned by a God everyone believed was good and loving. The dirty little secret of religion had been revealed: God was finicky. Prayers were boomerangs we threw heavenward. Hope was vanity. When the curtain was pulled back, God was less than the Wizard of OZ.

For the next few months, I went to church and watched my volunteer youth leaders share Bible stories while I sat in the back row, weighing if it was all bunk. Though I remained cordial, I was in a dangerous place, refusing to talk to anyone about the monster inside.

But there was a flaw in my theory about God's abandonment. The youth leaders, my friends, were gracious, continuing to love me quietly despite my melancholy. Their extravagant love never ceased. Several took turns throughout the week to visit our home to care for Cheryl and Coeli. Cheryl's hip injury kept her couch-bound. A few steps to the bathroom with a walker were agonizing. She could not care for Coeli. Although potty-trained, Coeli was back to diapers placed on her through a hole in the bottom of the casting. We moved her from room to room, propping her up like a piece of modern art. If we left the house with her, she was pulled in her red Radio Flyer wagon.

When Cheryl needed meals, our friends made them. When she needed help getting to the bathroom, she leaned on them. The house stayed clean and warm, and a meal was always waiting when I came home after work.

There was one disturbing moment I observed daily. Like strange psychic clockwork, Cheryl started quietly crying right before I walked in the door around 5:00 pm. I chalked her tears up to the slow healing of her throbbing muscles and stinging nerves. I was mistaken. She did not reveal why she cried. I avoided asking her about her tears for a couple of weeks until I could not take it anymore. Her explanation brought me no comfort.

After a day at work, I sat on an overstuffed chair and waited for her to wipe her eyes. She smiled at me.

"I have a question for you," I asked sheepishly.

"I've been waiting for you to ask me about the crying." She had grown familiar with the broodiness clinging to me after I came home from the church offices. Cheryl continued.

"This is hard to explain. I wake up every morning in pain. Every time I move, my hip feels like it explodes. I can handle the pain, but it increases throughout the day. Usually, around 4:45 in the afternoon, the pain is unbearable. By that point, the meds stop working. Maybe that's my tolerance point. I don't know. All I know is I feel the car accident all over again."

She saw me wince at the mention of the accident. She grabbed my hand and looked into my eyes, but I looked away.

"Like I said, around the time you come home, my physical pain feels unbearable. That's when the touch happens."

Into the Wonder

I sat up, trying to understand where she was heading with her story.

"Do you remember the IVs in the hospital, the ones with a small button for me to push to release a controlled painkiller to take the edge off?" I nodded. "That's what happens at the same time every day. Just when I am at my worst, I feel a touch from God flowing into my body, like I hit the button on the IV."

My confusion came out in frustration.

"You're telling me that God takes your pain away at 5 pm every day?"

Cheryl let go of my hand and thought carefully.

"No, Shawn. The pain does not stop. It's as bad as always. What I do experience is a tiny touch of His love. It's hard to put into words. At my lowest, I get this drop of God's overwhelming love. The pain remains, but I feel an overflowing sense of God's presence in that pain. At that moment, I grab hold of hope. At that moment, I feel the peace of God that passes all understanding. Instead of removing my pain, He enters into it with me. I know Christ is here, with me. And that's why I cry. I know He is here beside me."

This strange miracle Cheryl had been experiencing every day for weeks kicked at the pit of my stomach. Wasn't it God who allowed her pain in the first place? Why not just remove the pain? Did He abandon us, or was there some sovereign reason behind the head-on collision? My thinking was muddled. I wanted—no—I demanded answers to all my questions. I became manic as I tried to piece together a cosmic mystery. I was afraid that if I discovered the answer, I'd pull the mask off the Holy Spirit, like the Scooby Gang catching the villain at the end of the cartoon: a pitiful, desperate criminal trying to scare and manipulate people in the direction he desired.

In early April, the orthopedist released Cheryl to drive. Several weeks of grueling physical therapy brought healing to her body. We celebrated her progression from a walker to crutches. Watching

Cheryl gain independence, even on a minuscule level, was exhilarating. When she advanced to a cane, the doctor said it was time to leave the house. Walking and stretching her muscles was the next step in her physical therapy. The wires for Cheryl's jaw were removed, and she was back to solid food. I do not know what she enjoyed more, the freedom to move or the act of chewing.

We picked one of the first Wednesdays in April for her to drive to our evening youth gathering at the church. Cheryl put Coeli into a car seat designed for her body cast, loaded her red Radio Flyer wagon into the car's trunk, and drove for thirty minutes.

When Cheryl pulled up, I saw her out of the large plate glass windows forming the youth sanctuary's back wall. I remained in the back row, watching the room of singing and swaying youth. Cheryl pulled into a front space saved for her. Knowing she was reveling in her independence, I decided to wait until she was out of the car before I met her. Coeli would be out of a body cast in a couple of weeks. I had physically healed except for a ragged scar over one eye, and Cheryl was no longer housebound. I said a prayer of thanks. A tiny moment of thanksgiving to a Higher Power is dangerous for a stubborn agnostic wanna-be. Christ had sneakily knocked on the door to my heart, and I had cracked it open, if only a sliver.

As I stepped outside, an unexpected scenario unfolded. Cheryl was on the sidewalk holding her cane like a battle club as she stood over a thirty-something woman cowering on the ground. Open-mouthed, I tried to make sense of what I was witnessing. Cheryl turned toward me. Her facial expressions transformed from a stern glare to a warm smile. Once Cheryl's eyes were off her, the woman scampered back to her car and zoomed away.

"Can you get Coeli out of the car?" she asked calmly.

"Sure…but what just happened?"

"I will tell you later. Let's get into the service before the youth wonder what's taking so long."

Shaking my head, I grabbed Coeli. Cheryl entered the church to the cheers of dozens who had missed her like a mother long separated from her children. After church, with Coeli in her wagon, we stopped at Cheryl's favorite Tex-Mex restaurant to celebrate her newfound freedom. I was about to burst as I waited to hear her story.

An unknown woman, apparently a Word of Faith church member, had parked near Cheryl and watched as she attempted to maneuver Coeli out of her car seat. Exiting her car, the lady walked up behind Cheryl and spoke. Her tone was critical.

"Excuse me," the woman said, "I have a question for you."

Cheryl shut Coeli's car door before turning toward the woman.

"What did you do that caused God to take His hand of protection from you?"

The question was outlandish. There was a damaging theology the more extremist prosperity gospel folks propagated. These people believed that as long as you were under God's protection, nothing bad could happen to you. Bad things happen to people who are in sin, ignorant, and out of the will of God. The woman must have come from this theological camp.

Cheryl, who has the rare gift of saying what she is thinking without delay, walked to the woman, calmly hefted her cane like a baseball bat, and hit her square in the upper left arm, knocking her to the ground. The woman fell with a squeal of terror. Standing over her like an Amazon warrior, Cheryl calmly spoke as the woman cowered below.

"What did you do that caused God to take His hand of protection from you?" I spit out my Pepsi, spraying the table. This was Cheryl at her finest.

Throughout her agonizing months of recovery, she never grew angry at God. In her mind, the accident had nothing to do with God. Something bad happened. We were caught in a snowstorm. Our brakes locked up. Trying to piece together a spiritual puzzle for why bad things happened to our family was a waste of emotion, time, and energy. Bad things happen to people all the time.

Throughout all the agony, isolation, broken bodies, and lonely nights, Christ had been with us through the abundant love and care of our friends, families, and medical staff. There were moments of grace and kind deeds. Our friends' extravagant love was beyond calculation. Those daily doses of God's presence were enough for Cheryl to say, "Christ never left us. We were never abandoned."

I hiked out to the lake. There was a lone elm tree anchored into a sandstone cliff over Lake Grapevine that I loved to sit under. I watched as the full moon reflected off waves stirred by the spring winds. I wanted to talk to God, but months of stubborn resentment clamped my mouth. I lay down in frustration, looking up at the moon rings. A memory from the day of the head-on collision knocked loose in my stubborn mind. It was the memory described earlier when I was tasked with keeping Coeli awake, even if she thought I was angry and cruel. This was all her limited perspective allowed. I was saving her life. I knew it. She did not.

I sat up below the elm in a swirl of divine epiphany.

My perspective on why things happened, fortuitous or ruinous, was severely limited. In my pain, I assumed God had abandoned us. But had I seen God's face as He entered my pain, I know there would have been tears. God understands our questions, our pains, and our weaknesses. Wasn't it the Jesus I serve who said while dying a horrible death on the cross, "My God, my God, why have you abandoned me?" (Matthew 27:46 NLT). He knows what abandonment feels like on a level I will never understand.

My faith went down the toilet on Thanksgiving when the cold shower water hit my chest. In seven seconds, my world imploded. Everything I held on to vanished like smoke when those two cars collided head-on, and I heard the painful cries of my wife and child. In that clear physical reminder of what we experienced, I entered months of self-isolation wondering if I'd ever be whole again.

My doubts and anguish were unresolved through theology, philosophy, or psychology. My resolution started with acceptance. I will never know why horrible things happen. I have an unshakeable understanding: God walked next to us through our pain, just as He had many times before and after—this tragic season led to the destruction of my stick-and-mud house of faith. The freedom of not knowing the whys, just the One who walked with me wherever I went, allowed me to walk through the Valley of the Shadow of Death and fear no evil.

I love how British Author Susan Howatch puts it.

"So in the end every major disaster, every tiny error, every wrong turning, every fragment of discarded clay, all the blood, sweat, and tears—everything has meaning. I give it meaning. I reuse, reshape, recast all that goes wrong so that in the end nothing is wasted and nothing is without significance and nothing ceases to be precious to me."[18]

Sitting beneath that tree, I was overpowered by gratitude. The most extraordinary moment of anguish in my life led me back to a wonder that was foundational to my faith. Wonder is possible despite tragedy.

---

18 Susan Howatch, *Absolute Truths* (New York: Ballantine Books, 1994).

Chapter 17

Leap

Belize Barrier Reef - December 2008

Standing on the starboard plank, I let the irresistible splendor of Belize's Barrier Reef wash over me while its scariest predators swirled beneath my feet. All of the eyes staring at me from beneath the limp sails of the Ragga King were willing me to jump. I was okay with the danger, but when people took out their cell phones hoping to record blue waters turning crimson, I thought, "At least let me meet my doom with a little dignity."

The ship's captain had invited me to join a "Swim with Sharks" excursion while scouting for future Belize trips. Unable to pass on the adventure, I sailed with 20 passengers who had paid for a two-hour escapade. The invigorating breeze, Calypso music, and Jamaican rum made the voyage to the dive site festive. But as we slowed to a stop in the shallow waters of the reef, the celebratory mood dramatically shifted.

Six feet under the boat, several charcoal-colored nurse sharks and stingrays frenzied through the waters waiting for the daily snack the crew of the Ragga King provided. Once anchored, Charlie, our Jamaican captain, chuckled.

"Dem sharks sure look hungry todeh. I don't tink I've ever seen dem so agitated."

No one on the deck moved. Every passenger had paid money to swim with the sharks, but primordial fears won the day. As I laughed at the unfolding comedy, the captain turned to me.

"You tink it's funny? Well den, come on, big mon. Show dem ow it's dun. Time to be a hero and lead da way. Da beasts await!"

Knowing I led adventure trips, he had called me out in front of everyone on board. Though death as shark bait was unlikely, maiming was possible. I moved my hefty body to the tiny starboard plank and breathed deeply. I had come to swim with sharks, and by Poseidon's beard, I would do just that. I cautiously moved to the edge and caught a movement, really just a shadow, below. I stepped off the plank.

There are moments in life when time dramatically slows down, allowing you to perceive minute details with maddening accuracy. For a nanosecond, I saw enough to absorb the surprise below but not enough to stop the impending disaster. The exact moment I began my drop, an eight-foot nurse shark lazily swam under the boat into the path of my rapidly descending mass. A few screams of alarm from the passengers were the last thing I heard before I hit its sandpaper surface and stuck the landing, leaving my head held above the water.

I had pinned the monster onto the reef bed. My feet were straddling its dorsal fin like I was standing on a predator-shaped surfboard. As the shark stiffened in shock, I wondered if there was any truth about sharks attacking swimmers when they smell urine in the water. My fellow passengers looked down on me wearing panicked faces. I heard their thoughts: *Goodbye, you big, brave, foolish man*. The funniest expression was on the face of the weirdly amused captain. This was a first for him.

With one swoosh of its muscled body, the shark tossed me off its back, sending me end over end as it whooshed away. After I resurfaced, the captain broke the silence.

"Hey, mon. Don't be fraid. Dat shark is wid his family right now sayin' 'My back! My back! Wat landed on my back?'"

The bewildered observers erupted with laughter. Over the next half an hour, the passengers dived in, enjoying their swim with the sharks.

Standing in the reef, contemplating the beasts lazily swimming past me, I watched wonder nullify the fears of people who, ten minutes earlier, had refused to enter the water. Those nurse sharks were no more dangerous than the imaginary monsters stalking us. They appear terrifying, and it's easy to be convinced they will gobble us up. But when one is willing to leap into the adventure and face the beasts, wonder is reignited, transforming terrifying creatures into marvels of the sea.

At the end of the summer of 1992, Mike Yengo returned home from an exhausting trip to post-Communist Romania. As we sipped tea on one of those rare August evenings when the temperature dropped into the low seventies, I heard about Romania. The bloody dictator, Nicolae Ceaușescu, had been overthrown four years prior, opening the country to democracy and freedom of religion. Mike's mission team had been welcomed with open arms. When Mike exhausted his tale, he asked how my summer had been progressing. I sheepishly looked to the ground. It was time to share my frustrating confession: I was done with youth summer camps.

In America, churches pivoted their annual youth programs around the hallowed summer camp experience. In the 80s and 90s, the success of a youth group depended on how cool of a camp experience was provided. Word of Faith was no different. Our summer camp was one of the best. We had perfected the camp experience by creating an amalgamation of a theme park, rock music festival, outdoor adventure playground, and a hyped-up, emotionally packed charismatic revival.

Summer camps were a fun distraction, but for our camp team, it necessitated 19-hour workdays, leaving us in puddles of sweat. By Friday, the team was emotionally and physically wasted. The payoff was positive press. Hopefully, there was enough pious PR to hook kids into buying into another year of youth group participation. By my sixth year of reworking the grueling annual event, the insularity of the camp experience ate at me. These week-long spiritual festivals were self-contained with little connection to the real world. Summer camps were fun events wrapped in spiritual hype. Some kids' lives were impacted, but it was a spiritual country club for most participants.

We always told the kids to bring their "unsaved friends" with the hope that between water balloon fights, capture the flag, chubby bunny, and other competitions, they might catch Jesus like a virus. Everyone was on fire for Jesus while they were sequestered in the woods to play and pray for a week, but a month later, after the realities of the world overtook them and the spiritual steroids wore off, they were back to life as usual.

I needed a change. I wanted to invest my energy into exposing them to the world in a heart-opening way, something experiential and experimental, where there was no predetermined outcome. I wanted an organic flow that fostered a broader view of the world, designing adventures where wonder was discovered.

Mike waited until I ended my rant. "Shawn, we've talked about this for a couple of years. It's time you take your youth on a mission trip."

I had not been out of the U.S. since my Israel pilgrimage, and the travel bug tugged at me. I'd been uneasy about the responsibility of leading young people to another country. Listening to Mike's stories had drawn me closer to leaping. His mission trips were not crazy street preaching excursions where the team holed up in American-esque hotels, quarantining themselves from the culture. Mike was leading young people to places they'd never have visited if he hadn't provided the opportunity.

In his wildly popular book, *Into the Wild,* Jon Krakauer captured the revolution I longed for. "So many people live within unhappy circumstances and yet will not take the initiative to change their situation because they are conditioned to a life of security, conformity, and conservatism, all of which may appear to give one peace of mind, but in reality, nothing is more damaging to the adventurous spirit within a man than a secure future. The basic core of a man's living spirit is his passion for adventure. The joy of life comes from our encounter with new experiences, and hence there is no greater joy than to have an endlessly changing horizon, for each day to have a new and different sun."[19] The time to sacrifice the sacred summer camp cow and move in a new, radical direction was upon me.

I decided that the next summer we would travel to "The Land of the Eternal Spring." Guatemala has the highest indigenous population in Central America, an essential aspect of the cultural immersion I wanted the students to experience. We had an

---
[19] Jon Krakauer, *Into the Wild* (Albany: Anchor Books, 1997).

in-country contact who opened doors to the rarely visited southwest mountain town. Mike had never led a team to Guatemala. This allowed him to teach me the trip creation process. The new frontier for the youth group lay in Central America.

A few days after my newly determined course of action, Mike gave me a copy of Brennan Manning's *The Ragamuffin Gospel*. Inside the front cover, he inscribed, "To my nervy and endlessly curious friend. Let this book prepare you for the doorway of wonder you are about to enter. Turn to chapter five, and you will see my prayer for you as we plan our adventure to Guatemala."

I thumbed through the book until I came to a highlighted prayer. "Dear Lord, grant me the grace of wonder. Surprise me, amaze me, awe me in every crevice of Your universe. Delight me to see how Your Christ plays in ten thousand places, lovely in limbs, and lovely in eyes not His, to the Father through the features of men's faces. Each day enrapture me with your marvelous things without number. I do not ask to see the reason of it all; I ask only to share the wonder of it all."[20]

We landed in Guatemala with 27 high schoolers and adults in July. Leaving my family was the most challenging part of the journey. Cheryl was gaining strength and mobility even though she continued to walk with a noticeable limp, the combined effect of her hip injury and carrying a baby through her last two trimesters. Three weeks before the Guatemala mission trip, she had given birth to our second child, Kayla. I was in Guatemala only at Cheryl's insistence. She knew how much I needed this adventure after my months of wrestling with God.

---

[20] Brannan Manning, *Ragamuffin Gospel* (Colorado Springs: Multnomah Books, 1966), 91.

Into the Wonder

At the same time, Robert Tilton had started to unhinge. For three years, he had been doggedly pursued by Ole Anthony, the founder of the Trinity Foundation and the editor of the Christian satirical magazine, *The Wittenberg Door*. A shady character and dubious religious leader of a small Christian commune in East Dallas, Anthony made it his mission to expose the deceptively salacious fundraising techniques of televangelists.

The tides turned in Tilton's life when the ABC network's hidden camera exposé show, *Primetime Live,* teamed up with Anthony to produce a couple of episodes exposing Tilton (along with mega-pastor Larry Lea and evangelist W.V. Grant) as con artists. Though the majority of the evidence Anthony had revealing Tilton as an insincere huckster was debunked months later (much to the chagrin of TV reporter Diane Sawyer and *Primetime Live*), the damage was done. Investigations of Robert Tilton and *Success-N-Life* by the Texas Attorney General, IRS, FBI, U.S. Postal Service, and U.S. Attorney Office followed. Although Tilton's ministry was spiritually unbalanced, unhealthy, unethical, and manipulative, it was not technically illegal. Eventually, Tilton was cleared of all legal charges, but his mind deteriorated. He had started down a road that would carry the church and his program *Success-N-Life* into obscurity.

Guatemala was my chance to escape the Word of Faith media circus and see a different perspective.

Totonicopan, Guatemala - June 1993

Our Guatemalan home, nested in the Sierra Madre Mountain range, was the city of Totonicapan. It took a couple of days for us flatlanders to acclimate to the 8,200-foot elevation. K'iche' Mayans populate Totonicapan, the one-time rulers of Central America until the European conquest. The K'iche', descendants of a proud and ancient people, lived in the red-cobblestoned city where the Mayan military genius Tecún Umán reigned. They are tiny people, most under five-foot-five, brightly dressed in clothes woven from yarn that looked to be harvested from rainbows. Today's Totonicipan is an agricultural hinterland abundant with crops and livestock: maize, beans, potatoes, and herds of sheep and goats. Toto, as the locals call her, is Guatemala's breadbasket.

The drive to Toto was electrifying. We passed smoldering volcanoes coughing ash into the atmosphere and gut-clenching swaying bridges. I admired the plucky farmers who hung by ropes to the sides of mountains, like skyscraper window washers, as they harvested crops.

Our caravan arrived in Toto as guests of the mayor who personally unlocked the door of the Town Hall, our men's dorm, for the next two weeks. The girls were taken to the picturesque home of a wealthy widow living on the mountain behind us.

If there is one commodity the K'iche' have in abundance, it's their hospitality. Men, carrying loads of firewood on their backs taller than their bodies, stopped to grin, shake our hands, and say, "Buenos tardes." Ropes, attached to a cowhide brace shaped like a slingshot, held the stacks of wood in place. Several team members attempted to use the brace to lift a load. With the help of others, a few stood up, but after a few shaky steps forward, they were flung backward like an overturned turtle, much to the delight of the locals who gathered to inspect our strange group.

Our time in Toto was split between performing *Tale of Two Kingdoms* in schools, public markets, and churches or carrying out necessary service projects at schools in and around Totonicapan. When the work was finished, we explored.

In the evenings, we worshiped in small churches. We sang songs in our limited Spanish and danced on dirt floors and under corrugated roofs with families surviving on financially meager existences, yet they emanated spiritually prosperous lives. At the end of every service, we held hands and ping-ponged prayers in Spanish and English, not understanding each other's language but absorbing the love sown into every open heart. The words of Christ expanded beyond our thin understanding. Our world, our beliefs, and our once-narrow possibilities were expanding.

Into the Wonder

The transformation of our young people was evident. Thrown into a place as foreign as any they had ever visited, they entered the opportunities and came alive with the gift of discovery.

Our last moments of the day were circling up so that team members had time to share their daily experiences. Hours passed each evening as they told the stories of their daily encounters.

One student learned that in a pinch, a cornfield was a good substitute for a toilet. Several of the team said bathing in buckets of cold water in the morning gave them a deep appreciation for their hot showers. Our youngest team member was grossed out that toddlers often used chicken feet as teething rings. Graveyards, immaculately landscaped and full of fresh floral arrangements to honor the dead, became a rich cultural learning moment for all.

On our final night in Totonicapan, 90 people gathered on the rooftop of the Jehovah Shalom church. Our team and 60 local youth sat under a brilliant night sky, heavy blankets covering many as the cool air poured into the valley from the surrounding mountains. The gray-headed pastor, Señor Juan, and I shared words of encouragement through our interpreters. At the end of a lovely evening, Señor Juan spoke of a dream he had received 40 years ago.

In the dream, he had climbed into the Sierra Madres until he came to a cold highland brook. As the swift waters swirled around his knees, he noticed precious stones in the riverbed glinting from the dazzling sunlight overhead. He knelt and gathered opals, diamonds, emeralds, sapphires, and rubies until he could carry no more. Walking back through the mountains, he came to a jasper throne where Jesus sat. He laid the precious gems at the feet of his Lord.

Juan began to cry.

He told us that his Lord touched his cheek and said, "These stones are the youth of Totonicapan. Continue to visit the stream and pull them out. They are precious to Me."

Señor Juan stopped and said nothing for a minute. He looked deep into all of our eyes with grandfatherly love. Then he spoke.

"There is nothing more precious to Jesus than your hearts. Listen, my precious stones. There is nothing you can do, or not do, that will separate you from His love."

These rare moments are when words fill the air like a thousand hummingbirds. You no longer just hear the words. You feel the wind from their wings brushing your face. The simplicity of Juan's message, and the spirit in which he conveyed it, had us all blubbering like babies. Our youth had experienced a moment of wonder they would never forget.

As the sun rose over the mountains, pushing through summer clouds crowding the overhead peaks like fluffy-headed giants, I climbed to a generous overlook of Toto. In a few hours, we'd depart, and I wondered if I'd ever revisit. My chest thumped with the thunder rolling off the mountainside as I watched the villagers buzz like a miniature diorama a hundred feet below. Everywhere I looked, life was pulsating.

I had come to Guatemala seeking an adventure. I had discovered a world filled with wonder, and I knew my leap had altered the trajectory of my life. I agree with what Twain wrote in his article, *Taming the Bicycle*. "I started out alone to seek adventures. You don't really have to seek them—that is nothing but a phase—they come to you."[21] Looking down from the mount on the valley below, I acknowledged adventures came to me. All I needed to do was to leap.

---

21 Mark Twain, "Taming the Bicycle," *StoryOfTheWeek.lou.org*, 1917

Chapter 18

Mama Val

The Fisher Projects, New Orleans - September 1993

As I coughed up a lung, eyes looking out of darkened corners and shaded windows of New Orleans' most notorious housing project followed me. My guardian angel, Darren, a hulking ex-football player turned inner-city missionary, afforded me safe passage to a place I shouldn't have been entering. Outsiders were not welcome in Fischer during the daytime and never after dark. I was here to meet a formidable lady, a queen of sorts, to implore safe passage in the neighborhood. I wanted to bring a mission team into Fischer. Valeria Hawkins was the Godmother of Fischer, and without her blessing, my endeavor would fail.

Fischer was unusually quiet, which was a good sign. The dominant clamor came from me. My obnoxious coughing echoed off the graffiti-splattered walls, warning all folks in the building to stay as far away as possible. When Darren knocked on Ms. Val's door, I sounded like a bag of bolts dropping into a concrete mixer. Before I saw her face, I heard her strong voice.

"Honey, that cough will be your death unless I get you some of my special medicine. Get inside and let Mama Val take care of you."

I entered a one-bedroom apartment, packed floor to ceiling with a lifetime of mementos, furniture, knick-knacks, clothes, and cookware. The aroma was a grandmother's kitchen on Thanksgiving Day. Val cleared a stack of magazines off a green vinyl chair. A trio of TVs competed for attention, playing three programs in different rooms. Darren started into a rowdy conversation with our host. Just out of sight, Val opened a small pantry, pulling out liquid-filled jars and spices to mix into her secret potion. I was sure this was Big Easy voodoo, passed down through generations, to heal a nasty cough. Darren hovered over her as she performed her alchemy. Once satisfied, she picked up a long

Into the Wonder

lighter and waved it like a magic wand over the glass. *Whoosh*. She walked over to me with a half cup of liquid on fire. Val gave me the kind but serious look only a mother can give her frightened child about to receive a shot.

"Baby, when I blow out this flame, you need to drink this down in one go. It will burn, but trust me, that nasty cough will disappear quicker than one of my sweet potato pies at a church picnic."

Ms. Val was a woman without a speck of guile. She was a truth-talker, one of those folks you never have to wonder how they feel. Her charisma was fierce; my trust was instantaneous. She blew the flame out, and I swallowed liquid dynamite. As my throat ignited and my stomach felt the drop of a cannonball, I barely uttered four words.

"What…(hack)…was… (hiccup)…that…(breathe, just breathe)…medicine?"

Darren and Val broke into laughter.

"Son, that was the oldest of medicines. A honey-laced hot toddy."

Darren explained to this young teetotaler that a hot toddy was made out of cheap bourbon, lemon, honey, cloves, and a couple of mystery shots of alcohol. Within an hour, my cough had disappeared.

The three of us enjoyed a home-cooked meal. With touches of southern hospitality, Val served up gumbo so scrumptious that I thought my tongue was going to explode, sweet potato pie that, once I bit into it, stirred up my best childhood holiday memories, and what I hold to as the best fried chicken in the history of the south. Eating Val's Cajun fried chicken is the closest I've come to culinary Nirvana. The way she spiced the batter, just shy of an uncomfortable burn, opening my taste receptors to max capacity, made her chicken dangerously addictive.

Val asked me why I wanted to bring a bunch of Dallas kids to Fischer. "We don't need any more preachers. There's plenty of them around us. I just don't understand why you'd waste time on these people who won't care a bit about what you are doing.

They might be angry that you're here. We barely trust our own in Fischer. We don't trust outsiders."

Under Darren's supervision, we wanted to serve the community, learn what their lives were about, and eat Val's sinfully delightful chicken. I wanted our Dallas kids to soak in the Big Easy vibe and live in a different world from their own. Val and I talked until I could barely keep my eyes open. The hot toddy was winning the night.

"Baby, you come back after a good night's sleep, and I'll let you know if your crazy idea is possible. And also, you need to call me Mama." A few months later, we were back in Fischer.

In Guatemala, wonder disrupted my path and revealed my future direction. I had decided to take a group on a mission trip during fall break, a chance for another disruption. To pull it off, I needed the help of a good friend.

Obtaining a full-ride sports scholarship, Darren Bruce was bright, charming, and, at times, volatile both on and off the football field. While drinking with some buddies in downtown Dallas, a girl handed Darren a religious tract. As he stood looking down at her, she asked if she could pray for him. Something about her eyes sobered him. He let her pray. Back in his dorm, he read the little booklet. The words took him to his knees. He asked Christ to grab ahold of his explosive nature and replace it with one of peace. That holy moment changed Darren.

After completing Bible School, Darren joined the Word of Faith staff where he was ordained. The once fierce linebacker was now a gentle children's minister. Darren became my best friend at Word of Faith.

Raised in the projects in Pennsylvania, Darren never forgot how tough life had been for his family. In 1992, after years of service at Word of Faith, he asked the Lord to take him to a place in America's inner cities where no one else wanted to go. Darren heard New Orleans. When he started researching, he learned about the devastation of the inner city of New Orleans, with Fischer being its most desperate corner. Darren resigned from his well-paid pastoral job and moved south. Many of his friends questioned why anyone would want to give up a life of safety and security for one full of threat and insecurity. Darren had an answer.

"I'm going where Jesus lives."

Mama Val was one of Fischer's first residents after its completion in 1965. The Mississippi River Bridge, which connects the French Quarter on the East Bank to Algiers on the West Bank, looms over the Fischer Projects, a concrete reminder of the heaviness constantly hanging over their heads.

Housing Projects in major U.S. cities began with mass clear-outs of the underprivileged minority sections of a city so that they could be commercially developed. The city of New Orleans built more than ten projects. These dehumanizing superblocks became a symbol of urban poverty and despair. Val told visiting groups, "The projects keep low-income black people separated and walled off from the white folks in the city." As the cheaply constructed buildings deteriorated over the years, so did the hope of the tenants.

"This is a hard place. It is a sad place. Fischer is where people come to hide, to exist out of sight. This is where we live, but it's no home."

By the early 1970s, Fisher was a notorious battleground. The drug trade, gang violence, robberies, and multiple murders turned Fischer into one of the deadliest neighborhoods in America. Violent crime in Fischer was 25 times more prevalent than the national average. Val told me stories of shootings, gang warfare, and retaliation against the N.O.P.D. that set my heart racing. Police, fearing for their lives, refused to enter the neighborhood. Fischer felt apocalyptic.

Darren moved into a small apartment on the edge of Fischer. He was determined to call Fischer home. Starting each day, walking around the perimeter of the forty-eight-acre property, Darren asked God how to serve the community. One morning, a resident asked Darren if he'd ever met the sixty-two-year-old feisty woman many looked to as the matriarch of Fischer.

Valeria Hawkins was born September 10, 1930 as her mother lay on a few sheets thrown on the hard-planked floors of a tiny cabin. Like all their neighbors, her family was poor, but the household was filled with love. Valeria adored her parents. Her mother taught in an all-black school across the river in Louisiana, while her father, a soft-spoken pious man, raised the kids on the banks of the Mississippi. The Hawkins family did what black families in Natchez had to do: whatever it took to provide for their families. This meant Val joined her dad working in the cotton fields. When her mother came home on the weekends, she educated her preschool children and sewed clothes for the family, including drawers and dresses made from Red Squirrel flour sacks. She took them to the daylong Sunday services at the Pentecostal Church. To Val, nothing was more tortuous than sitting still in church on a hot summer day while your potato sack underwear started itching your backside.

The strong-willed girl did not make life easy for her family. She had a formidable way about her. If somebody did her wrong, she was as mean as a feral dog, and she guaranteed they'd pay for their transgressions. By the time she was nine, she had cussed well enough to make a grown man blush, and smoking tobacco came as easy as chewing gum. Whippings, which she received in spades, had no effect. Though she was an intelligent girl, the only way her father motivated her to go to school was to pay her a weekly stipend. Her favorite time of the day was the five-mile ride to school. Val pumped the pedals of her bike while her two younger siblings rode on the back pegs and the front handlebars.

If Val heard a youth complain about their hardships, she'd say, "Shoot, boy. You do not know what the word *tough* means. Have you ever scrubbed a wood floor with a brick or had to wake up before God to feed the chickens and clean the hog pen? And let's not talk about picking cotton." Her queries were always met with bewildered silence.

The night I met Val, and she learned that I was a minister, she felt comfortable enough to explain her complicated relationship with religion to me.

"Son, there are a couple of types of folks I can't abide with; dumbasses and hypocrites."

Sundays meant one thing: church. The First Pentecostal Church of Natchez was the week's liveliest community event. Val's constant verbal mutinies did not stop her parents from dragging her to Sunday school, followed by a four-hour morning service. All attendees were expected to stay for midday prayer, a huge potluck lunch, and an evening service. Church went from 7:30 am to 7:30 pm. Val didn't see the point. She often kept her nickel offering given to her by her mother as a tax on her parents for forcing her to go.

"Shawn, I remember my mom smacking my butt when I asked her why God, who created all the wonders in the world, wanted to spend so much time with us on Sundays. Certainly, He had better things to do. I certainly did."

After a few years of friendship, Val revealed substantial trauma she had experienced from churches that had soured her view of Christians.

When Val was 15, she was impregnated by a man in the church 14 years her senior. When he left town to avoid the responsibility of being a father, Val went to her church looking for a safe place to receive help. As the morning service ended, there was an altar call to come forward and be filled with the Holy Ghost. Desperate for peace, Val came forward. Kneeling in the front, she poured out her pain and fear. Val begged for God's mercy, wondering how she would tell her parents she was pregnant. The preacher came to Val, asking the Lord to fill her with the presence of the Holy Ghost. He asked her to speak in tongues to prove God's work in her heart. She waited, but no words came. An hour later, after the preacher prayed, rebuked, cast out, and did whatever a desperate preacher does when he feels the crowd anxiously waiting for a miracle, he told the congregation Val couldn't receive the Holy Ghost because she had sin in her heart. Val was gutted. She did not need to speak in tongues. Val needed help. She needed a safe place. She needed love.

"I walked away that day convinced I was nothing but a disappointment to God. I was too stubborn, too mean, and certainly full of sin. When I miscarried my baby at eight months, I knew God was punishing me for my sinful heart. I stayed out of church for the next 40 years. I don't know why I am telling you this, Shawn. I haven't talked about it to anyone."

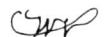

Over the 40 years that Val lived in Fischer, she earned the community's respect. She had witnessed the degradation of the projects, but she helped her neighbors survive as the world crumbled around them. When her seven-year-old grandson was hit by a ricocheting bullet as rival gangs fought for territory, Val, enraged about the pointless violence, faced the local kingpins. She shamed them to their faces for how the deadly skirmishes affected the innocents of Fischer. From that point forward, when Val gave the word, things quieted down.

Val was our doorway to serving the residents of Fischer.

By November, I was back in NOLA with 35 high school students on fall break. Our first two eventful days in Fischer set the tone for how I would serve communities across the globe for the next three decades.

Into the Wonder

Darren had posed a question to Val. "What is the thing that drives you the craziest in Fischer, the project you want to be completed that we can help you accomplish?"

Mama Val knew the answer. She wanted Fischer cleaned up. At the time, it was not unusual for the residents to throw their trash everywhere. Fast food bags flew out of car windows, trash piled up in the middle of courtyards, junk filled the dilapidated playgrounds, and people tossed garbage bags off their front porches onto the ground below. Val was done with it all. The three of us devised a clean-up plan—but it didn't go as we had hoped.

Val asked the dominant gang in the area to leave us alone. They went above her request and promised protection for the Dallas students. Armed with trash bags and gloves, we stood in a circle before Val's high rise for a pep talk before our first trash collection day. Val gave a cheery hello and thanked the students for coming from Dallas to serve the residents of Fischer. She was an inspirational communicator. She told a couple of stories and had the students laughing and clapping. With a final prayer, we broke for our assigned tasks.

For the next six hours, we moved throughout the complex, filling our bags with dirty diapers, rusty needles, old newspapers, used food containers, broken toys, damaged furniture, and every imaginable type of refuse. Most of the residents avoided us. By the end of the day, after filling three huge dumpsters, we circled up to pray for Fischer. Mama Val stood with us, somber with what had been accomplished by a gaggle of high school students. We celebrated the day's work with shrimp po' boys as the students shared their impressions of the mission. They could not wait to get back and tackle another project.

The chatty youth went silent the next day as we pulled up in our vans. The evening after we left, several young people in Fischer spread across the property much of the garbage we had collected, clearly communicating that we were not wanted. Val met the downcast kids in the parking lot. She told the kids what her neighbors did was wrong and that she'd meet with the Fischer Counsel later to discuss the offense. She gave us a choice. Either leave Fischer or start again and show them why we're doing this. She promised that the day would end with a special treat if we were willing to clean again.

The youth cleaned the debris and waste again but with an added twist. Walking in a straight line, from building to building to methodically pick up the trash, they sang old hymns at the top of their lungs. Their young, jubilant vocals rang off the walls and bounced throughout Fischer. Older folks gathered in the front breezeways and on the porches to sing the hymns with them. Conversations started as residents asked dozens of questions about why we were in Fischer. Some of the younger residents joined our cleaning crew.

As the sun dipped low on the horizon, I stood arm-in-arm with Mama Val looking at the expanse of grass, once hidden under trash, and watching young children play on the park grounds without the fear of contamination. Val smiled as our team picnicked on the lawn, losing their minds over her Cajun fried chicken and sweet potato pie.

Her meeting with the Counsel went better than she expected. She wagged her finger in their faces, daring them to speak against her assessment of the trash battle overcoming the community. "You should be embarrassed that a bunch of kids from Texas had to come to show us our shortcomings. It's time to get off our asses and take pride in where we live. Here's how we are going to do that." Val unfolded her plan.

By the end of the week, with a few calls to City Hall, the Housing Authority of New Orleans (HANO) provided cleaning crews, even employing residents, to keep the property clean so that the children of the Fischer Projects could play safely. Val, shrewd as any person I have ever met, had utilized our mission to benefit Fischer for years to come.

Val and many others around her worked tirelessly with HANO to expose the shortcomings of the Housing Projects throughout NOLA. HANO's failed experiment left people hopeless, drained their community pride, and caged them like dying animals in a failing zoo. Ten years after my first visit to the Fischer Projects, all the buildings were demolished and replaced with

Into the Wonder

neat, single-family, rent-to-own dwellings. A Fischer community coalition managed the residents, created guidelines for property ownership, and brought dignity to the Fischer. Val had been the catalyst for a miracle.

Our first voyage to NOLA in the Fall of 1993 was the starting trickle for a flood of hundreds of youths from across the United States who served in Fischer and throughout greater New Orleans for the next three decades. Val spoke to every group. Exposing young people to the Projects was an education in sacrificial service. Mama Val fed our teams over two-thousand pieces of her mouth-watering fried chicken and sweet potato pie. While they ate, she told true stories from her life, the plight of her people, and the realities of living in the Projects. Most students who joined these voyages lived in safe, stable, and loving environments. For many, New Orleans was their first realization that there were places in the United States operating like war zones.

To fully serve people, one must understand their plight, world, and reality. Empathetic education became a method for how I led trips to hard places around the world. The ability to open yourself up to the suffering of others is an element of experiencing wonder. It's comfortable and safe to swoop in and out of a place performing good deeds. It is quite another to purposefully live in a place for a few days, empathizing with the pain of those around you, learning the stories of those you serve, and departing with the seeds of compassion planted in your spirit. This is called *incarnational* service. You not only meet people in their pain, but you enter their pain with them—just as Jesus did when He came to earth as a human. Loving others means lowering our emotional barriers. This is not an easy discipline, and it takes years to learn.

In his book *The Divine Magician*, Peter Rollins writes, "To love is to experience a world come alive, but it also means opening oneself up to a poignant suffering. When we open ourselves up to love, we do not leave pain behind in favor of pleasure; rather we open ourselves up to an experience of depth and meaning that involves both pain and pleasure. For when life is infused with depth and wonder, we cannot help but experience our fair share of both happiness and unhappiness. It is only in protecting ourselves from love that we can hope to protect ourselves from suffering. By creating a closed circle around ourselves, where we care only for our own well-being, we create barriers that protect us from the storms of life, but that also shield us from life's summer days."[22]

Mama Val inspired hundreds of youths who heard her stories and pondered questions she posed about racial equality, the plight of blacks in America, public housing, and gang violence. If she invited you into her world, and you were brave enough to walk through that door, you grew and opened your heart to the wonder of compassion.

On August 29, 2005, Hurricane Katrina, the deadliest tempest ever recorded in the Gulf of Mexico, struck the Louisiana coast as a devastating demon bent on wiping the Big Easy off the map. After smashing the coast, it crept up the Mississippi River leaving New Orleans an underwater catastrophe. The floodwalls had failed, submerging 80% of the city in water that turned poisonous in the days following. Hundreds were dead, most of whom had either refused to leave or could not flee. More than half the city's population who had escaped ahead of the storm never returned. Days after Katrina, multitudes were unaccounted for, including our beloved Mama Val.

Val had fully invited me into her life. I was in New Orleans at least once a year with a team to serve Fischer, and she insisted I stay with her. We spent hours eating hearty meals at her favorite restaurants

---

22   Peter Rollins, *The Divine Magician* (New York: Howard Books, 2015), 78.

and swapping stories. I brought my family to NOLA, including my three children, all under six. While I served with the teams in Fischer, the kids stayed at Val's apartment. She loved showing off her adopted grandchildren in the local Walmart—her favorite haunt. At restaurants, stores, parks, and throughout Fischer, my kids called her Grandma Val, causing anyone around to do a double-take. Val ate it up.

Mama Val was a mother to Cheryl and me. Once a year, we flew Mama Val up to Texas to spend a week with our family. She called this her "high falutin' vacation week in the Big D." We joked we would only send her back home after we all gained ten extra pounds from her cooking. We sent her on a cruise to the Caribbean on her seventieth birthday. She was proud to show us her passport and tell us about her first time out of the U.S. She declared her cruise one of the happiest adventures of her life.

When Val disappeared during Hurricane Katrina, we were terrified. We had tried to reach her before the chaos, but the bedlam came sooner than anyone imagined. The telephone lines were dead as the brunt of the storm pounded NOLA. When the levees breached, we prayed desperately for Mama's safety.

Over the years, we had formed dozens of relationships across the city. Most of our friends had fled before the hurricane. A few, especially in Algiers, were determined to ride it out. A few days after the storm, we connected with someone and asked him to check on Val. Her place was locked up, and she was nowhere to be found. Scouring the internet for information, trying to work through our networks, and contacting rescue organizations, our efforts were dead ends in the aftermath of the killer storm. All we could do was pray.

Two weeks passed with no word of Val's whereabouts. We began to consider that she might not have survived. Our family was sitting in a restaurant when I received a call from my friend Blake, a youth minister in Dallas who had been to NOLA on one of my trips with his youth.

"Shawn, this is really strange, but I think my friend Matt found Ms. Val. I'll text you his phone number." The word was out in churches across the U.S. who had visited NOLA with me over the years that their beloved Ms. Val was missing. Blake had received a call from his friend serving in a first responder triage outside Baton Rouge.

My hands shook as I dialed the number. I introduced myself to Matt. The small talk ended quickly when he said someone wanted to talk to me.

"Baby, is that you?"

I started to cry when I heard Val's worn-out voice.

"Oh, baby. Don't cry. I'm okay."

Her story was both harrowing and miraculous. Val and a couple of busloads of the elderly Fischer folk were picked up and taken to the Superdome, joining 30,000 other citizens surviving the ferocious hurricane as it overtook the Big Easy. Val's next few days in the Superdome were, in her words, vexing. The conditions disintegrated quickly, becoming sub-human: no electricity, blistering heat, a lack of water, and backed-up sewage stinking up the Superdome. Val was trapped in the middle of growing madness. Her age, emphysema, and chronic heart condition allowed her to move to the front of the list for medical evacuation. Mama Val was taken by ambulance to the safety of a Baton Rouge triage. Matt, an EMT, had driven down from Dallas to volunteer. For a week, he took the vitals of high-risk patients, monitoring their medication administration and caring for their mental well-being.

On his last night before driving back to Dallas, he sat with a woman who was a deluge of conversation. While taking her vitals, she found out he was from Dallas. Then she asked an impossible question.

"Do you know my son, Shawn Small? He lives in Dallas, and I am sure he's worried about me."

Matt was stunned. Though he and I had never met, Blake had casually conversed with Matt about his trip to NOLA with me. Something clicked in the back of Matt's mind. The chances were impossible, yet Mama Val had asked the right question, to the right person, at the right time. An hour later, she was in Matt's car heading to our home in Texas. Our reunion was tear-filled.

Val lived with us for six months until it was safe for her to return to Fischer. She missed NOLA, her friends, the food, and the place she had lived all her adult life. Hurricane Katrina relief work motivated several teams we took to NOLA over the next five years.

In February of 2008, at 73, Mama Val quietly fell into the arms of Christ. After Hurricane Katrina, she had told me, in no uncertain terms, I was to speak at her funeral. The tone of her post-life ceremony was to be merry and irreverent. The message she wanted to leave behind was, "Life is tough, but laughter and love are priceless gifts. Look for them. They are all around you." She wanted those who attended to know that Jesus had found her even when she had run from Him. About 150 people stood in and around the little Baptist church that seated half that amount. Friends, family, government officials, gang leaders, and preachers roared with laughter as I told stories she had requested two years before her death. My adopted mama, Mama Val, Queen of Fischer, left me with her final instruction.

"Baby, if it's not as funny as a Night at the Apollo, I'll haunt you!"

Chapter 19

Gone

In 1992, faith healer Norvel Hayes introduced an emotionally fragile and spiritually shattered Bob Tilton to a charismatic sect known for their extreme practices in demonic deliverance. Sam and Jane Whaley founded Word of Faith Fellowship (WFF) in Spindale, North Carolina. The sect, which fellow members claim was a cult, was known for its paralyzing legalism. Since the inception of WFF, the Whaleys created a growing list of "dont's" for those who joined. Ex-members claimed congregants did not celebrate holidays, including Christmas and Easter. Church members had to get permission to attend college, choose a major, and purchase a house or car. Television, movies, newspapers, alcohol, and secular music were taboo. Members were even prohibited from buying Nikes because the swoosh on the side was considered a pagan symbol. These rules were strange, yet the weirdest doctrine they practiced was "demon blasting."

Many practices the Whaleys instituted were birthed out of twisted demonology. Extracting vague passages taken out of context throughout the Bible is the backbone of any cult. The Whaleys believed demons had overrun the earth. A few true "believers" were in an epic battle with those demonic forces for the souls of humanity. They believed throngs of evil spirits clung to non-believers and backslidden believers. Evil spirits entered a person through books, cigarettes, false teachers, restaurants, radios, magazines, sitcoms, concerts, television, bikinis, comic books, sermons, and anything the founders deemed unholy. In their teachings, the world was overrun by demonic entities, but the Whaleys had harnessed the revelatory power of God to set people free.

Tilton had become paranoid, believing the devil chatter he pushed on his television show, *Success-N-Life*. In his mind, Satan had targeted him because he was God's prophet. Looking for relief

Into the Wonder

from his outward persecution and mounting innermost torments, Tilton ran to the Whaleys for deliverance.

In early August, Tilton came to the church stage directly after Word of Faith's executive pastor, Don Clowers, resigned. Tilton had the live Sunday service cameras turned off before he announced to the four thousand attendees that he was divorcing his wife, Marte. He made his statement as she sat in the front row, straight-backed with a stoic look of defiance. Her two oldest children sat to her left and right. The following day, the massive WOF offices had been scrubbed of any item with Marte's image or name. Empty bookshelves, missing pictures, historical keepsakes; nothing remained to show she had ever been a co-founder in the ministry.

The Word of Faith lay leadership staff, Christian leaders worldwide, and close friends begged Tilton to reconsider his divorce. He ignored all of them. Over the next twelve weeks, the church lost two-thirds of its members. Eight months later, he married Leigh Valentine, a member of the Whaley camp. The marriage lasted three years before it ended in a messy, public divorce.

Then came the Twilight Zone service. To this day, I doubt I will ever sit through a church service that will equal the Sunday morning Robert Tilton imploded in front of 1,500 parishioners. Years later, a friend at the service told me, "It's a moment I would have never wanted to miss and one I would never want to relive."

Uneasiness hung as we walked into the sanctuary on an overcast mid-November morning. We sat near the front, where we typically roosted, joining a shrinking congregation of 1,500. Shadowed faces filled the front row on the opposite side of the cavernous 4,000-seat auditorium. Several prominent members of the North Carolina sect, including the Whaleys, sat in the audience. One of their ranks was the new executive pastor. We called him the Dark Raven as he lurked around, watching us and taking notes about our activity. During his preaching, Pastor Bob regularly took shots at the press, Ole Anthony, *Primetime Live*, or "enemies" who were persecuting "God's prophet." He did this while TV cameras were broadcasting live. But this morning, there were no cameras, a sign that something big was about to go down. My stomach pinched with anxiety.

An outwardly cheery Pastor Bob spoke as if he had no care. A few minutes into his message, Tilton began to dive into one of his usual us-versus-them rants. A prominent congregation member stood up and addressed Tilton. Everyone turned toward the impromptu public confrontation. In short, he questioned Tilton about the destructive nature of his messages over the last few months. Tilton called over two burly security guards to eject the naysayer from the building. He pleaded for Tilton's repentance as security pushed their way through seated congregants to drag him away. A reporter visiting the service and smelling blood in the air, made a call. Within twenty minutes, local news, camera crews, and reporters with microphones were waiting for disgruntled congregants to emerge and tell their stories.

The last congregants of the Word of Faith community held onto the hope their pastor would either repent of his wayward ways or leave the church. They wanted WOF back. But it never was their church.

After the man was expelled, Tilton walked through the congregation, pointing out those he believed were spreading slander and lies against him. Calling many by name, he spoke judgment before they were physically ejected from the building. One of our senior ministers, Dr. M, known for his wisdom and poise, had whispered something in Tilton's ear. He was ushered to the stage and handed a microphone. The congregation quieted. Dr. M stood silently for a few seconds, collecting his thoughts, while Tilton stood opposite him with a triumphant grin.

"Bob, I came on staff here because of the church you've worked so hard to build. I've loved you and have been a recipient of your abundant generosity. Look around. You did this. You built all of this. Your faith, your faithfulness, has touched people around the world."

Hearing these words, Tilton began to tear up. Dr. M had taken control of the microphone and shut down his accusers. But Dr. M wasn't finished.

"What has happened to you that you have run so far away from the Lord you say you believe in? Why have you allowed yourself to be led astray? You are hurting all of us."

The air was sucked from the room. Tilton, suddenly red as a tomato, yelled, "SECURITY!"

Security guards gruffly shooed Dr. M off the stage. People yelled back and forth throughout the auditorium. There were those in support of Tilton and those who could no longer sit silently. By the dozens, they stormed out, never to return.

I wanted to protest. I wanted to yell like an Old Testament prophet, rend my garments, shake the dust from my feet, and walk away. But I sat still. I was too afraid to make a move. I had a family to think about. What I was sure of was that my time at the church was coming to an end.

Our pastoral staff was down by 50%. Tilton came into the office Monday morning saying it was time for the staff to fervently seek the Lord. For a couple of hours each morning, we were to gather in staff "deliverance" sessions led by the Whaleys until we broke through to God's blessing. This is where the "demon blasting" practice emerged like maggots from rotten meat.

I went to the first session, curious how this strange group had gained a tight hold on the charismatic Robert Tilton. After a brief sermon about the innumerous evils of the world, people were invited to come forward for prayers of deliverance. I sat near the front. The Dark Raven came and stood before me. I looked into his empty eyes. He started to put his hand on my shoulder.

"Don't touch me," I said flatly.

"Brother, I am here to free you from the demons tormenting you." He reached again for my shoulder.

Looking at him with a hard stare, I said, "I'll break your fingers if you touch me."

He backed away, then whispered into Jane Whaley's ear. I'm sure he was convinced I was possessed. I got the hint and moved to the back of the room.

A few people came forward for prayer. Each person was placed in a chair while the North Carolina crew circled them. They started their deliverance session by boisterously rebuking the devil and all his minions. After a few minutes, they shifted into loud tongues. The bellowing ruckus grew in pitch and force to a crescendo. The frightening "demon blasting" then commenced. Speaking in tongues turned into ear-splitting roars and screams. It was a prayer akin to an enraged *Jerry Springer* audience.

The spectacle was jolting. Those who submitted to this spiritual abuse sat shaking, crying, screaming, or holding their eyes shut, waiting for the ordeal to end. Plastic bags were given to those being prayed for. According to the Whaleys, one being purged of a demon will often spit or vomit up the evil entity. Though they continued for the next several weeks, I never returned to the deliverance meetings.

Cheryl and I agreed on my resignation date. We had spent months saying goodbye to dozens of families fleeing the crumbling church. We referred to that season as our lifeboat ministry. We compassionately lowered students we loved out of the sinking Titanic and into lifeboats taking them to a safer harbor. Churches for twenty miles in every direction were absorbing WOF's spiritual refugees. I reminded the students that, no matter where we go, God is always close at hand. God was with them when their spiritual role models failed miserably.

By the end of November, the youth group was down from hundreds to a sad handful of hangers-on. Cheryl and I were no longer attending church services, so trying to run a youth service was useless.

We decided to take an extended vacation through the Thanksgiving holidays to look at our future. On the first Monday in

Into the Wonder

December, I would put in my two-week resignation with the veiled hope I might be instantly let go with a severance package attached.

We placed the children in their car seats. Coeli looked up at me with that "too tight" grimace as I double-checked her shoulder straps. It was hard to believe she had spent months trapped in a full-body cast. Outside of the small circular scars on her left knee, she was a work of healing wonder. Only five months old, little Kayla slept as we placed her in the car.

We were celebrating our years at Word of Faith with one final holiday bash. Invitations were sent to the leadership team we had pastored at WOF. Even though the last couple of years had been tumultuous, our season as youth ministers had been exceptional. We had learned how to spiritually encourage others in their faith journey, dipped our toes in cross-cultural missions, and served the best we knew how for hundreds of teenagers. Despite the absurdity of Word of Faith and Robert Tilton, a close, dynamic community had developed.

Several couples were a part of our leadership team. These couples were mentors and lifelong friends. The authenticity and openness with which they lived revealed aspects of God's love to us. The whimsical VanSinderens taught us to stay childlike in our adult pursuits. The Ericksons, ever curious, displayed the infinite possibilities of the imagination. Our marriage was steadied and strengthened through the wise and compassionate counseling of the O'Briens, and the Grosses never left a hug hanging in the air. These couples, who had already left the church, and dozens more were coming to a Christmas party to remember all that had been good in our time at Word of Faith.

We drove down a stretch of road under heavy construction as the winter sun descended below the horizon. We were three miles from home, where the mammoth Grapevine Mills Outlet Mall footprint had just been poured. The lack of light on the four-lane motorway made it challenging to see. Flipping on my signal,

Gone

I turned left to cross the northbound lanes. In the center of the crossing, still looking to the right, I was blinded by high beams unexpectedly illuminating the inside of my vehicle. A driver heading northbound was driving without his headlights. He turned on his lights thirty feet from our car before t-boning us at 70 m.p.h.

His car smashed into Cheryl's door, bulldozing our vehicle 40 feet down the road and onto the embankment. Glass fragments burst onto my right side, accompanying the all too familiar sound of an explosive metallic meat grinder. The driver who hit us remained up the road, slamming on his brakes after the initial concussion. Stunned, I looked back at the girls. They were shaken and crying but safe. Cheryl was not. She had taken the full impact of the hit. Her door had crumpled like a soda can, the window shattering to dust. She was unconscious and breathing sporadically.

A guttural wheeze crawled from her throat before her chest stopped moving. Afraid to touch her, I screamed for her to wake up. The girls in the back seat cried, hearing the fear in my voice. Cheryl did not move. Suddenly, she sucked in a painful rush of air into her lungs. Barely coming to, Cheryl asked about the sudden flash of light before she coughed up blood and went unconscious again. A sickening gurgling came from her throat as she started into a death-rattle.

The ambulance arrived mercifully fast. Several EMTs rushed over. When they saw Cheryl, a call was made for a CareFlight helicopter. The next few minutes were a blur as they pulled the girls into the back of an ambulance to check their physical state. I stood sinking into a despairing madness as an EMT asked me questions.

"This was not supposed to happen again. How is this happening again?" The EMT, confused by my ramblings, tried to calm me down.

"She's dying all over again. I can't lose her a second time."

He continued probing, convinced I had hit my head in the accident. The thump-thump-thump from above stopped my ramblings. A medical emergency helicopter landed in the middle of the road. Knowing time was short, the EMTs lifted Cheryl's gurney into the chopper.

As it headed into the sky, I snapped. Convinced I would never see Cheryl again, I walked toward the south side of the road, directly into oncoming traffic. A hand grabbed my arm and tugged me back before I walked into the path of a Mack truck. A police officer, having no idea of my mental state, grabbed me to lead me to the ambulance where my daughters waited for me. I snapped out of my disorientation.

We were taken to the local hospital and given a quick look over by the ER doctor who declared us unharmed by the impact. By then, friends had arrived. The Ericksons whisked the girls to their house while Jim O'Brien took me to Cheryl. She had been flown to the Parkland Trauma Unit. When I arrived, one of the doctors pulled me aside to steady me before I entered Cheryl's station.

"Your wife is in critical condition. She will need immediate surgery to stabilize her. She took a major blow to the head. All the right side back ribs are broken. One of her ribs has punctured her right lung. Her right hip appears to have been shattered. Before you can see her, we need to insert a chest tube to re-inflate her lung. Once we stabilize her, you can visit her briefly before we take her to surgery."

Thus began the darkest night of my life.

Without anesthesia, the ER doctor cut through Cheryl's side, attempting to insert a tube into her chest cavity. The procedure was designed to empty the excess fluid that kept her right lung from inflating. I sat on the other side of the curtain, going out of my mind, as I heard Cheryl's agonizing groans. I blubbered into my hands, wishing I could take her place. Why was this happening again? After fifteen tormenting minutes, I heard the doctor.

"This isn't working. We need to change the angle."

And like some hellish Groundhog Day, the process started over this time with a periodic pitiful yelp from Cheryl. Death waited to pounce and take her out of my life. Mercifully, the second procedure worked, and Cheryl breathed without gasping. A few moments later, they ushered me to her side. She lay under a sheet. A tattered pile of cut-away clothes crumpled in the corner. Bruises were forming on the right side of her body. I gingerly touched her hand. It was enough for her eyes to flutter open.

"Hi," she whispered.

That one word released a deluge of tears. Trying to compose myself enough to talk, I told her she was about to undergo surgery. She was so broken and physically wracked that I doubted I would see her again. I tried to wear a brave face.

"The doctors are going to take good care of you. Everything is going to be all right."

She looked at me, discerning my untruth. She reached up and touched my face like a butterfly wing drying my tears.

"If I don't live, remind the babies how much I love them. I will always love you. It's okay for you to live life once I am gone." She suddenly grimaced in pain and let her arm fall to her side.

"I'm so sorry," was all I could muster.

"Mr. Small, we need to take her now." An ER nurse came behind me, shaking me out of my stupor.

Then she was gone.

Cheryl was in serious but stable condition. They were monitoring her closely. Everyone was amazed at the grit she displayed. Her ribs would take time to mend. The right hip, like her left hip the year before, had been rebuilt in surgery. She suffered a mild traumatic brain injury that would have minor effects on her for the rest of her life. An EMT, in full gear, had just landed with another car accident victim. He had inquired about Cheryl and was coming down to see if the rumor was true. The nurse had pointed at me, and he had approached with a beaming smile.

"Mr. Small, I had to see your wife for myself. When we picked her up in the copter, she was in a dangerous place. We lost and revived her three times on our 12-minute flight to Parkland. I was shocked when they told me she made it and was growing stronger every hour."

Into the Wonder

After some small talk and my undying thankfulness, he walked away, saying, "This is what makes what I do worth it."

Cheryl spent ten days in Parkland Hospital. Though her injuries in the second accident were more severe than the first, our accident a year prior had mentally, physically, and spiritually prepared her for an energetic recovery. The key was physical therapy that she tackled like a training Olympic athlete. Cheryl recovered in a fraction of the time she had with the first accident.

My heart was also in a different place than it had been a year ago. The accident happened because a guy was driving without his lights. I did not see him. He did not see us. He walloped us. And we were still alive. During my night of agony, I sensed God's presence surrounding me, comforting me, and weeping when I wept. I slept beside Cheryl in the hospital, and we talked about family, friends, love, wonder, peace, and how nothing could separate us from God's love.

We agreed that the Word of Faith mess was small potatoes in the vast scope of our lives. The last year's trials had acted like a life filter, separating the essential from the dispensable. Magician Nate Staniforth, in his book *Here is Real Magic* writes,

"Once in a while something happens—and I have become convinced that it absolutely does not matter what—and we see the cracks in our convictions, and through them a sliver of that larger, wider world outside the one we have constructed. The vision we see there either assaults our sense of control and sovereignty and drives us cowering backward to the world of our making, or it exposes that world for the illusion it really is and invites us upward and onward toward the real thing. So if your goal is to bring wonder back into your ordinary daily life, start by recognizing that it's not ordinary daily life, start by recognizing that it's not ordinary if you don't want it to be, that it never has been ordinary even if you do want it to be, and that the whole world waits for you to open your eyes and look around you and really see it."[23]

Our life was extraordinary. Those things we once fretted over, including the end of our time at Word of Faith, were the husks of our existence. God was not the author of our pain. He was

---

23 Nate Staniforth, *Here is Real Magic* (New York: Bloomsbury, 2018), 229.

Gone

the author of our healing. He walked beside us no matter where our next steps took us.

As I sat in my office on my first day after our accident, I found that writing my resignation letter came quickly. I was a lame-duck pastor. The Dark Raven continued to slink around the church like Frankenstein's Igor. While I had been caring for Cheryl, he had replaced me with another person to run the youth group, now down to a handful of kids. He considered me spiritually compromised since our little encounter a few weeks back. My interaction with Robert Tilton on the night of the accident was the strangest and most disturbing of my five years of employment.

When Cheryl was rushed into surgery, an ICU nurse said I had a phone call. I was hoping it was my family, and I shuddered when I heard Tilton's voice. Not unlike his television persona, he began, in his bellicose manner, to pray aloud for God to save Cheryl's life. He began rebuking hit-squad demons sent to destroy us, asking God to forgive us for the doors we had left open for the enemy's attack. Then came the groaning and screeching of his demon blasting.

There was not a hint of compassion in his voice. He was a general speaking to his troops, readying them for battle. I stayed silent.

"Pray like me, Shawn, or Cheryl will die!"

I hung up.

The day I returned to the office, I submitted my resignation letter. For two weeks, I waited for the memo to pack up my belongings and hit the road. It didn't come.

On my final day, mid-January, Tilton popped his head into my office. After small talk, he asked me to stay on for a few more months: double pay and the opportunity for a big future. I thanked him for his offer and then told him that I did not agree with what was happening in the church. He asked me where I was going next. When I told him I had no idea, he shook his head.

"Shawn, you are missing the opportunity of a lifetime. But you're entitled to make any stupid decision you want. Lord bless you in your pursuit to nowhere."

Robert Tilton hung on to Word of Faith for a few years. By 1996, now divorced for a second time, he put a puppet pastor in charge of the church. Tilton sporadically showed up a few times a year to preach. The congregation of 130 eventually faded away like invisible ink. Tilton relocated to Florida for a few years before landing in California, where he met with a dozen congregants, his rendition of Word of Faith, in a hotel conference room. Tilton continues his online presence, asking for donations with his fundraising schemes.

When people discover I worked for Tilton, I'm often asked to give my opinion of him. They assume that Tilton is a con man. I don't believe that. I never observed anything about him leading me to believe he was out to steal money from the ignorant and innocent. He wasn't a snake oil salesman running the long con. There was something much more tragic about Robert Tilton.

He believed everything he taught.

Robert Tilton wholly gave himself to the doctrine he peddled to others. He believed he was God's conduit for people to obtain physical, spiritual, and financial prosperity. Thus, people should give to him generously. The most frightening possibility for any preacher is when they are unequivocally convinced that they speak for God, holding an exceptional understanding of the Bible. I think Robert Tilton was blinded to the message of Jesus by embracing his interpretation of a gospel he desperately wanted. And that is how the Bible identifies a false prophet.

Red Rocks, Colorado - June 2007

On the outskirts of Woodland Park, Colorado, I hiked to a rare gem called Red Rocks. The 30 to 70-foot red sandstone monoliths can be seen for miles. There were subtle cuts and grooves in the rocks, created through a millennium of rainstorms and harsh weather, forming subtle magnificence, a divine showcase of monumental sculptures. Awestruck by their beauty, I circumvented each monument, exploring how they were individually shaped on the meteorological pottery wheel.

Those towering beauties, formed through violent weather, are reminders of our lives. The greater the intensity of climate, the deeper the splendor. Pounding rain, ferocious winds, and deadly lightning were nature's tools of choice when fashioning these sandstone giants.

My odd years at Word of Faith were formative to my spiritual journey. I learned and grew amid the absurdity. The storms of those years were God's hammer and chisel, forming me into the person I am today. Nothing I experienced or witnessed was wasted on my spiritual journey. "We know that God makes all things work together for the good of those who love Him and are chosen to be a part of His plan" (Romans 8:28 NLV).

Sitting atop a sandstone giant and reading a quote by G.K. Chesterton, I thanked God. "How much happier you would be, how much more of you there would be, if the hammer of a higher God could smash your small cosmos."[24] As my time at Word of Faith closed, my small cosmos had been obliterated, laying the way for a richer life. What came next was anyone's guess.

---

24   G.K. Chesterton, *Orthodoxy* (Chicago: Moody, 2009), 46.

"I jumped at the opportunity to pilgrimage to the Holy Land, and I invited Mike to join me." (Israel October 1991)

"I can recall the crunch of 4000 pounds of plastic, glass, and steel." (Iowa November 1991)

"My kids called her Grandma Val." (2006)

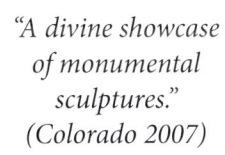

"A divine showcase of monumental sculptures." (Colorado 2007)

"Keith, the Cross Carrier." (Solomon Islands 2006)

"Antonio took to NOLA with gusto." (New Orleans 1994)

"A stone carving was embedded in the wall over the altar." (Inis Ofrr Ireland 2001)

"Coumshingaun Lough might have been the dwelling place of dragons." (Ireland 1996)

"Immrama played a considerable role in my life." (Ireland 1998)

"A wisp of a girl begged me for a bite to eat." (Madagascar Africa 2001)

"Mauritius' smudge-blue mountains thrust upwards like daggers." (Mauritius Africa 2001)

"You must fulfill your vow and wear Chief's shoes." (Comoros Africa 2001)

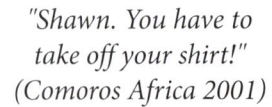

"Shawn. You have to take off your shirt!" (Comoros Africa 2001)

*"The structure was constructed around the
stone, the chapel's altar." (Wales 2001)*

Chapter 20

Wantok

He stood before the fiery preacher, a tear-stained face divulging a lifetime of pain and aching rejection. The 40 companions watching him were silent in the tension. In all his years of attending church, he had never stepped forward for prayer, rejecting the spiritual beliefs of others as silly, cruel, and vindictive. He had no time for such notions. The visiting preacher, at the end of his soul-stirring sermon, invited anyone who wanted to talk to God to come forward. Antonio was the last person anyone expected.

As he stood by himself, eye to eye with the preacher, the angels paused for the unexpected. The preacher looked into the face of a young man barely old enough to get a driver's license and asked him a hushed question:

"Son, do you have something you want to say to your Father in heaven?"

Antonio breathed, gathering himself. Looking toward the Almighty, he raised a fist and roared, "God, I hate You!"

Guadalcanal, Solomon Islands - March 2006

The wiry black man with the million-dollar smile had walked barefoot on the wisp of a rumor that he might find us at our hotel. On a small island nation, word of strange visitors circulates on the ocean winds. Solomon Islanders, or SI-ers, prefer being barefoot. They believe it is easier to connect with the earth's life flow. Isaac had walked five miles to ask if Keith, the Cross Carrier, might share words of encouragement with the Anglican Church of the Transfiguration's Sunday School class.

Into the Wonder

Keith and I were on one of our edge-of-the-earth adventures in the South Pacific. The Solomon Islands, specifically the big island of Guadalcanal, had been the setting for Operation Watchtower, the first major land offensive by Allied forces against the Japanese Empire in World War II. The costly battle lasted seven months. Allied forces succeeded in wrestling Guadalcanal free from the Japanese invaders because of the intelligence and stealth of the SI resistance. They are tough, rugged people, once head-hunters, now heroes.

The 992 islands of the SI are part of Oceania's Pacific Ring of Fire. People have inhabited her tiny coastal villages and ancient lands for 30,000 years. A complicated tribal system passed down through the millennia holds the ruling cords that create a binding peace between diverse tribal groups speaking over 100 dialects.

Guadalcanal has a ragged, worn-out feeling, like a once opulent garden overrun with weeds. The country's hectic disrepair resulted from a depressed economy that never sufficiently recovered from foreign invasion. Guadalcanal was one of those atypical travel locations that made me homesick, not because it reminded me of the things I was missing but because it accentuated the reality that I was a stranger. The appearance of the shoeless, blond-haired pastor Isaac derailed my perception. Up for the unknown adventure, we climbed into our vehicle and headed outside Honoria's capital city.

Our one-hour journey was on roads that were peppered with rain-filled holes that almost swallowed our vehicle, lasted an hour. We parked near a steep emerald hill with steps hand cut from the earth. Keith and Isaac raced up the rise while I clawed hand and foot. As I huffed and puffed over the last rise, I saw a blood-red steeple standing on a promontory overlooking the verdant fruit-filled valleys of the island's interior.

The Sunday School class met in a tin-covered circular structure without walls. It provided a clear view for miles in all directions. An escalating harmony relieved the emotional melancholy I had been holding for the last couple of days. Thirty young people from the church's youth choir were punching the atmosphere with resurrection songs in Pijin and English. We arrived as they were finishing their rehearsals for the upcoming Easter program. I was overcome by the beauty of the moment. In the words of Abraham Joshua Heschel, "Unless we know how to praise Him, we cannot learn to know Him. Praise is our first answer to wonder."[25] The praise of these young people opened my despondent heart to the surrounding wonder.

Pastor Isaac introduced us. The group gathered around, giving us generous hugs as if we were visiting relatives. We shared stories of faith. They shared friendship and tenderness. We laughed, prayed, and exercised our taste buds over a table filled with sweet island fruit.

As we readied to leave, Isaac spoke a blessing over us. We sat while the young people surrounded us, their affection overcoming any of my outsider imaginings. In a deep, sing-song voice, Isaac spoke.

"You, my friends, are no longer strangers to our island. You are part of our clan, our family under Christ the King. You are *wantok*. We speak the same language. We obey the same Chief. We love the same Lord. We are your *wantok*. Our land is your land. Your needs are our needs. Your God is our God. You will forever have a family in the Solomons."

The Pijin word *wantok* is an adaptation of the English phrase "one talk" or "of the same voice." When you are *wantok* with a community, you serve under the same chieftain; you practice the same customs and are entitled to all tribal resources. In return, you are compelled to aid another *wantok* in whatever they ask, such as food, shelter, helping to build a house, cutting wood, or giving them a ride. To refuse is to disgrace yourself, the community, and the chieftain. In naming us *wantok*, we were invited into the clan with benefits as community members.

The longing to be *wantok* is one of the aches of humanity. We want to be wanted and accepted into a community we call our family, our people. The small gathering at the hillside church welcomed us *wantok* under Christ. There is a hopeful promise found in the Bible. "There is one body and one Spirit—just as you

---

25   Abraham Joshua Heschel, *Man is Not Alone* (Harper Torchbooks, 1966).

were called to the one hope that belongs to your call—one Lord, one faith, one baptism, one God and Father of all, who is over all and through all and in all" (Ephesians 4:4–6 ESV). Galatians also tells us, "For in Christ Jesus you are all sons of God, through faith. For as many of you were baptized into Christ have put on Christ. There is neither Jew nor Greek, there is neither slave nor free, there is no male and female, for you are all one in Christ Jesus" (Galatians 3:26–28 ESV).

That afternoon, we were no longer strangers but a part of a family, even though that family lived on the other side of the planet. We were, and would forever be, *wantok*.

A few months after leaving Word of Faith, I was offered a job as a youth minister in Dallas. This was as familiar as I could hope for. Unfortunately, choices based on comfort and familiarity can blind the desperate. That was certainly the case for me when Cheryl and I met with Don to discuss the church he was starting.

The implosion of Word of Faith caused aftershocks. WOF had been a unique place, albeit stained by the foibles of Robert Tilton. If someone discovered you had been a member of WOF, you either received an eye roll, a muffled snicker, or a look of confusion. Thousands of ex-members who had once defended Robert Tilton searched for a new spiritual home. A cluster of churches filled with WOF outcasts emerged throughout the Metroplex.

The pattern for these Sunday pop-ups was predictable. Disenfranchised ex-WOF members met to discuss what the perfect church should look like. They approached an ex-WOF pastor asking him or her to shepherd this imagined spiritual Shangri-La. Self-appointed leaders ironed out the financial details, meeting location, and leadership structure that trumped all other concerns. A Sunday meeting began in a hotel, school, or strip mall.

Six fellowships within twenty minutes of the old WOF sanctuary cropped up in a year. They were filled with wounded, cynical, yet sincere spiritual refugees. Unfortunately, these groups were created out of woundedness. The newly anointed shepherds, my ex-compadres at WOF, were as confused as anyone else. However, like me, there was a strong pull to the familiar. Most of the insta-churches did not survive five years.

Don had been the executive pastor at WOF. He had started as a preaching phenomenon at age 15, traveling with well-known circuit faith healers and evangelists. He led tent revivals worldwide before starting a church in his Tennessee hometown. His friend, Robert Tilton, had sought him out to become the Executive Pastor at WOF during the difficult days of *Primetime Live*. Don, with his wife, accepted. Don did well with the WOF pastoral staff and mentored me, the youngest minister. Seeing my potential, he was patient, and he challenged me. Under his encouragement, I experimented with mission trips. His hands-off management allowed me to take the youth ministry to exciting places.

When Don discerned the inevitable implosion of Tilton's divorce announcement, he stepped down, even when others encouraged him to hijack the church. If anyone had a chance to wrestle control of WOF from its unstable pastor, it would have been Don. Instead, he returned to his evangelistic roots.

When WOF dropped to a few hundred parishioners, and Don saw the spiritual refugees wandering *en masse*, the temptation to take a piece of the crumbling mega-church pie became fierce. He gathered a handful of ex-WOF pastors, including me, to form Grace Fellowship Family Church (GFFC). Our church, housed in an office complex, landed three miles from the WOF sanctuary.

By the fall of 1994, GFFC had a congregation of 300 the majority being ex-WOF members. Everyone felt as if life was steadying. In reality, there was an underlying current that anyone who has experienced the trauma of a church split understands. Silent questions tore at the edges of our protective walls. *When will the bottom drop out? Will this pastor fail? How will I trust spiritual leadership again?* Those thoughts were thrown into a subconscious bag of doubt and dread. We buried them in a shallow grave of forgetfulness. Our leadership team did not address the existential undercurrents. How could we? We struggled with those questions ourselves. Our new coping method was Avoidance 101: put your nose to the grindstone, let the dead bury the dead, and move on. Compartmentalize the past and bury it as deep as possible.

Over the next year, the GFFC youth ministry took off. There was a healthy mixture of the WOF kids and new youth. Within a year, 20% of the church were youth. Our regular mission trips and travel adventures were a considerable part of the draw.

We took teams to visit Mrs. Val and Darren in New Orleans, inviting other youth groups to join the fray. In the summer of 1995, I led our first trip to Alaska. The Alaska trip fed our youth's longing for exploration and the grit to make it happen. We raised our funds, budgeted well, and had money left in the account to subsidize our next journey. All in all, my new position at GFFC was going gangbusters.

Our voyages to New Orleans became a rite of passage for our students. Several aspects, like the rich cultural stories, impactful times of service, a unique Big Easy culture, and Mama Val's chicken, motivated students to raise funds and come along. When it was time to sign up for the trip, we always had people on the standby list. There was one particular youth I was excited to bring, above all the others.

I met 12-year-old Antonio while at Word of Faith. His older half-sister dragged him into the church youth group. "He is a difficult boy," she said when she dropped him off.

Antonio was a kid of extremes. A fierce competitor and standing a bare notch over five feet, Antonio ran circles around his basketball opponents. Usually reserved, he became the coolest kid in the room with the flip of a switch. He was easy to love and pleasant as long we observed one rule: Antonio did not want to be hugged. Affection was foreign to him. If you tried to hug him, he disappeared like the Invisible Man.

Antonio's mother raised several children in Honduras. When her first husband died, her adult children relocated to the U.S., some legally and others illegally. She chose to remain in Honduras, finding employment as a housekeeper for a wealthy construction company owner. Seduced by the man, she became pregnant with Antonio.

Antonio had dim childhood memories of his father and a life of ease, but his mother had a different experience, one frightening enough for her to flee Honduras with her six-year-old son. With the financial aid of her children in the states and in desperation for Antonio's welfare, she entered the U.S. illegally. She moved in with her oldest daughter in Dallas. For the young boy, this was a confusing time. He easily picked up English and, with fake documents, began attending the local elementary school.

Antonio's sister treated Antonio as a bastard. An angry, bitter person, she justified abusing Antonio through the filter of her Christian faith. His strong will and sharp tongue placed him under relentless physical, emotional, and spiritual wrath.

When Antonio was forced to attend the Word of Faith youth group, he was angry, understandably mistrusting, and cynical about God. For three years, he cautiously engaged but kept at arm's length from any spiritual entanglements. He was a delightful kid, and our adult youth leaders adored him.

The last time I saw Antonio at Word of Faith was our students' graduation into the high school group. Every student, dressed to the nines, was on their best behavior. After speeches and earnest accolades, the evening ended with each of the 50 eighth-grade graduates walking past 20 youth leaders, receiving hugs and words of encouragement. Antonio stood last in line. We all assumed he was going to avoid the hugs. He had been reticent during the festivities. His face was clouded. Mike was the first leader in line. Antonio reached out a hand. Suddenly, breaking into inconsolable tears, he stretched his arms around Mike as if he would never let go. For the next 20 minutes, Antonio moved down the line, hugging every leader as if it was the last time he would see us. The leaders were a blubbering mess by the time Antonio finished. A week later, Antonio disappeared.

Into the Wonder

When I was on staff at Grace Fellowship, Antonio moved in with a sibling a few minutes from where I lived. He was a 16-year-old high school dropout working at a fast-food restaurant. We met for a meal, and he filled in the missing pieces from his years away.

Growing up, Antonio's world had required an escape plan. When he was registered for school, a family member convinced the administration that Antonio's paperwork, such as a birth certificate or health records, was lost in the move. When the school inevitably forced the requirement, his familial guardian promised to track down the appropriate documents. Months went by before the school authorities figured out something was wrong. When the heat of suspicion became unbearable, Antonio moved to another school district.

Antonio was an intelligent kid who learned to navigate the system. During his last week at Word of Faith, as he was about to enter high school, the authorities became suspicious he was an illegal immigrant. Antonio was shipped off to a half-brother in Tennessee and eventually a half-sister in Florida.

The sister he was currently living with was kind, but there was significant substance abuse in the home. He had heard I was at a new church, and remembering his time at WOF fondly, he asked if he might attend the GFFC youth group. We were ecstatic. Antonio always participated in every service while remaining spiritually agnostic. Every Wednesday evening after church, he joined our family for dinner.

When Antonio heard the youth were going to New Orleans, he asked to join. I kept a straight face, nodding in a cordial yes while exploding in thankfulness.

Antonio took to NOLA with gusto. He was a workhorse in the Fischer Projects, wholeheartedly diving into every project. Mama Val clicked with him when she watched with glee as he ate her fried chicken, his fingers and lips covered with grease. Antonio had matured. He was outgoing, and the other students, many of whom he had known in his junior high years, were delighted he was back. But all of his enthusiasm dried up when the students engaged in worship. During those moments, Antonio became part of the wallpaper. His distrust and resentment during these times caused fellow students to avoid him like a chained pit bull.

Everyone was shocked when Antonio walked down for prayer on our last night in NOLA. A guest preacher, Bishop Reggie, had given a fiery sermon about God as our ever-seeking Father. His cadence, filled with authentic love, stirred, convicted, and convinced. His messages compelled us to fall on our knees and weep for the goodness of God. As he came to a close, he ended with an invitation.

"The Father longs for you. He waits for you to come and permit Him to embrace you in His arms. If you need that embrace, come forward." The atmosphere was fiery and freeing as Reggie spoke. I thought there might be a holy stampede.

Antonio moved fast. No one else moved. Everyone knew where Antonio stood on the subject of God. Exponentially more shocking was Antonio's indignant response.

"God, I hate You!"

Reggie, unmoving, whispered something in Antonio's ear, then stepped back. Antonio fell to the ground, curled up like a baby, and sobbed for 30 minutes. We sat in that holy and unexpected moment, unsure of what to do.

Antonio sat down with Cheryl and me after everyone cleared out. He was as surprised as anyone else. For the first time, Antonio shared about the extreme abuse he had experienced under his oldest sister, the struggle of never having a home, and his consuming sense of abandonment. He longed for God's love, but his circumstances made it hard to believe. His outburst of "God, I hate You!" was his final attempt to distance himself from this mythical Father in heaven. But what he experienced dropped him to his knees. He was overcome with a Presence. A physical sense of peace wrapped around him like the arms of a loving father. At first, he was shaken by the intrusion of love. After a couple of minutes, exhausted, he stopped fighting, stopped running, and succumbed to the presence of Love.

We can all understand that sense of loneliness. Are we alone in the vast universe? That question opens us to the possibility of God's presence in our lives. If there is no presence, nihilism is our only choice. If God's presence is real, then meaning and wonder undergird our whole existence, no matter what happens in our lives.

Antonio, abused with the Bible, abandoned by his family, on the run from the authorities, and alone in the universe, encountered a God who longed to embrace him, and he finally succumbed to the pursuit. What I watched Antonio experience was the nearest I'd witnessed to my encounter in the little Assembly of God Church in New Jersey when I was 17. There was an undeniable connection between those two sacred events.

As Cheryl and I talked to Antonio, we knew we had a part to play in his story. A week later, Antonio moved in and has remained a part of our family. Happily married, a business owner, brother to his adopted siblings, and a legal U.S. citizen, Antonio leads groups of students on pilgrimages and mission trips so they might have an opportunity to encounter wonder as he had so many years ago. Antonio is one of those unique gifts from the Father we never intended. He is *wantok* with the Smalls. And being *wantok* is a wonder.

My time at Grace Fellowship Family Church defined who my people were and who they were not. My adventures over the next couple of years set the course for my future. I was *wantok*, but not with whom I assumed.

Chapter 21

Otherworld

Inis Oírr, Ireland - May 2001

The trinity of the Aran Islands, sitting at the mouth of Galway Bay on the west coast of Ireland, draws a few thousand visitors each year. The smallest of the islands, Inis Oírr (Inisheer in its anglicized form), is the least visited, making it ideal for unhindered exploration. Legend says the Aran Islands were the last sanctuary for the fleeing Fir Bolg after losing Éire to the invading bright beings, the Tuatha de Danna. DNA testing reveals the generational residents of the Aran Islands have the oldest Irish bloodlines. Even though Gaelic Irish is the first language of the islanders, the locals speak English when outsiders are within earshot, a byproduct of their hospitable nature.

The Inis Oírr ferry had fewer than a dozen passengers the day I first traveled to Inisheer. Departing the Galway Coast, the skies dumped barrels of summer rain, blurring the world for miles inland. As we crossed the intimidatingly named Foul Sound, the skies cleared. I enjoyed a hot drink on my passage with an older gentleman, Mr. McCormick, who looked as though he'd been raised by Poseidon. He said if I bought the coffee, he'd add the Irish. Pulling out a ruddy flask from a well-worn tweed jacket, he topped our coffees with firewater. I only had a few hours on my first visit to Inis Oírr, so I asked him where I should go. In his sing-song brogue, Mr. McCormick spoke.

"You go where your feet lead and heart tugs. Since you're a spiritual boy, my prayer is that the Lord above leads you in the footsteps of Cavan."

"What does that mean?" I asked.

Mr. McCormick chuckled. "Young people today. Where's your sense of adventure?"

Into the Wonder

I felt a pull as my foot landed on the Inis Oírr jetty. Trusting in Mr. McCormick's prayer, I turned left and walked through the tiny streets toward the edge of Baile An Lurgain. A grand mound hovered between the island's football pitch and the ruin of a 14th-century castle above.

The clip-clop-clip-clop of passing horses added rhythm to the choral of swirling sea birds, ocean breakers, and soft westerly winds. On the outskirts of the village, I came to a hummock covered with seagrass rolling in the wind.

From the bottom of the hill, I spotted dozens of stones peppered across the rise like the slanting teeth of a stone giant. A short, sloped concrete climb veered off the main road ending at a black, Victorian gate. I had come to a graveyard. What might cause the islanders to pick such an unusual place for their dearly departed? The gravestones multiplied as I worked to the top of the hill. The oldest of the memorials, any trace of engraving long gone under years of weathering, leaned, unable to take a firm root in the sandy soil.

The hill came to a peak in the center of the graveyard. I climbed wooden steps to a marvel hollowed into the earth. Below me, surrounded by 20 feet of sand held back with stone retaining walls, was the perfectly preserved 10th-century Celtic church of Teampall Caomhán.

St. Cavan (anglicized version of Caomhán), the hallowed saint of Inis Oírr, established his monastery on the island in the ninth century. For centuries, sand, blown in by sea winds and the depth of the ever-growing graveyard surrounding the church, swallowed the sanctuary under the mound. Time erased the building out of the memories of the islanders. They had forgotten for a few hundred years that the earth contained a sacred treasure.

In 1885, a fierce storm battered Inis Oírr for days. Unremitting torrential rain and gale force gusts uncovered three stone peaks now standing like one-dimensional pyramids in the center of the hill. The peak of the pre-Romanesque church of Teampall Caomhán had been rediscovered. Since then, the locals have gathered annually on Saint Caomhán's Day to clear the relentless encroachment of sand. Once the sanctuary is cleared of sand, the islanders partake of the Lord's Supper at the ancient altar.

I worked my way around the roofless building to the low stone lintel entrance. I had to duck to enter a roofless nave only 15 feet across and 45 feet long. The sands had preserved the intricate stonework as if the church had been constructed only 100 years ago. Entering the sanctuary, my curiosity morphed into a divine rendezvous. I had entered a thin space.

Over the years following the initial car accident, I was struck by the phrase "eternal life" as I read the Holy Scriptures. Eternal life is typically defined in Christian circles as what happens to you when you die. Christians spend a lot of time and energy on the premise that eternal life is the afterlife. Preachers beg believers to fight for the souls of men, women, and children to obtain eternal life when they die. In the evangelical world, saving souls from hell underlines and informs the worth of most endeavors. This idea is a grossly incomplete understanding of eternal life.

When Jesus spoke about eternal life, He equated it with a spiritual kingdom as real as our world. Eternal life is an existing state of being, not a future location; it is our connection with God opening the door to the spiritual kingdom into our tangible world. It is not some far-off heavenly Shangri-la but a reality Christ wanted us to engage in now. Eternal life hugs the invisible edges of this reality, ready to break through when we are willing to allow God to meet us where we are. When Jesus taught His disciples to pray, He said, "Thy kingdom come, Thy will be done on earth, as it is in heaven" (Matthew 6:10 KJV).

Heaven is a divine reality straining and reaching to engulf our world with beauty, love, wonder, compassion, joy, and peace.

The Christian Celts of Ireland adopted the term *otherworld* from their pre-Christian past to explain the relationship between this hidden eternal world that was both transcendent and intertwined with our world. The famous Celtic knotwork in Gaelic art represents the intertwining of the seen and unseen worlds, the eternal and the physical. The *otherworld* is our true home and the source of wonder in our world.

Another term used in Celtic Christianity explains places where the eternal shines into our world. Those sacred spaces were called *thin places*. They are known in every culture. Like the Wailing Wall in Jerusalem, the mountain hermitage of Eremo in Assisi, Mother Teresa's Missionaries of Charity house in the slums of Kolkata, the communion table in your church, or the rising sun on the horizon as you sit atop a mountain, thin places seep wonder into our world. These are physical spots where the spiritual realm and the natural realm kiss. They come so close together they can usher a person into sublime awe. Thin places evoke a spiritual response. Donald Miller, in his memoir *Scary Close,* describes thin places.

"There's no rational explanation for that kind of emotion [in response to a thin place] except perhaps, at times, we accidentally tear a little hole in the fabric of reality so something on the other side shines through, exposing the darkness of our routine existence."[26]

Most of us have experienced moments when we are overcome by a sense of wonderment, where we want to fall to our knees and embrace something bigger than anything we've found in this world. These portals into wonder are sometimes as wide as barn doors, sometimes as small as keyholes. Thin places remind us that wherever the Spirit dwells is our home.

As I passed under the thousand-year-old arch in the center of Teampall Caomhán and moved toward the unadorned stone altar, I was overcome with a sense of homecoming. A stone carving was embedded in the wall over the altar. Several images, slightly worn and glistening with a dark sheen created by the natural oils of thousands of pilgrims who had traced the complex carving with their

---

26   Donald Miller, *Scary Close* (Nashville: Nelson Books, 2014), 181.

fingers, begged closer inspection. I joined the cloud of witnesses through the ages as I gently traced my fingers over the images.

> *A circle of sunlight surrounds the*
> *image of the crucified Christ.*
>
> *He is above and before all creation.*
>
> *Archangels hover at steady attention*
> *over the sacrificed Savior.*
>
> *Witnesses and mourners.*
>
> *The crude, torn image of Christ*
> *on the cross is central.*
>
> *He is in this world and the*
> *otherworld at the same time.*
>
> *His head was crowned in gnarled thorns.*
>
> *Both a King and a criminal.*
>
> *The shining Ark of the Covenant*
> *sits on the ground to his right.*
>
> *Presence and life.*
>
> *The dreaded spear of the soldier*
> *lies on the ground to his left.*
>
> *Sorrow and death.*
>
> *The wound in his side flowed, releasing*
> *the Bride in a bloody flood.*
>
> *Seed and sacrifice.*

As the noonday sun poured down upon the altar stone, lighting the church with brilliant sunbeams, I experienced the closest I have ever known to pure wonder. Dumbstruck, I stood in the thinnest of places, tipping into the eternal. When I traced the altar stone, feeling the images as if I were reading braille, I became Thomas, feeling the wound in His side, and I believed. This mystifying convergence of physical touch and my realization of the otherworld shone through begged poetry; it begged praise. Still, I could only remain silent as the minutes faded, like sand in an hourglass.

When I removed my hand and looked at my watch, I had been standing at the altar for an hour. I would have sworn I'd been there for five minutes. There was no other place I wanted to be. At the altar of Teampall Caomhán, I came face to face with Jesus. In the words of C.S. Lewis, "But now, for the first time, there burst upon me the idea that there might be real marvels all about us, that the visible world might be only a curtain to conceal huge realms uncharted by my very simple theology."[27]

I had looked into the eternal *otherworld*, into the eyes of Jesus, and I walked away changed.

Thomas Cahill's *New York Times* bestseller, *How the Irish Saved Civilization*, became a publishing phenomenon in the mid-1990s, adding to the budding Irish Renaissance. The eyes of the nations were watching Ireland because of bands like U2, The Cranberries, and Clannad, the explosively entertaining *Riverdance* stage show, and an economic boost from the European Union, which allowed the advertising catchphrase "Discover Ireland" to blanket the United States. Ireland became the world's hottest tourism location and the jewel of the EU.

I picked up Cahill's book and consumed it thrice in quick succession. *How the Irish Saved Civilization* is a historical work filled with a compelling narrative of Ireland's role in preserving Western culture while the Dark Ages enveloped Europe. The book shares the nail-biting story of St. Patrick, a British Roman citizen captured and enslaved as a youth under a cruel Irish master, his

---

27   C.S. Lewis, *Surprised by Joy* (San Francisco: HarperOne, 1955), 61.

miraculous conversion as a follower of Christ, and his harrowing escape back to Britain. But it was his staggering decision to return to the land of his pagan captors that started into motion 600 years of history, ultimately saving a European civilization overrun by barbarians in the Dark Ages.

Ireland's conversion was unique. The Irish tribes embraced the Gospel of Christ as their own and became known as the "Isle of Saints and Scholars." Cahill showed how this little nation of barbarians on the edge of the Roman Empire was uniquely prepared for the Gospel in a way not seen since the missionary travels of Paul 400 years prior. The Irish missionaries, zealous for the Gospel of Christ, traveled around the known world in fearless pursuit of sharing the Good News with anyone who might listen.

For most readers, Cahill's book was an entertaining read. For me, *How the Irish Saved Civilization* became a manifesto of a Christianity I longed to experience: Celtic, holistic, fearless, emotional, poetic, full of wonder, and adventurous.

I landed in Ireland a year later.

The plans for an Ireland voyage started shortly after our youth's successful foray to Alaska. I had no idea what we might do. I had no connections in Ireland, but the stories of the Celtic saints in *How the Irish Saved Civilization* rang in my ears. After several dead ends, false starts, and disorganized research, I was introduced to a young man who was the first Irish student to attend Christ for the Nations where I spent my first two years of college life.

Nick was a tall, muscular soccer player with a brush of blond hair, a million-dollar smile, and bushels of Irish wit. His accent made the girls swoon and the boys envious. After an hour of our first meeting, I knew Nick would be in my life for a long time. Though ten years his senior, we clicked like blood kin. We decided that Nick and I would take a pre-trip to his family to see what we might create for our summer adventure to the Emerald Isle.

Nick and I visited his parents, John and Sonia Spencer, in New Ross, a nondescript town in southeast Ireland, sitting on the crossroads of County Kilkenny, County Wexford, and County Waterford. The Spencer family was amused when I disembarked the plane in shorts and a t-shirt, unbothered by the 50-degree temps.

Within a couple of days, the celebrated Irish hospitality the Spencers displayed made me part of the family. Ten years my senior, John Spencer looked like an 18-century sea captain: barrel-chested, strong as an ox, and with a perpetual three-day shadow across his cheeks. John was an entrepreneur during the week and the pastor of a small, local, evangelical fellowship on Sundays. He was garrulous, not in an overpowering way, but in a manner that caused you to hope he never stopped talking. A human encyclopedia of history, architecture, farming, sailing, and whichever subject filled his bottomless curiosity, John was pure joy. When I departed Ireland, I left with an unexpected *anam cara* (soul friend).

Sonia was a lightning rod of a woman. She might stand invisible in a room, taking in the conversations, her artistic sensitivities absorbing an idea for a future painting. Or she might explode with passion and energy, leaving any standing around floored by the sheer force of her words. At the time, I had no idea the Spencers would be key influences in my life over the next three decades.

On the second day of my visit, to the stunned disbelief of John, Sonia, and Nick, I asked if their home could be our base of operations for our youth team at the end of July. I latched onto something prophetic about their home, The Ferry House, named so because it sat on the River Barrow, the border waters between County Wexford and Kilkenny. The 400-year-old farm was the historic dwelling place of the ferryman who boated passengers from one side of the river to the other. In a spiritual sense, I was crossing from one place to the otherworld. I had discovered a home I never knew existed.

The Spencers have avowed that I was uncannily Irish in my mannerisms, the way I carried myself, and my humor. When I visited holy sites, specific locations I wanted to take the team, hill walked, or pub crawled, I was Irish.

Everywhere the Spencers took me, I had an overwhelming sense of being surrounded by *thin places.* The Land of Saints and Scholars was living up to its name.

I wanted the team to bring an unusual gift to the Irish. Mike Yengo and I had spent a couple of years writing a 40-minute production inspired by our favorite book, *The Divine Romance,* by Gene Edwards. We spent hour upon hour attempting to crack the code, using all the intellectual and creative power we possessed to conjure art, cross-cultural in its presentation, mythical in its appeal, and sacred in its message. Our ideas were solid, but our execution was zilch.

Over the few previous months, Mike had grown weirdly distant. The animated and passionate missionary was turning cantankerous. Whenever I asked him what was happening, he grew irritated with his inability to communicate his emotional struggles. His bodybuilding physique was slowly shedding. Mike was stubborn and did not have much money, so he avoided doctors. I begged him to seek medical help, but he was convinced he was going through a rough spell that would turn around. Eventually, we stopped working on our stage piece.

After a lovely feast with the Spencers of golden baked shepherd's pie, warm brown bread smothered with the best butter I had ever tasted, and the perfect hot cup of Barry's tea, I retired. The spark of an idea that had started to burn on the day I landed in Ireland was beginning to blaze.

After reading Cahill's book, I studied Celtic Christianity, roughly from the third to tenth centuries. I came across an Old Irish word that transfixed my imagination: *immrama* (or Wonder Voyage). The term described oral stories passed down throughout Éire's (the ancient name for Ireland) history concerning a hero's journey to the *otherworld.* These tales told of the exploits, dangers, sacrifices, and sense of destiny defining a journey where the protagonist might have to die for his people as he leads them to the *otherworld.* The monks of the Christian era preserved these stories. They defined the Irish missionary journeys that cost them their lives with the word *immrama*.

Immrama was such a vital element of the pre-Christian Celtic consciousness that they absorbed the story of Christ as a divine *immrama*: where the perfect myth became a reality. Hearing about the Son of God taking a fatal journey, where His death for mankind brought the *otherworld* (the eternal) to all, was the primary reason the Irish embraced the Christian narrative. The story of Christ was the fulfillment of all Celtic stories. Within a few decades of St. Patrick's initial mission to the Irish, the Celts of Éire were so changed by the story that they prohibited human sacrifice. Jesus was the final and perfect sacrifice.

I sat down after supper, breathing in the lovely aroma of a peat fire, and began to write. I was a bard of old as a fire seed of inspiration burst into a creative inferno. A hand-written story flowed as if it was coming from a source beyond. By 3:00 am, with a cramped hand and a sore back, I had finished the first draft of a short stage production titled *Immrama*.

The forty-minute play captured the heart of a bridegroom who longed for a fallen bride. *Immrama* was performed as the bard Taliesin, the story's narrator, spoke the tale of one man's love for one who had rejected his love. Expressed through Celtic folklore and accompanied by a soundtrack of haunting Irish music, the stage play was filled with surprises.

The hero, Jeshua, Ard Ri (High King), battled Crimthan, the rebel leader of the *fianna* warband. The brothers who played the lead roles in *Immrama* were black belts in karate. They trained with a professional who taught stage swordplay. Their intense sword battles, bordering on risky, were a crowd favorite. The entire cast was trained in Irish dance, delighting audiences wherever we performed. Based on the book of Hosea in the tradition of Celtic lore storytelling, the allegory was designed to leave a lasting impression on the hearts of those in attendance. No heavy-handed morals. No altar calls. Just a solid, entertaining story that begged for conversation later.

When I returned to Dallas, I started to prepare our GFFC team for our upcoming voyage. John had booked several venues across the south of Ireland, including churches, theaters, and outdoor stages. *Immrama's* cast was comprised of volunteer high school and college students passionate about theater. We spent eight weeks in rehearsals, perfecting our performances for our premiere in Cork in June. All was going better than imagined except for one issue.

Mike Yengo was dying.

On the highest point of Inis Oírr, the crumbling ruins of O'Brien's Castle gave me a superb view of the island's patchwork landscape. Hundreds of thousands of ashen rocks, once covering the land like a stone desert, were stacked as walls, creating small parcels of green. The island was a giant mosaic. Sheep were moved from field to field by the tedious chore of tearing down a wall section, then rebuilding it to hem them in. Openings appeared at the will of the shepherd.

The miracle of those emerald fields is the knowledge that each green patch was created by hand. When the fields were first cleared, those who had lived on Inis Oírr painstakingly hauled seaweed up to the areas, building a compost base that allowed grass to grow. There is not a great depth to the soil, but it is exceedingly fertile. The people on this island have always labored hard, whether they cultivated the land, fished the seas in their curraghs, or built their simple churches. Every view from the top of the castle was rapture.

After my look into the *otherworld* in Teampall Caomhán, I climbed the hill above the church to O'Brien's Castle, the crumbling remains of the 14th-century tower house stoically sitting atop the small island. Ignoring the "Do Not Climb" sign, I scrambled up the rough-cut walls to the top of the roofless hold to drink in the beauty. I transcribed the details of my day into my journal. When I first arrived in Ireland five years prior, I was visiting home for the first time. Inis Oírr was a home within a home. She was a place I would come back to again and again.

I caught sight of a person carrying an unwieldy bag on his back as he climbed the hill to join me in the ramshackle keep. He waved and then greeted me with his thick Aussie accent.

"Hello, friend. How's the view up there."

"Splendid. You should come up. You won't be disappointed."

His name was Trevor, and he told me that this was his first visit to Ireland. He was booked in the local pub as a musician that evening. Trevor was a fourth-generation Australian and the first in his family to return since the days his great-grandmother was shipped away to Australia. We shared bits and bobs about our lives, but time was pressing. I told him I had to get back to avoid missing the ferry.

"Mate, you have to stay for five more minutes. I wrote a song about my great-grandmother. This will be the first time I've played it on the island she was from. An audience of one will help me prepare for tonight's performance."

Nothing could move me from the wall after his invitation. Unwrapping the gangly bag on his back, he revealed a set of uilleann pipes. The Irish version of the bagpipe is more subtle, gentle, and numinous with a broader range of notes than its Scottish cousin. Played with bellows attached to the arm, the uilleann pipes allow the musician to sing instead of blowing into the instrument.

Trevor found a place to stand atop the castle wall and let his fingers release angelic notes from the pipes. As I closed my eyes, I saw his song. Like the primordial bards of Éire, his music became a vibration on the wind, magically producing images.

A young woman, the prodigal of Inis Oírr, was caught in a compromising position with a wealthy Galway nobleman who had seduced her. The man's wife discovered their affair. The nobleman accused the girl of stealing his wife's dress to save his reputation. The wife had caught him during his attempt to get it back. The young girl was arrested, condemned without trial, and banished to Australia. She would never see her family of her beloved Inis Oírr again.

As the last of the notes drifted away on the wind and into the *otherworld*, the unfortunate prodigal of Inis Oírr was bound to her homesickness. At the same time, I discovered a way to relieve my own. I longed to utter the words at the end of *The Chronicles of Narnia*, "I have come home at last! This is my real country! I belong here. This is the land I have been looking for all my life, though I never knew it till now….Come further up, come further in!"[28]

---

[28] C.S. Lewis, *The Last Battle* (New York: Harper Collins, 1956), 170.

Chapter 22

Sublime

Ireland - June 1996

Flying over the United States into a rising moon, I stared out the window of a Boeing 747 unable to coax myself to sleep. In a few hours, our team would land at Dublin International Airport for another adventure. I had completed the *Immrama* script and produced a 42-minute soundtrack. The narrator, Taliesin, told his story while accompanied by several Celtic musicians. We focused our cast on a complex choreography, including Irish dancing, precarious sword fights, and playful interaction. Sparse set pieces were engineered to be compact and quickly assembled for travel. *Immrama* costumes, created by a professional ren-fair clothing designer, brought authenticity to the production. Our cast members spent over 200 hours preparing and learning their roles, including our small stage crew, sound person, wardrobe master, and photographer. By the time we departed for Ireland on June 23, we had become a semi-professional theater company.

June 23 has inexplicably been an important date in my life. This was the date I encountered Christ in 1985, the day I got married in 1988, and now the day I left for a place of destiny: Ireland. This was also the date Mike Yengo, my best friend, died.

Over a relatively short period, Mike had grown uncharacteristically short-tempered. He had stopped engaging in the endeavor central to his life, traveling with mission teams and serving in challenging places. The focus necessary for planning his globetrotting adventures was out of his grasp. At times, he forgot simple details like his home address. When I landed from my pre trip to Ireland,

I was stunned to learn that Mike had been admitted to Parkland Hospital, the same hospital where Cheryl had fought for her life after our second car accident.

Mike's mother had found him sinking in a near catatonic state. She called 911. At first, the doctors theorized Mike had picked up an obscure brain-attacking parasite during his travels. An early blood test revealed the truth: Mike Yengo was in the late stages of AIDS. He was dying, and nothing could be done to save him. Excessive drug use via needles in his teens was the point of entry. Twelve years later, Mike's body and mind had succumbed to the deadly disease.

I drove to Dallas and found Mike in an HIV unit. He lay in a darkened room, hushed by sensory aggravation. His transformation was fearsome. Down 40 pounds, his once-healthy muscles shrunk in defeat. During the month gap since our last conversation, he had lost the ability to speak, but I knew he understood me because the spark still shone in his eyes. I held his hands in mine and cried. My best friend was slipping away piece by piece. Mike smiled, answering my questions with blinks and eye movements. At the time, AIDS was not only a death, but it was an anathema to those who believed it might be contagious. Few people had visited Mike, fearful of contracting the disease. I was thankful that I was with him.

Over the next few weeks, as I furiously prepared the *Immrama* team, I visited Mike one night a week. I read the first draft and, eventually, played the produced soundtrack of *Immrama* for him. He was half the reason it existed. One windy evening, we listened to the three-hour *Les Misérables* soundtrack. On another night, while a thunderstorm shook the windows, I read him his favorite book, *The Divine Romance*. By June, he remained unconscious during most of my visits. On those evenings, I held his hand and prayed. I cherished my final weeks with Mike. Before effective treatments were discovered, AIDS was a wicked killer, a vampire slowly draining its victims of life. Every week there was a little less of Mike and a deeper wound in my heart.

A week before we flew to Ireland, Cheryl and I visited Mike, now an 88-pound skeleton, in hospice. The skin on his face was pulled back against his cheekbones, giving him an expression of terror, though I do not believe he was fearful. Cheryl and I spoke about our love for him, knowing this was the last time we'd see our friend. He had led hundreds of young people to over 30 countries, loving and inspiring countless people to share Christ's love with abandon. Mike Yengo was the initial catalyst for my discovery of pilgrimage.

Looking out the airplane window at the world below, I sensed his passing. Bowing my head, I thanked the Creator for Mike's stories, sacrifices, and courage to follow God wherever He led him.

After a night of jetlag-deepened sleep, we traveled down the road from the Spencers' to the tiny village of St. Mullins. One of the original Christian settlements in the south of Ireland, St. Mullins was founded by St. Moling in the seventh century along the River Barrow as a lighthouse to the tribes of Leinster. Over 1,500 years, several churches were established in an area barely larger than two acres. Wandering through hundreds of years of church history in such a compact place brought the saints of Irish history alive. We placed our hands on rough, stone-hewn, ninth-century Celtic crosses, drank from a holy well established by St. Moling, where the refreshing underground spring still flows today, and climbed atop the mound of the Kings of Leinster. Starting our voyage with a thin place set the tone.

Immrama premiered in Cork in a local church. There is nothing like an Irish audience. They stood and clapped as they watched our American youth perform traditional Irish dances. A musical and poetic people, they were transfixed by the soundtrack and the story. I was floored when the crowd shouted for joy as Jeshua and Jeru united for the first time. They hissed and booed at the devious Crimthan, the Ard Ri's (Ard Rye) treacherous leader of the Fianna, as he seduced and kidnapped the High King's bride. They hooted and hollered as the Ard Ri fought Crimthan, flashing blade upon blade, for the release of his kidnapped bride. The most surprising moment came when Crimthan thrust his sword into the heart of Jeshua as he shielded his beloved Jeru.

"*The blood gushed forth from his heart. Pulling Jeru close, he whispered in her ear. 'I did this for you - simply because I love you. Do not despair; the ransom is paid - the Immrama fulfilled. Three days my love...new life...restoration...the mystery revealed...'*"

At every performance, Jeshua's proclamation of sacrificial love hushed the room. Both sobs and stunned silence met us. The moment always came as a surprise. Something of the *otherworld* entered the atmosphere wherever we performed. This added weight to the Ard Ri's resurrection, Jeru's restoration, and the destruction of Crimthan.

Immrama, a simple allegory of the Gospel presented in the Celtic storytelling tradition, toured for five years with four different casts. We performed across Ireland, Canada, and the United States. Word got out as we performed in parks, schools, theaters, malls, and cathedrals. The Fringe Arts Festival in Toronto, Ontario gave us our first paid gig. We became regulars at the North Texas Irish Festival and the Texas Scottish Festival. We even took *Immrama* to the Fischer Projects in New Orleans. By the time I retired *Immrama*, we had completed 40 performances to 7,000 people who heard its final words:

> *A blood ransom has been paid.*
> *The Bride is restored.*
> *The mystery revealed.*
> *Thus begins a new Immrama.*[29]

Immrama played a considerable role in my life. But before our final performance in June of 2000, I experienced another death,

---

[29] Shawn Small, *Immrama* ©1996

Sublime

obliterating everything I had worked for in the thirteen years as a professional minister.

⁂

Near the end of our emerald isle adventure, John took us to a place unknown to most Irish. We packed our lunches and grabbed our hiking sticks for an outing to the Comeragh Mountains. After a sleepy drive, we parked on the side of the road near a gently sloping, non-descript field. There was nothing particularly stunning about the scenery. John prepped us. We would hill walk for the next few hours. Our team was bursting with energy from our jaunt into the unknown.

    We went up, up, up through fields and meadows. The Texas flatlanders were winded as we followed the ascending Irish billygoats. Stopping to catch our breath, we wondered where the heck we were heading. Our elevation increased, as did the size of the granite rock formations. Sighting the final rise of the climb, a student, Thumbelina-sized in the distance, froze at the top of the hill, then leaped for joy with a barely audible "whoopee!" before disappearing over the rise. As the last in line, I watched this scene repeatedly. A person came to the top of the climb, froze for a minute, then yelled joyfully before disappearing. Speeding up, I topped the hill and lost my breath.

    I stood in front of a natural amphitheater scooped out of the eastern slopes of the Comeragh Mountains by an earth-crushing glacier 10,000 years ago. Coumshingaun Lough is the finest example of a glacial lake in Europe. Inky black, pear-shaped, and a mile long, the lake is dramatically framed by 700 to 1,200-foot granite cliffs around most of the water's edge. Coumshingaun Lough might have been the dwelling place of dragons. Held up by a sizeable black moraine, the lake, when rippled by the wind, gave the appearance of something massive swimming in its unmeasured depths. Occasionally, a fish would break the surface with a tiny jump begging the question, "How did any fish end up in the lake?"

Over the hours we explored Coumshingaun Lough, the weather changed from clear and sunshiny, causing the cliffs to dazzle in polychromatic glory and the waters to reflect a steel blue hue, to a cold rainy drizzle creating shrouded mists from above, eddying up and down the cliffs like threatening spirits warning us not to get too close. John led the heartier team members up the precarious rise. After an exhausting climb, I sat atop a 1200-foot cliff, the most stunning spot of natural beauty I have ever visited. I sat on the edge of terror and ecstasy, unable to fathom the depth of beauty and awe below me. I had slipped into the sublime.

In his superb book about the psychology and compulsion of mountain climbers, *Mountains of the Mind*, Robert Macfarlane writes, "In 1757 a young Irishman with a bright future published a short work with a long title. *A Philosophical Enquiry into the Origin of Our Ideas of the Sublime and Beautiful*, by Edmund Burke (1729-97), tried to account for the passions evoked in the human mind by what Burke called 'terrible objects.' Burke was interested in our psychic response to things—a rushing cataract, say, a dark vault or a cliff face—that seized, terrified and yet also somehow pleased the mind by dint of being too big, too high, too fast, too obscured, too powerful, too *something*, to be comprehended. There were sublime sights—hectic, intimidating, uncontrollable—and they inspired in the observer, said Burke, a heady blend of pleasure and terror… At the core of Burke's thesis was the proposal that these sublime sights caused terror, and terror was a passion which, he wrote, 'always produces delight when it does not press too close.'"[30]

Sitting on the edge of the cliffs above Coumshingaun Lough, knowing a step forward would end my life, I was overcome by God's presence. God permeates nature. The Spirit comes through it as electricity comes through a wire. The God who created creation blesses us through its beauty. Nature is a sacrament in which we enjoy Him in all His goodness. I had experienced unhesitating, unflinching awe in a state of sublime grandeur. Sitting between earth and sky, I was silenced by this moment of wonder.

---

[30] Robert Macfarlane, *Mountains of the Mind* (New York: Vintage, 2004), 74.

We were blissfully lost in the present, our exploration, and our community. Our wonder was indelible in potency yet impossible to grasp and keep a hold of like a physical object. They were spiritual. They disappeared like smoke when we tried to grab them and hold them tight to the chest. What did remain was a fading aroma lodging into our brains. Those moments of wonder remained a memory drawing us into the perpetual fullness of the present.

Varanasi, India, November 2014

Rambling through the streets of India's largest cities is like negotiating your way through crowds entering a stadium for a sold-out concert with a few additions: you cannot read the signs, you do not know the language, and you are not sure what event you are about to attend. Eventually, you ignore the nose-stinging body odor and the pressure of humans touching every part of your body.

I led a group of senior adults into the center of religious India: the holy city. Varanasi is where Hindus come to spiritually recharge. A pilgrim town for 4,000 years, Varanasi is one of the oldest continually inhabited cities. Situated along the western banks of the Ganges, Varanasi came to prominence in the eighth century when the philosopher Shankaracharya established the worship of Shiva, "The Destroyer," as a prominent sect of Hinduism.

The legends state Shiva founded Varanasi to maintain the cosmic balance of the universe. The Ganges River, holy throughout India, finds its prominence in Varanasi. The Ganges flowed from the right toe of Vishnu, "The Preserver." The flow was transformed into the mighty river Ganges by Shiva with promises: the Ganges will never leave; she will remain gentle, and she will harbor no dangerous aquatic animals. Thus, this river of renewal flows along the bank of a city associated with the goddess of death. Those two realities can never be separated. According to Hinduism, they are eternally tied together, creating a cycle of birth and death that

Into the Wonder

is mankind's spiritual imprisonment. These are oversimplifications of a complex religious system, but they capture the essence of Hindu theology.

The most exciting and dangerous way to travel through the streets of Varanasi is by rickshaw. The men who pull these pedestrian chariots have the gift of an internal GPS, the strength of a horse, and the ability to weave and dodge like a prizefighter. I have taken a lot of rickshaw rides. Nothing can compare to a Varanasi outing. As we began with a slow trot, touts (people selling anything they could, thus "touting" their wares) yelled at us to make a purchase. Suddenly we were at full gallop absorbing the visual overload of hundreds of booths filled with flowers and food, clothes and religious reliquary, color bombs, and jewelry. The driver-puller picked up the pace a notch. I held my heart in my throat as we nearly collided with screaming pedestrians, honking cars, humming motorcycles, sacred cows, towering trucks, mutilated mopeds, and terrifying child-sized monkeys that could crush my skull with one hand. When my adrenaline-packed ride ended, I was shaky-legged. Our team looked tipsy as we stood back on solid ground, relieved to stand near the River Ganges.

In Varanasi, 84 ghats, or sacred steps, lead down to the River Ganges. Pilgrims bathe in the river at all hours to wash away their sins. They long to be liberated from the tyrannical cycle of birth and death played out through reincarnation. According to Hinduism, visiting Varanasi brings one closer to overcoming this cruel cycle established by the gods. To come to a ghat in the holy city is to worship the gods, cleanse the soul, and illuminate the mind. But there's one primary reason pilgrims come to Varanasi: they come to die. Dying and being cremated in Varanasi allows the Hindu to attain moksha, freedom from the cycle of reincarnation.

We boarded a boat on the River Ganges. The large disk-shaped sun sat behind a flat curtain of pinkish-orange clouds accentuating our view of the Manikarnika Ghat, one of the holiest. According to mythology, this ghat sprung from the earring of Mata Sati, goddess of longevity, who sacrificed herself by setting her body ablaze. Scores of elderly folks spend the last days of their lives absorbing the mysticism of this holy hospice, pondering the end of their suffering. Once they die, their bodies are cleaned and prepared with ritual spices, a secret kept by the generations of Manikarnika cremators. Off-white linen is wrapped around the body, overlaid with colorful flowers or material. The corpse is placed on a bamboo stretcher carried by four men who chant, "Only in the name of the god is everlasting. All else is perishable." The men dip the body in the water at the River Ganges and then let it dry.

The chief mourner, typically the first-born son of the deceased, receives a ritual shave, removing all the hair on his head as a sign of mourning. He dips himself in the Ganges and then dons himself in the white clothes.

Once the deceased body is dry, the Doms, a tribe cursed by Shiva to be the Keepers of the Flame, take over. The Doms are from the lowest Dalit caste, already at the bottom of all Hindu castes, including the Untouchables. Shunned as a tribe, Doms are not allowed to receive medical help, public education, or establish themselves in society except to manage the crematorium. Sixty bodies a day can come through the Manikarnika Ghat. The Doms say the foul smell of dead bodies never leaves their nostrils. It is a tough life serving the dead in Varanasi.

The body, lying on a four-foot-tall pyre of wood, is given to the flames. Cremation costs are determined by social status, the calculation of the fuel necessary to consume the body, and the quality of wood used. The rich prefer sandalwood, while the poor are happy with any type they can get. The body is covered in bamboo and dried grasses. The chief mourner brings the sacred flame, fire-red coal, in a torch, and he lights the pyre from five points around the body, signifying the five elements: fire, water, earth, air, and sky. The deceased's ashes will be released into the Ganges.

Ten days of mourning are observed, binding the soul to the earth until day eleven, when a Brahmin priest, for a fee, frees the soul. The deceased's name is recorded in the temple, and on day thirteen, the family holds a celebration feast ending the days of mourning.

We sat in the middle of the Ganges as dusk turned dark. From where we were anchored, a dozen pyres holding the dead looked like a flower market. Another nine pyres, burning with bright oranges, yellows, and greens lit up the ghat and shone off the faces of the dozens of family members saying goodbye with low groans. I was mesmerized by the reflection of the burning pyres in the water. The smoke of the dead raced toward the sky, turning invisible in the ensuing darkness of the moonless night. We smelled, saw, heard, and tasted death.

Gathering with 10,000 people standing on boats and on the shore to watch the grand celebration of the Ganga aarti, a ceremony where several Brahmins offer sacrifices to Mother Ganga, my mind wandered back in time. I thought about the death of Mike Yengo and how his life was a catalyst for who I was and what I did. As followers of the Way, one of our foundational truths is that new life, resurrection, springs from death. Jesus' death brought new life to the creation.

The death I walked through my last two years at Grace Fellowship Family Church would be gut-wrenchingly painful and beautifully sublime.

Chapter 23

Shadowlands

The morning church service was another one for the books. Pastor Don wielded his message like the hands of a slaughterhouse worker on the kill floor. He aimed his sermon toward two families sitting near the front of the sanctuary. Don stood with a crooked finger, pointing at them, as his southern preaching bravura reached a fevered pitch.

"A couple of men, members of Grace, visited me this week. They don't like the way the church is governed. They have trust issues with me and the way I lead. Well, I can tell you now—if you don't like the way I run the church, feel free to leave. Nobody's forcing you to stay. There's the door. Don't let it hit your backside on the way out. Amen? Amen!"

As I watched my friends and their families, humiliated in front of the congregation, rise from their seats and depart, I shook my head and whispered to Cheryl, "I can't believe it's happening again." If only I had listened to the Spirit months before.

Grace Fellowship Family Church did not skyrocket to the Christian mega church success its pastor believed was inevitable. Like a dozen other churches birthed out of the Robert Tilton Word of Faith implosion, GFFC did better than most, maintaining 300 congregants. It had generous giving and consistent attendance for a small church. On the outside, the church appeared healthy. Behind the scenes was a different story.

By 1996, over half of the paid staff were family members of the senior pastor. Nepotism was the norm. The non-family staff members were constantly questioned about why the church was not growing beyond the 300-member mark. Tension strained the atmosphere. As family staffers' paychecks increased, non-family staff pay raises froze. A general sense of unease and frustration brewed, and our pastor began to rule with an iron scepter.

He came from a religious tradition where the senior minister was the hand and the word of God for the church: prophet, priest, and king. Where he led, we were supposed to follow. By year four, our lack of success in becoming a charismatic powerhouse triggered something disturbing in Pastor Don's leadership style. Control of the money, the direction of the church, and the methodology of staff and volunteer management grew unhealthy. Don's increasing chokehold of the church was the impetus for the meeting my friends asked to have with him in the spring of 1998.

I was close to both of these men. Their children were part of the youth group and participated in our mission trips. They and their wives were our friends and mentors. Sensitive to the "lone pastor" leadership style, as both men had survived the Word of Faith debacle, they went to Don in gentleness to ask when a broader diversity of church government, promised at the inception of GFFC, would be instituted. There was no elder board outside of Don, his wife, or another person. The senior pastor listened quietly to their apprehensions, giving the impression he was seriously considering their questions. With an, "I will prayerfully consider your thoughts before getting back to you," he walked them out. What I observed after they left was a man chagrined with resentment. The following Sunday, he furiously answered them from the pulpit.

The following Monday, I sat in my boss's office. Heartbroken, I tearfully asked what had happened. His version of the confrontation was born out of the lens of paranoia and insecurity. He believed a coup was brewing to take the church from him. I begged him to consider the concerns of the men he had publicly humiliated. They had come with pure motives. Neither wanted anything to do with taking control.

From my perspective, Don was burned out, depressed, and growing irrational in his attempt to navigate the church, his legacy, and the future he believed he deserved. A spiritual mid-life crisis was in full bloom.

In his mind, I was ignorant and too trusting. He had been through church takeovers. These men were dangerous and needed to be cut from the vine. My face portrayed that I was not buying his theory. I left his office with a target on my back. My time at GFFC was running out.

I had entered the Shadowlands.

My doubts began months earlier with a deep dive into Psalm 51. This sung poem, penned by King David, was written when the eyes of the world viewed Israel as a superpower. One day, while holding royal court, David was confronted by his trusted friend, Nathan, a prophet of Israel. David, a man after God's own heart, the fearless shepherd boy who became a giant killer, and the anointed King of Israel who wrote a hefty portion of the Psalms, had grown soul-hardened, prideful in his victories, and complacent to his heavy responsibilities as the shepherd of Israel. As his heart turned from God's presence, he became spiritually blind. His entitlement led to adultery and the pre-arranged murder of the husband of the woman he slept with. Putting his neck on the line, the prophet Nathan confronted David about his sinful heart. Nathan exposed a hard truth: David's actions had brought judgment down upon his children, his household, his ancestors, and the kingdom of Israel.

King David was wrecked. As his heart was made naked, raw, and tender once again, David entered a time of mourning, seeking the face of God he had forgotten and ignored as the anointed king. Psalm 51 was David's lament born out of his repentance.

C.S. Lewis called these seasons of humility, raw spirituality, elevated self-awareness, and sacred cleansing the Shadowlands, dark times of turmoil in which all things are shifting shadows. But out of our darkness, when we lay bare before the Creator and patiently wait for clarity only found in humility, we come out as new creations on the other side. The Shadowlands are purging epiphanies where we let go of our pretenses, the emotional bastions we've constructed against others, our skewed views of the world, and our carefully fabricated constructs to shield us from pain. The Shadowlands force us beyond our false narratives into the truth.

I spent the whole of 1998 poring over those words of poetic penance in Psalm 51. The pinnacle of Psalm 51, falling dead center of the psalm, anchors all the surrounding words.

Lord, take the raw materials of my life and create something new,
An uncontaminated heart, a spirit established
exactly where it should be.
I don't want to wander from Your presence,
nor lose the embrace of Your Spirit.
I long for Your transcendent joy and liberty
that flows from knowing You.
Embrace me with Your generous, willing and loving Spirit.
Psalm 51:10–12

My perception of God's will, in which I had been confident, became foggy. Deep into the Shadowlands, the road I walked upon crumbled away. A resurrected heart was only possible with the deconstruction of the old heart. I wrestled with my past and present to discern my future.

One of the first foundations in my life that started to crumble was the theological community I'd been a part of since I was 18. I questioned the black-and-white religious fishbowl of the charismatic evangelicalism I had called home for 15 years.

Don surrounded himself with a group of men he called his "spiritual sons," disciples of his wisdom and benefactors of his leadership. He drew in men like me who longed for the approval of a fatherly figure, and he took advantage of our emotional needs. When I watched my friends ejected from the church, I started to crumble like a cracking mud wall in an earthquake. I was under leadership that was poisoning my soul.

As Psalm 51 fused into my heart, I recognized that during my decade of pastoring, travels outside of the church community had reframed my view on God's love, spirituality, the nature of humanity, and how the word *church* was defined. I found myself standing outside of the fishbowl. I had been looking in another direction, but I was not courageous enough to walk away. Yet, wonder sang from the edges of my world, daring me to follow.

The more the Spirit whispered for my obedience to move beyond GFFC, the deeper my fingers went in my ears. I grasped the apostle Paul's words to the Romans about struggling with God's will. "What I don't understand about myself is that I decide one way, but then I act another, doing things I absolutely despise. So if I can't be trusted to figure out what is best for myself and then do it, it becomes obvious that God's command is necessary" (Romans 7:14–16).

Our second voyage to Ireland had been a smashing triumph. Joining with another youth minister duo from New Jersey, Juan and Tracy Galloway, our two groups double-billed a tour of *Immrama* performances during the day, and a Christian punk band performing in clubs at night. Our unorthodox mode of sharing the love of Christ gave us an audience of those who wouldn't usually be open to religious content.

When John Spencer suggested I come to help with the church in Ireland and start a travel company with him, I shivered with excitement. Still, the fear of change was a frozen lock in my imagination. In the name of staying loyal to Pastor Don, I politely told John I must continue where I felt God had placed me.

When Don brought on an executive pastor, Dave M., we questioned if he was positioning himself to walk away from the church. Our new boss, an up-and-coming prosperity preacher with a propensity for shiny suits and oversized rings, was gifted with a baritone voice that he used to preach vapid sermons with Pentecostal sizzle. He jumped at the opportunity to grab the reins of GFFC and steer it into charismatic glory.

David's staff adjustments, backed by Don, were rapid. New staff members, friends of Martin, were brought in. Some old staff members were cut. While the senior pastor made six figures, our paychecks were significantly cut, including the loss of medical benefits. My pay dropped to two-thirds of its original amount. It was our fault the church was not growing. Our paychecks needed to reflect our failure.

It only took a few weeks before my family was in desperate financial straits. Even though Cheryl implored me to consider other options outside the church, I remained loyal to GFFC. Surely Don wouldn't hurt our family on purpose. I was dedicated, did my job faithfully, and served his vision. The pay cut was a sacrifice I needed to make. These were my flimsy defenses as I avoided the truth. They wanted me out of GFFC. I had outlived my usefulness. But I clung to the hope that circumstances would change.

My justification was that our youth ministry was healthy. 20 percent of the congregation was in the youth group. My likeability amongst the congregation made it hard for the new executive pastor to justify laying me off. In many ways, I was an ideal employee. But my inability to keep questions to myself was a huge negative.

The Shadowlands were revealing my deep insecurities. My only job throughout my twenties had been a youth minister. My identity was wrapped in my position and title as pastor. Who was I away from the ministry, away from the church world? The thought terrified me enough to ignore the guttural growls from the dark corners of the Shadowlands. I didn't want life to change because I couldn't conceive another life.

My prayer from Psalm 51, "Create in me a clean heart and renew a steadfast spirit in me," was unmasking the person I had morphed into during my five years at Grace. I was a person I did not like. I had yielded and made excuses for the unhealthy and toxic workplace I had served under. I was a coward, unwilling to leave when the Holy Spirit shouted at me to get out.

At the end of the year, Grace Fellowship purchased an empty church building in south Irving, a few miles away from their church offices. On Sunday, January 17, 1999, I returned to my office after the morning service to pick up some items. The youth room was filled with men listening to Pastor Don passionately campaigning for the church's future. I stood around a corner, out of sight, wondering why I had not been invited to the impromptu meeting.

"So, as you can see, gentlemen," Don cleared his throat, "this is why we must let a staff member go." I walked around the corner, looking directly into Don's eyes.

"Who?" said one of the men. Don stopped, unsure of how to proceed.

"We'll have to make that announcement later. Thanks for coming and supporting the future of the church."

As the men filed out of the room, confused and uncertain, my stomach tightened like I was about to get into a fistfight. My time at Grace Fellowship Family Church was coming to a sudden end. In my desperation to keep the status quo, my career had failed. I was about to be cast outside my protective wall into the scary world beyond.

Chapter 24

Blessed Disillusionment

Rome, Italy - July 2013

A gifted storyteller leading you through the time-worn avenues and alleys of the Eternal City grants you the gift of visualizing the opulence and shining glory of the nexus where, at one time, all roads started and ended. Paolo, our spirited tour guide, threaded us through the jumbled streets on a sticky July afternoon, stopping at strategically planned places of interest. He drew out stories of historic hindsight from ancient Rome's cool-to-the-touch marble façades.

The 20-something dark-bearded Paolo began our day-long journey with tales from the emperor's bloodlust arena, the Colosseum. We ambled our way to the Arco di Costantino that was built as a war trophy after the merciless, take-no-prisoners victory of Emperor Constantine over Maxentius for the supreme power of the empire. We walked the Palatine, centermost of Rome's Seven Hills. This had been the axis of the Western world for 900 years.

Silence overtook us as we stared skyward inside the architectural wonder of the Pantheon, the most expansive dome in the world. We were rambling our way to our stopping point of the day, the glorious and over-touristed Trevi Fountain. Before we reached our end point, Paolo stopped for one last story.

The Temple of Hadrian, dedicated to the deified emperor, stands today as a massive inner chamber wall with eleven external colonnades. Paolo took off his sunglasses with a dramatic sweep, stopping us at the outer wall. He furrowed his sweating brow as he pointed at the wall and dramatically spoke.

"Hail, Hadrian, betrayer of Rome!"

Paolo's impromptu street performance brought the sidewalk of summer tourists to a halt. His impassioned history lesson told of how Hadrian, to the shame of his Imperial predecessors, immobilized the expansion of Rome. Hadrian's fear of the outside pressures squeezing in upon the Empire's borders caused him to react in a way previous Emperors would not have considered. Hadrian built walls and fortified borders, effectively killing the millennium-long expansion of the Roman Empire. Hadrian's sweeping decision of Roman preservation turned Rome in upon itself. For the next 200 years, Rome's primary battles were civil wars rather than territorial conquests. And Rome's enemies took notice.

Without Rome's outward military pressure, eager barbarians pressed back with bolder and bolder invasions into the Empire. Hadrian's decision to maintain the status quo was the Empire's death knell. Rome collapsed on top of itself.

Paolo paused, wiping his brow with a handkerchief before putting his sunglasses back on. His voice, finishing in a desolate whisper, stopped his history lesson with, "And that, my friends, is the death of the undefeatable Roman Empire."

During my final days at Grace Fellowship Family Church, I learned how I desperately built walls to keep out the danger of change. I grew so concerned about the stability of my little world that I lost sight of the possibilities and wonder that called from the edges of my life. To move forward, those walls had to be destroyed.

The emotional blow of Pastor Don informing a couple dozen church members about my sacking triggered a pent-up volcano. As the men filtered out of the Sunday morning meeting, I asked Don's son, the staff administrator, to come to my office. I reared up and nearly chest-bumped him.

"I guess someone's getting fired. Do you think you can quit being a coward and tell me to my face that it's me getting let go before your dad tells everyone else in the church?"

The shock of my abrasive stance caught David off guard.

"Yes, Shawn. You're being let go."

"Finally, some honesty. When did you plan on letting me know?"

I deflated my chest and sat behind my desk, defeated.

Blessed Disillusionment

David spoke a few insufficient details before briskly exiting my office. What I was assured of was my firing. On Monday, I'd find out the specifics, the final dirge of my full-time pastoral church work. Though I felt betrayed, a whispering voice told me I should not be surprised. I was experiencing another gift of wonder: disillusionment. In his book *Learning to Speak God from Scratch,* Jonathan Merritt writes about this boon the Holy Spirit longs to grant us.

"Disillusionment is, well, the loss of an illusion. It is what happens when you take a lie—about the world, about yourself, about those you love, about God—and replace it with the truth. Disillusionment occurs when God shatters our fantasies, tears down our idols, and dismantles our cardboard cutouts. It is the result of discovering that God does not conform to our expectations but rather exists as a mystery beyond those expectations."[31]

I understood months later that my *disillusionment* was not designed to hurt me. In that moment of being fired, I entered a sacred experience, a moment of wonder that refused to let me live a lie that had kept me bound for months. These disillusioning experiences are often painful but never destructive because they make us shed the lies we've mistaken for truth. I had accepted the unacceptable for months because seeking a new path was terrifying. I wanted to hide behind safe walls. Wonder is always outside the walls. Sitting at my desk, with no one around and knowing my time had ended, I knew what was true. It took me time to realize the God breaking down the walls was exponentially more wonderful than the God I had believed in at GFFC.

There had been a stirring in my heart for months to break the boundaries of this GFFC existence and seek a new horizon. I had never fit into the world Don was trying to realize at the church. I had been too afraid to walk away. In avoiding launching out, I'd allowed myself and my family to experience unnecessary emotional, spiritual, and financial hardship. In the name of some

---

[31] Jonathan Merritt, *Learning to Speak God from Scratch* (New York: Convergent, 2018), 121.

Into the Wonder

twisted version of biblical loyalty, I had clawed to stay in a place in which I didn't belong and that no longer wanted me.

Earlier in the year, John Spencer had asked me to consider bringing my family to Ireland. My fears buried all possibility of something rife with prospects. In the fall of 1998, three months before I was fired, my good friend Anthony Does sat with me over coffee and said he believed the Holy Spirit had given him a message for me. God longed to release a creative force within my soul. If I dared to allow the Spirit to move freely, and if I were willing to place my fears, my questions, and my burdens at the feet of Christ, a dream would grow through my adversity. The suffering and pain I'd spent years avoiding would lift me like a kite in the wind. At the time, his words scared me.

Sitting in my home, darkened with the reality of getting fired, Anthony's words were a trickle of courage.

I sat in a stupor as David laid out my exit plan. I'd remain on the payroll for a couple of weeks as the church moved into its new location. I was to transfer youth leadership to a volunteer staff member. When Pastor Don was ready, I would join him on stage during a Sunday morning service and announce that I had decided to leave Grace.

I looked at David and said, "But that's not true."

He made it clear that if I didn't follow this plan, I could kiss three months of severance goodbye. I was no longer Pastor Shawn.

Northumbria, England - August 2014

As I sloshed around the carved stones on the northern English frontier, I regretted my disdain for Wellies. My socks, soaked from the boggy ground and a few extra gallons of water in my clothes, reminded me how rare a sunny day is in this part of the world.

Historians call Chester's Roman Fort, a semi-preserved barracks, one of the four similar forts along the once 73-mile Hadrian's Wall. Chester's Fort allows historic nerds to visit sec-

Blessed Disillusionment

ond-century Britannia. I was walking along the physical proof of the story Paolo told me in Rome a year prior.

Hadrian's predecessor, the ambitious Trajan, emptied the empire's coffers through massive war campaigns that gobbled up new territory for the glory of Rome. When Hadrian, a practical and notoriously neurotic man, visited the edge of the Roman Empire in northern England, he revoked the philosophy of past Emperors. Taxing the Roman Empire with costly wars was a waste. Instead, he commissioned the construction of an enormous snaking wall, nine feet by five feet, across the narrowest portion of Britannia, to hem in the untamable and troublesome, blue-goaded Picts, the irritatingly relentless plundering scourge of the southern Roman citizens. Hadrian erected borders to separate the refined from the wild, the familiar from the strange, and safety from risk.

Those "protected" by the walls were now plundered by the government taxes used to safeguard them from the monsters on the edge of the Empire. And like that, Rome experienced gridlock. The Roman world changed from aggressive expansion to dire defense. Instead of keeping invaders out, the walls tempted those outside the walls to treasure within Roman territory. Over the next few hundred years, Rome shrank in upon itself, desperate but unable to keep its financial and governmental stability. Building walls has never been the ultimate safety solution. In 395, only 273 years after Hadrian's wall was erected, Rome, in power for nine decades, was sacked by Germanic barbarians crossing the frozen Rhine. Rome was no more, and the Dark Ages descended upon Western Europe.

Ironically, Celtic and Pict missionaries, carrying the light of Christ, those Hadrian's Wall had intended to hem in, became the bearers of the Holy Gospel back to Europe a few centuries following.

Hiding behind the GFFC walls smothered my sense of wonder. I spent the previous several months defending my borders and abandoning imagination and possibility in exchange for safety and stability. Rote worship took the place of sacred communion. My prayers had been reduced to a list of to-dos instead of an unpredictable, uncontrolled, unhindered connection to the Spirit. In defending the wall, I was becoming deafened to the prompting

Into the Wonder

of the Son and blind to wonder. No one was to blame but me. But by God's grace, my self-preserving choice had been stripped out of my hands. Banishment beyond the wall was at hand.

~~~

Two weeks of forced silence became strained, not just for me but for the church. Phone calls to our home were constant.

> *"Where are you?"*
> *"Are you still at the church?"*
> *"Has there been a falling out?"*
> *"Are you leaving Grace?"*

Cheryl found a full-time job while I stayed home with the kids. She was thrilled with the swap, and I needed sanctuary. Lost in a cloud of insecurity, my world had been thrown into a no man's land of self-loathing, confusion, and loss of purpose. I was a ghost hovering above my frail ego. Getting fired is a psychological scourge.

The one conviction crystallizing in my mind was what I'd say on the Sunday Don wanted to bring me up on the church stage to announce my transition. He was sure I'd follow his orders. Three months of severance pay lay on the line. Surely, I was not foolish enough to jeopardize my family in the name of my pride. Feeling the vice-grip I was under, Cheryl declared her support of me, no matter what I decided to say.

"Just make sure you follow your heart. Be the man of conviction I know you are, no matter the cost."

On Sunday morning, after a somewhat lowkey sermon in GFFC's new sanctuary, Pastor Don invited me onto the stage for an announcement. Word had spread that I had not been around the office for a couple of weeks.

As I stood next to Don, he threw on a mile-wide grin. He placed his hand over my shoulder as an outward sign of solidarity in what he was sure I had tailored to be an encouraging pronouncement. I held the mike in my shaking hand and prayed for the Spirit to strengthen my words.

"I do have an exciting announcement."

The usually talkative crowd sat still.

"Pastor Don has asked me to step down from staff."

Don's talons bit into my shoulder.

"I want to make it clear that I agree with Don's decision. For quite a while, I felt that my time at Grace was over. I just didn't have the guts to be obedient to God."

I looked at Don's face. A slight twitch in his smile and sweat on his forehead began to crack his polished veneer.

"Don is just helping me make a move I was too afraid to make myself. I don't know what is next; I just know it's not here. Pray for us as we journey on." A confused murmur filled the sanctuary as we left GFFC for the last time.

Don called me the following morning, a booming volcano venting fire at my insolence. There were consequences for my disobedience. I was severed from the fold. No funds. No friends. No future. Forget severance pay. I would not see the final paycheck owed to me. We were lied about, causing most of our closest church friends to cut ties with us. Now labeled *persona no grata,* all we'd known for the last five years was wiped away in my decision to be truthful one Sunday morning. *Pastor* Shawn was in the past.

I'd been faithful to my church and Don, yet, like my nine-year-old self sitting in a storm-battered car overlooking Lake Michigan, "Dad" had rejected me. Only this time, it was real. Old wounds opened, and the old monster I once feared was ready to pounce, threatening to maul my soul.

I wrestled with my emotions for months, yo-yo-ing between anger and rejection or taking responsibility for avoiding the voice of the Spirit, trying to be someone I wasn't by embracing something I no longer believed. I wanted justice or, at least, my last paycheck. The ridiculous demands of my boss and things I had been required to do for "the good of the church" caused my life to be out of whack.

Two decisions helped me navigate the Shadowlands I was stumbling through. The first was not to throw spears. This lesson came from *A Tale of Three Kings* by master storyteller Gene Edwards. David learned to avoid being hit by deadly spears thrown by Saul, the king he loved and attended. As a spear-dodger, David determined to hold back from throwing spears at those he served under and (eventually) those he ruled over throughout his reign. One passage from the book became a daily read for months after I was fired.

"You can easily tell when someone has been hit by a spear. He turns a deep shade of bitter. David never got hit. Gradually, he learned a very well-kept secret....One, never learn anything about the fashionable, easily mastered art of spear throwing. Two, stay out of the company of all spear throwers. And three, keep your mouth tightly closed. In this way, spears will never touch you, even when they pierce your heart."[32]

I was determined not to spread vindictive words about Don or GFFC. On the other hand, I was honest when people who deeply cared about me asked me questions to help me walk through the healing of my soul.

My second decision was to seek out those who would walk beside me and provide sound counsel, loving support, and clarity that I did not possess in my distress. Every few weeks, I flew somewhere in North America to declutter my brain full of emotional junk I'd built up over the last ten years of church work. I visited a handful of friends who had suffered similar trials and came through with renewed hearts and a deeper understanding of Christ's peace and love.

The more I faced my pain and learned to let go, the more I rediscovered wonder. As Jesus implored, I let the dead bury the dead, and I followed Him. In this case, I was both the deceased and the follower. The suffering I endured was never outside of the loving, caring hands of Jesus. In his book *Drops Like Stars,* author Rob Bell defines suffering as a gift.

"Michelangelo said that his David was in the stone clamoring to be freed... sculptures were in there the whole time. All these sculp-

---

[32] Gene Edwards, *A Tale of Three Kings* (Carol Stream, IL: Tyndale, 1980), 24.

tors really did was remove. Sculptors shape and form and rearrange, but at the most basic level, they take away. And there is an extraordinary, beautiful art to knowing what to take away....Suffering does that. It compels us to eliminate the unnecessary, the trivial, the superficial. There is greatness in you. Courage. Desire. Integrity. Virtue. Compassion. Dignity. Loyalty. Love. It's in there—somewhere. And sometimes it takes suffering to get at it. It's in there."[33]

By August, six months after my pastoral existence ended, I had settled into a new rhythm. Cheryl was our household provider. Her only issue was why it had taken her so long to return to work. I had lost my identity; she found her own. As a stay-at-home dad, I discovered a joy I'd overlooked in full-time ministry. I loved being a dad: waking the kids up and getting them ready for school, making lunches, putting them on the bus, cleaning the house, and making dinner for the family. My crowning achievement was potty training Hunter.

My home was my monastery, giving me time to be still, pray, and drain my head by thinking through the last ten years of pastoral ministry. I read, journaled, and planned the future I wanted to build. These moments, filled with everyday wonder, helped me find my footing beyond the walls.

I believed, at the time, my anger had subsided. The truth was different. I was earning a master's degree in compartmentalizing pain. I was healing in degrees, but whenever some innocuous moment triggered a wave of anger, I dumped a load of denial over it, like a murderer burying a body.

I knew I had to deal with the magma bubbling under the rock bed of my emotions, but confronting the insecurities I used to shield myself was the opposite of what I wanted to do.

---

[33] Rob Bell, *Drops Like Stars* (San Francisco: HarperOne, 2009), 37.

Chapter 25

Toss the Hat

West Ireland - June 1999

Creating an organization that led voyages worldwide, seeking God's abundant wonders, felt as realistic as manning the first mission to Jupiter. If this, my first solo exploit imploded, I'd be burned by defeat. If I succeeded on my next Ireland voyage, the improbable dream in my heart might work. With my spiritual and emotional shackles off, I was free to create, experiment, take risks, and share my vision.

On a bright West Ireland afternoon, our team, in need of filling their lungs with fresh Gaeltacht air, strolled down a swerving farm road. The farmer who put down the lane may have had a wee bit of whiskey while on the job. The road was umbrellaed by an army of ancient oaks on one side and a tall stone wall one the other. During their 400 years of conquest, the English stripped Ireland of her mighty forests to construct the English Navy. To come upon a cluster of old-growth trees was unusual. Only the English could have saved the trees from the English. Our guide told us of an English estate hidden behind the stone wall.

One of the young men in our group, an avid rock climber, felt along the wall for a grip. "Can we see the estate?"

"Can you scale this wall?" our guide replied. The smile on the guide's scruffy jaw meant a tale was coming our way.

"It's time to toss our hat over the wall."

This unusual phrase, used by President Kennedy in a speech inspiring the American people to the impossible dream of landing a man on the moon, had an interesting origin. JFK cited the Irish writer Frank O'Connor who lived in this region where many of JFK's ancestors were born.

Like most Irish boys in the mid-1800s, Frankie endured his school lessons with an ear toward the end-of-the-day bell. His adventures usually began on the way home from his classroom. Frankie and the lads cut across a lush farm field one fair afternoon. A little wandering helped push away the inevitable farm work waiting at home.

After butterfly chases, slingshot practice, and a spitting contest, Frankie and the lads approached the unscalable walls of a spectral estate sprawling on the edge of the village. Generations of penniless village boys and girls wondered what was hiding behind the soaring stone walls. The boys surveyed the barrier for half an hour, scanning the granite-flecked rock with their fingertips.

Frankie's fervent curiosity drove him to investigate. He imagined aloud how he might climb the wall for a peek into the veiled kingdom beyond. The only visible way through the wall was a locked gate. No one outside of the estate staff crossed that barrier.

"Frankie, it would take a ladder the size of an oak tree to make it to the other side. It's hopeless. Leave it alone, boyo. You'd never make it."

Furrowing his brow, Frankie calculated. Determination set in his eyes as he looked from the gravel below to the stones on the top searching for a solution. Then, just as it appeared that he might have been beaten by the wall, Frankie made a move that caused bugged eyes and a collective gasp from all the boys.

Frankie took his expensive hat off his sweaty head and tossed it over the wall like a frisbee. His father had given him the felt bowler for his fourteenth birthday. It was his pride and joy. However, all his friends knew Frankie's handsome hat came with a warning from his father.

"Lad, your mother and I saved for a year to buy you this hat. You best not come home if you lose it because you'll receive the scolding of your life. Happy birthday, son."

The gang hushed and looked at Frankie like he had lost his ever-loving mind. Then, with the confidence of a seasoned explorer, he smiled as he looked into the stunned eyes of each boy.

"Now I have to find a way over."

And he did.

As the team members looked for ways to climb the wall, I whispered to the Spirit.

"I hear what you are saying. You've placed an impossible dream in my heart, a dream only You can bring to pass. Though I lack the finances, I will toss my hat over the wall. Though I have no business training, I will toss my hat. I don't even have a computer. All I have is this ridiculous desire to lead these voyages. I will toss my hat! Now Lord, what is my hat?"

Leading these voyages was my unique expression of worship to the Creator. Leading others in a life of spiritual exploration was a gift I longed to give. I wanted to stand at the doorway of wonder and invite others in. My prayer came easily. "Yes, I will be obedient and follow the call You've placed in my heart, regardless of all the reasons it seems impossible." My decision was a make-or-break moment for my life.

A journal entry Meriwether Lewis wrote when he turned 31, the same age I was, sums up my mood. "This day I completed my thirty first year, and conceived that I had in all human probability now existed about half the period which I am to remain in this Sublunary world. I reflected that I had as yet done but little, very little indeed, to further the happiness of the human race, or to advance the information of the succeeding generation…and resolved in future, to redouble my exertions and at least endeavor to promote those two primary objects of human existence, by giving them the aid of that portion of talents which nature and fortune have bestowed on me: or in future, to live for mankind, as I have heretofore lived for myself."[34]

Like Meriwether Lewis, I dedicated my life and talents, which God had bestowed upon me, to live for humankind by pursuing

---

34 Meriwether Lewis, "August 18, 1805," *LewisAndClarkJournals.Unl.Edu*, 2023.

Into the Wonder

the dream clawing to get out of my head and heart. A doorway opened to a future beyond measure.

But there was one last piece of unfinished business.

A pilgrimage to Ireland and a mission trip to New Orleans convinced us that starting a travel organization was feasible. Both trips were financially viable, thrilling to create, and enjoyable to lead. By September, a handful of churches contacted me to develop and lead trips during the summer of 2000. The word was getting out.

Cheryl enjoyed full-time work as much as I enjoyed being a stay-home dad. I jumped whenever a side gig arose, like manual labor or consulting at a local church. Several of our friends found temporary jobs I could do to help pay the bills.

An intimate group of generous friends with whom I shared my "toss the hat" moment encouraged me to take the risk. Learning I had no technology, Kim and David showed up at my house with a new desktop computer and printer. A few folks sent regular financial gifts that, to the dime, covered our monthly office expenses. Jim and Doug covered the legal costs of starting a non-profit organization. Everything was going better than I had hoped.

Before I was 25, I had obtained a handful of wicked scars. Each jagged healing contains a story.

My first childhood scar sits dead center on my left thigh, the last stand for a king-sized wart. The doctor froze it and knocked it off like an icicle. I kept it in a small jar and eventually traded it with a neighborhood kid for a plastic soldier, a torn comic book, and a pack of Chiclets.

My lower abdomen holds one of my worst mutilations. I dove into a flooded lake without checking the depth of the water. As a result, my stomach caught a shallow underwater cliff edge, scraping away my flesh to the muscle and sending me into instant shock. My Siberian husky, Tanya, jumped into the water and pulled me out before I drowned.

As I thought about my future, I fixated upon a nickel-sized scar below my left knee resulting from a brown recluse spider bite. The dangerously venomous arachnid left a gruesome hole in my leg for months.

My trip to the ER was the first place I'd heard of this tiny, deadly creature with a nasty reputation. Its small body and characteristic fiddle markings are usually unseen. I woke up one morning with shooting pain in my lower body. By mid-morning, my left leg had swollen to a ghastly size and turned a shade of purple. The shy spider had most likely crossed my sleeping body. When I shifted, Browny panicked. I never saw the perpetrator. The only evidence of its crime was the nasty hole left in my leg.

The doctor identified my wound and told me to prepare for a lengthy recovery. Every victim of the brown recluse responds in various ways to its venom. For some, it's as nasty as a rattlesnake bite. I had a moderately severe reaction to the spider's hemotoxic poison. Necrosis, or the death of living cells, sets in. Two pinprick bites turned into a painful purple and black open wound. The venom released by the brown recluse spider contained a complex collection of enzymes rupturing my blood cells. My leg was being consumed from the inside out. With proper treatment, the wound healed, and I avoided a skin graft.

I traced the old scar. There was no feeling in the area. The venom had penetrated deep like the bitterness eating away at my heart that summer of 1999.

Bitterness affects the soul, like brown recluse venom on the body. If allowed to penetrate, it leaves open wounds vulnerable to infection. In some instances, it can lead to amputation or organ failure. And it always leaves scars. I thought I had forgiven those who had hurt me. Yet, a quiet, self-justified bitterness hid within my heart. When someone mentioned Don's name, or I passed a church while driving, or heard certain religious songs, I became melancholy. Weights and chains, invisible and unassuming, kept me pinned to my past. I put on a brave face, lying to myself and everyone else, but the bitterness and unforgiveness remained. There was no way I could toss my hat with unforgiveness tying me to the ground.

Grabbing a yellow legal pad, I began to write down the wrongs I held on to, and then I took a moment to forgive. Starting on the left side of the paper, I began a list, first an offense followed by forgiveness. Each carefully pondered "I forgive" cast a piece of my unforgiveness into an ocean of divine absolution:

1. I was lied to. I forgive them for lying.
2. I was manipulated. I forgive their manipulations.
3. I was used. I forgive their selfishness.
4. I was stolen from. I forgive their meanness.
5. I was ignored. I forgive their callousness.
6. I was cut off. I forgive their fear.

I confessed and forgave for the next two hours. When I finished, I filled up all 34 lines on the sheet of paper. Emotionally exhausted, a rush of relief poured over me. Broken, I cried. For the first time since being fired, I was honest about the pains and scars I had inwardly collected like a glass menagerie.

I could finally move forward. I sat up in bed with the dramatic intention of burning the sheet of paper as a visceral offering of my act of forgiveness.

The Spirit of God whispered in my ear. "You are not finished." I froze. The interior voice of the Spirit had rarely spoken so sternly. The impression of those words had an impact on me as if my father was telling me, a six-year-old, to stand absolutely still because a rattlesnake was about to strike.

An action was dropped into my mind. I drew a line down the center of the yellow pad page. The left side of the page was filled top to bottom with my grievances and words of forgiveness.

I understood what the right column was for, and I dreaded the exercise. I began to fill in the corresponding right side with the name of a person I had hurt similarly. My stomach tightened.

Forgiveness had taken an all-too-personal turn. I was no longer the victim. I was the assailant. All those good vibes of forgiveness melted in my admission of guilt.

> I was lied to. I forgive them for lying.
> I lied to William M.
> I was manipulated. I forgive their manipulations.
> I manipulated Brent B.
> I was used. I forgive their selfishness.
> I used Sandra K.
> I was stolen from. I forgive their meanness.
> I stole from Robert T.
> I was ignored. I forgive their callousness.
> I ignored the Caters.
> I was cut off. I forgive their fear.
> I cut off the O'Daniels.

Wonder is both a clarifier and a cleanser. When we allow God's presence to hold our stubborn and sinful hearts like clay under the hand of the sculptor, we are transformed and transfigured into the story He has gifted us. As Juan de Pascaule wrote, "If attended to, the experience of wonder gives birth to self-examination and to a mindful awareness of the world. In time you come to know yourself as you have been and are—and this gives you the possibility of choosing how to be. Through the experience of wonder we become true individuals and true citizens of the universe."[35] This challenging moment of wonder was revealing the real me.

My absolution turned into a journey of forgiveness. For the next two months, I sought a face-to-face audience to ask for forgiveness from everyone on my list. These conversations were hard. People were gracious but also honest. They let me know how I had wounded them or how they had forgiven me for my offenses against them. Often, my confessions and their subsequent forgive-

---

35 Juan De Pascuale, "A Wonder Full Life," *Magazine.ND.Edu*, 2003.

ness left us in a tearful hug. By December, I started to grasp what forgiveness was—a pilgrimage, not just words.

As I named it, The List was a map of my freedom. Every one of my interactions was the chisel of God upon my hardened heart. Serving people, loving people, and leading them on spiritual journeys of transformation were internal and emotional movements. I engaged in the ancient Irish practice of the journey of *Immrama*, challenging others to join me on a Wonder Voyage.

I had tossed my hat into wonder. Where I might land was limitless.

Chapter 26

An Unconventional Pilgrimage

Seychelles, Africa - October 2000

Much to my surprise, the atmosphere in the market had transformed from a bustling ant colony of energy into a street performance. The crowd pressed in, eager to touch the rough-hewn wood. The folks surrounding us craned their necks to hear Keith speak. Smiles slowly dawned on concentrating faces. Parents planted children atop their shoulders to get a better look while small claps of joy popped like fireworks. Just as I began to feel at ease about being a central part of the odd spectacle, an irritated police officer bulldozed through the crowd. Pulling out his nightstick, he nearly bumped Keith's chest in a show of authority.

"Who permitted you to do this? You need allowances from the commissioner to do such a thing."

The more Keith explained why we were in the market, surrounded by a crowd of 200, the more indignant the officer grew. The crowd, agitated by the interloping officer, started yelling in protest.

One man, frustrated at the intrusion, stood nose-to-nose with the officer.

"Let him be! He is not harming anyone. Go do some real police work and leave these two alone." In a final burst of intimidation, and witnessing the crowd turning against him, the officer shouted to Keith.

"Pick up your cross and follow me!"

Although I found his order ironically amusing, I was alarmed. We'd been in Africa for less than 24 hours, and we were being arrested.

Into the Wonder

Cheryl and I launched into my holy hunch with a few hundred dollars in the bank, three monthly donors, a computer, no staff, no advertising, and no business knowledge. The few gifts I held, the practical know-how to build and lead trips, savvy budgeting, spiritual zeal, and love for explorative travel gave me the courage to start a truly unique organization. On January 1, 2000, Wonder Voyage was certified as a legal non-profit dedicated to leading pilgrimages.

Our mission has remained the same since our inception: *Wonder Voyage is an extraordinary non-profit organization that creates personalized pilgrimages and mission trips. Our voyages encourage an encounter with the heart of God through exploration and sacrificial service to distinctive communities around the globe. Through Wonder Voyage, each event becomes a journey, and every participant becomes a pilgrim.*

During our first official summer operating as Wonder Voyage, three volunteer interns, who had been in my youth group at Grace, joined our family in Ireland to run trips through June and July. We settled into our temporary home, a dairy farm near the Spencers, as we hosted five teams. Taking my family to Ireland meant a financially profitless summer, but the adventure and memories outweighed all other fiscal considerations. The entire endeavor would've been impossible without Cheryl by my side. My children, aged three, seven, and ten, lived a magical summer, free to explore and learn about a wider world.

Wonder Voyage was more than I had hoped. Our teams, diverse in personality, denomination, and background, were eager to explore. We hill-walked in sublime natural wonders, partook of Eucharist in ancient Celtic chapels, sailed to empty islands for a day of frolicking in the sea air, and encountered abundant wonder in every setting in which we landed. Every day was a new adventure, often with our plans giving way to sudden moments of inspiration.

We were figuring everything out for the first time. The leadership skills I'd developed over a decade of pastoring were not adequate in these new waters, any more than a mountain climber is prepared for scuba diving. New skill sets were tirelessly developed. All necessary adaptations were made by trial and error. And there was a whole lot of error. The pressure of running my organization revealed my leadership deficiencies.

I did not account for mental and physical exhaustion, an inevitable component of launching a new endeavor. One of my interns, tired of my barking, left halfway through the summer. Worse yet, a rift was forming with the Spencers. Still sensitive about my scars from my time at GFFC, I reacted, rather than responded, to the challenges of creating a new organization.

By the end of the summer, although the trips were the realization of a dream, I seriously doubted my ability to move forward with Wonder Voyage. I wrestled with lacking the professional skills it would take to make this my career, to care for my family properly, and to love people well in such an extraordinary endeavor.

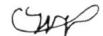

I was neck-deep in an emotional swamp when I received a fortuitous phone call from Ken Janke, one of our founding board members. Promoting and preparing for our 2001 summer trips was essential as September approached, but my emotions and blistering doubts paralyzed me. Although the summer had been more than I had hoped, I fixated on my laundry list of blunders. I was not making money, and we were sinking into debt. Wonder Voyage needed clients, a website, and lots of word of mouth. My ability to develop a staff was suspect as I was unlearning a decade of baked-in leadership ideas I'd picked up through my pastoral ministry under unhealthy senior ministers.

Ken called with an audacious offer. He knew I needed to get out of my unhealthy headspace. The best way to cure my doldrums was by sending me on a pilgrimage. He had raised funds for me to visit Africa with his good friend, Keith Wheeler.

Keith has an eccentric mission. For decades, he has carried a 12-foot wooden cross around the world as a witness of God's abundant love. Keith had walked more than twenty-five thousand miles in one hundred countries at the time. I was to walk with him as he carried the cross across five islands off the East Coast of

Africa for 17 days. I did not know Keith, but the idea of such an adventure was both exciting and concerning.

Before I accepted the invitation, I questioned the wisdom of such a journey. Keith was drawn to locations where propagating Christianity was a crime worthy of prison, torture, and possibly death. Yet, I was intrigued by his mission. Keith might not have a problem experiencing war, jail time, or persecution, but the torture of my body for someone else's nervy witness was not on my wish list. I deliberated because, even with the trip covered by a generous donor, there was no way this could be the right thing to do at this time in my life. The risks were too high.

I sat down with Cheryl and methodically presented my rationale for not joining the journey. She laughed at my grave demeanor.

"Don't make me your excuse for not going. I think I can handle things on the home front. The real question you should ask yourself is, why are you afraid to go."

Cheryl pulled no punches. Although I was the founder of an organization that invited people to travel beyond the borders of their lives, my fear of the unknown stood as a roadblock.

The truth is, I felt the pull to the African pilgrimage the same way I had experienced a nudge to start Wonder Voyage. I heard a gentle whisper, filling me with peace. The voice in my heart said, "Continue forward. You are moving in My will."

Pilgrimage is a doorway to a world beyond yourself. My longing for an adventure was unexplainable. I knew this trip was necessary. I wanted—no, needed—to go on a pilgrimage, to connect with the Creator who dropped this vision in my heart through His still, small voice.

Fear was a monster that could consume my desire for a pilgrimage. A choice must be made. I could cower to the obnoxious ogre or obey the gentle Spirit. I decided to take Brennan Manning's advice. "To live without risk is to risk not living."[36] I wanted to live.

Two weeks later, I was heading to Africa as a reluctant pilgrim.

---

36   Brennan Manning, *Ruthless Trust: The Ragamuffin's Path to God* (HarperSanFrancisco, 2000) 21.

An Unconventional Pilgrimage

We landed in Seychelles, a group of islands known for its friendly population and Edenic climate. The Creole population, a beautiful mix of African, European, Indian, and Asian bloodlines, walk tall as if they descended from Atlantis. On the main island of Mahe, beaches drape the lush green mountains like a string of pearls.

After settling into our hotel, I drove Keith to the outskirts of the capital city of Victoria. Finding a quiet parking lot, he assembled his sturdy redwood cross with several screws and plates binding a wheel at the bottom. Before starting his walk, Keith lay on the ground, hands stretched above his head in a moment of silent prayer. This was his daily ritual.

I was self-conscious walking next to a guy carrying a massive piece of wood representing the most controversial religious figure the world has ever known. Within minutes of entering the marketplace, 200 people had gathered around to ask questions of the strange cross-walker. When I asked Keith how he overcame his discomfort with such an odd calling, he simply replied, "Who said I have? I am just trying to obey what God has asked me to do."

The primarily Catholic observers asked why Keith carried the cross outside the Easter season. As Keith answered, an irritated officer stormed through the crowd and shouted at Keith to pick up his cross and follow him.

We arrived at the nearby police station. Keith was taken through an unmarked door while I waited with angst boiling inside. Keith lugged his cross through the front door and set it upright in the cramped, block-stoned lobby. The handcuffed arrestees, sitting on benches around the walls of the austere room, bowed their heads.

After repeatedly pestering the front desk officer on the whereabouts of Keith, I was escorted to the office of Mahe's police commissioner. Taking my hand in a warm embrace, the commissioner spoke. Keith was sipping a soda as if he were enjoying a mid-summer picnic.

"I see nothing wrong in what you are doing. I am very sorry for the trouble our overzealous officer has caused, but I am happy he brought you in so I could meet you. I am a man under authority, and you, too, are under a greater authority, so who am I to stop you?"

My jaw hit the floor. Over the next few minutes, I witnessed the commissioner confessing as if he was sitting before his parish priest. He detailed his many shortcomings and besetting sins. Keith asked if he wanted us to pray with him.

"I do not need prayer. I need to make a decision."

After a tense moment of silence, the commissioner picked up his phone and spoke to his dispatcher to alert all the stations on Mahe that we would be visiting for a few days. Keith was to have passage throughout the island to carry the cross.

Before sending us on our way, the commissioner gave us three rules.

"Do not block traffic. Do not walk in the middle of the road. And do not hit anyone over the head while preaching about the cross."

We laughed, thanked him for his kindness, and departed. The strange stories I had heard from Keith about his cross adventures might be true.

A couple of hours later, Keith found himself on the wrong side of a busy street when the sidewalk ran out. I stopped the heavy traffic so Keith could cross the middle of the road. Two of the commissioner's rules were broken.

Continuing down the sidewalk, I noticed an old man hobbling toward us. Two small children dragged their aged grandfather by pulling on his hands, while a third shoved him from behind. He squinted at the cross-bearer heading toward him in an inevitable meeting. The scowl on his face revealed his uneasiness about having to cross paths with us. But his grandchildren pulled him directly in front of Keith by sheer will.

For a few seconds, there was a silent standstill. When the small children smiled at Keith, he gave a little wave. The old man bored his eyes into the ground. He decided to reward the children's determination with bright stickers. Keith carried a roll of ugly, orange, day-glow stickers that read: Smile, God Loves You.

Resting the 87-pound cross on his shoulder, Keith took the stickers and leaned down to the small children to give them their

An Unconventional Pilgrimage

gift. As Keith bent, the descending upper portion of the crossbeam met the stationary top of the grandfather's head with a decisive clunk that sounded like two coconuts being smacked together. I saw the old man's eyes cross with the pain of impact. When Keith felt the weight of the cross suddenly relieved off his shoulder as it rested on the old man's head, Keith stood up, taking the weight back upon his shoulder. He looked around, perplexed. Keith did not notice the palling man in front of him. Down again he went, and the cross came smack in the middle of the man's skull. This time the old man almost dropped from the blow.

Keith stood up with a sudden realization of what he had done. The glazed look in the old man's eyes was a clear indication. Keith's emphatic apologies didn't help; the man knew no English. But his scowl was gone, replaced with the goofy grin of one who had entered a blessed state of enlightenment. He moved down the road, pushed and pulled by bestickered grandchildren.

I burst into laughter. The commissioner's final rule was broken. Letting yourself enter a story, no matter its twists and turns, is vital to pilgrimage—and essential for wonder.

The second leg of our island-hopping pilgrimage was a 1,000-mile flight south to Mauritius. Enclosed in a coral reef surrounding the island's exterior, Mauritius' smudge-blue mountains thrust upwards like daggers through the center of the landmass. Massive volcanic stone walls dividing property throughout Mauritius revealed its geothermal genesis.

Mauritius is best known as the home to the legendary Dodo bird, the only place it was found on the planet. Sugar was the island's lifeblood. Thousands of Indian laborers came to Mauritius in the early 1800s to farm the fields, inadvertently creating her modern-day population. Shantytowns containing the ancestors of these workers are scattered across the landscape. Stillness on the island was as extinct as the dodo. As the busy pandemonium of Mauritius swirled around us, Keith's cross-carrying was considered a strange roadside spectacle. We passed temples galore, centers of religious devotion that were filled with seekers longing for a touch from the gods.

There was so much I did not understand. I was exposed to people and places that cracked me open like an egg. Trying to process radically different cultures, my brain deduced new categories of unconsidered questions, rethinking my prejudices and stripping away my carefully manicured world. Of course, the nuances of religion and faith, culture and ethics, practice and belief were infinitely diverse. Still, the core of the cosmos was a longing for the One who transcends our world. Everyone was seeking something or someone.

Pilgrimage affords you a rare opportunity to be surprised at every waking moment. As I took in a lively, new corner of the planet with open eyes, I learned about myself, endless human possibilities, our capacity for love, and the challenges troubling all of us. Traveling through these new places helped me define the places I thought I knew well, both externally and internally. This is a central result of the act of pilgrimage.

A short flight west brought us to the French island of Réunion. Her capital, St. Denis, looks like any mid-sized European port town, except the labyrinth of streets has no signs. This lack of clear direction became a theme for us in Réunion. The population comprises the Malabar sect, a synthesis of several religions mixed with indigenous voodoo. On the outside, it looks like an institutionalized Christian religion, but its true nature is animist. Unlike the highly communal nature of Hinduism, Islam, or Christianity, the Malabar religion focuses on the individual.

On our arduous walk through the island, we were branded as an abnormality to be ignored. As the hours passed, I drifted a couple of blocks behind Keith to avoid the blatant disdain of those we passed.

The island was dotted with shrines to Kali, the Hindu goddess of death. Her grotesque statue had a cross painted behind her, symbolizing death as the victor on this island. The image was a violent act against my senses. I was a foreigner, an outsider, the other. As the sun hovered between high noon and its ocean rest, the volcanoes on the island coughed up soot, forming a murky ash cloud. By dusk, Réunion's skies were a gathering of foreboding shadow-wraiths. Réunion had her own Mt. Doom. My mood darkened with the atmosphere.

Departing Réunion the next day, I realized I was starting to slip into a quagmire of despair. As I slogged through the maze of a confusing location, I found it too easy to lose sight of the Divine. I wanted to run from the cross instead of clasp hold of it for dear life. As I lost sight of wonder, I lost my equilibrium.

Réunion reminded me how precious and tenuous the gift of wonder was in my life. Sliding into my doubts, fears, and anxieties about how others perceived me choked out the whispers of Spirit. I had allowed my sense of wonder to be dulled and dampened by my surroundings. Réunion had as much wonder as any other place in the world. Without a sense of wonder, you are only a tourist.

On day eleven of our African pilgrimage, we landed in Madagascar, the fourth-largest island in the world. Madagascar was settled by Malay Polynesian mariners 1500 years ago. I came to the big island with visions of lemurs and lush jungles. I was greeted with red hills, dusty roads, and diesel fumes surrounding the sprawling capital of Antananarivo.

Within minutes of leaving the airport, we drove past lean-tos crowding the edges of roads. Women carried stacks of wood, baskets piled high with clothes, bundles of newspapers, or other items precariously balanced on their ironclad necks. They might hold a tool, a screaming baby, lively chickens, or all three at once.

The visuals were perplexing. Ribbons of raw meat hung from makeshift butcher stands. Covered in flies, the meat strips moved like snakes. Women and young children soaked their clothes in the lime-green sewage ditch before beating them on rocks. Looking out over a field of dry swirling dirt, covered with a patchwork of drying clothes, I wondered why they bothered with the process.

Smog, like a cloud of burnt coffee, sagged over Antananarivo. Broken sunlight struggled to punch through the haze. Occasionally, a rogue breeze rushed through, removing the dank air for a few minutes of relief.

Later in the day, while I wandered the penurious thoroughfares of the city, a wisp of a girl begged me for a bite to eat by putting her pressed fingers to her lips. She was probably six years old, but malnutrition made her appear much younger. The heartbreaking moment caused me to ache for my children. Seeing hunger in her eyes created an uncomfortable realization: I'd never experienced true poverty. My understanding of lack needed to be redefined.

Throughout my African pilgrimage, I was exposed to worlds I'd never considered, never wanted to believe possible. The shock of witnessing realities beyond my understanding were earthquakes shaking apart my prejudices and my idealism, and they reorientated my spiritual assumption, naïve platitudes, and understanding of unconditional love and unhindered cruelty.

As desperate as Madagascar appeared, our days there were defined by her kind, inviting people rather than her harsh realities. Though much of their world was filled with pain and poverty, Madagascar's men, women, and children freely gave friendly smiles, kind waves, and shouts of joy. There was always a world beyond my faulty perception. I needed to slow myself down to see beyond the veil.

The island's primary faith is Malagasy, the most foreign religion I have ever encountered. Malagasy is an eccentric mixture of the veneration of ancestral spirits. A Malagasy believer cries out to his or her ancestors for wisdom.

When my first Wonder Voyage summer had ended, I struggled with all the mistakes I had made in Ireland. Like the Malagasy ancestors, a crowd cheered me on, but I was not asking for help. I needed to change if I was going to make a go with Wonder Voyage. I needed to lean on a community, friends, and confidants. Pursuing this dream all alone was not an option.

An Unconventional Pilgrimage

As my African pilgrimage expanded, my desperation for spiritual clarity deepened. Being away from the familiar created more questions than answers. A religion without wonder is a book without words, an ocean without water, a song without a sound, and a marriage without love. This quest to lead others into wonder was solidifying.

One island remained, and it defined, more succinctly than any other experience in my life, our quest for the divine, for wonder.

It started with a disgusting pair of sneakers.

Chapter 27

Reluctant Pilgrim

The Comoros Islands, Africa - October 2000

As our flight approached touchdown, I was a ball of nerves. The passengers and flight attendants' staring eyes and wary whispers were disconcerting. The pointing proved that something was amiss. Two plain-clothes officers took us into custody as we disembarked onto the tarmac.

The senior officer took a minute to study our faces.

"Why have you come at such a dangerous time?"

Under the circumstances, I was confident Keith knew how to give a sensible and sensitive answer.

"We are on hajj. I have come to carry the cross in your country, and my friend is joining me."

My face drained of color. As I waited to be arrested and imprisoned, the officer laughed.

"Welcome to my island!"

We were swept away in a nondescript government vehicle and sequestered at a hotel until Officer Samir met us for a second, casual interview. Samir was a handsome man carrying rigid authority and a copious ego—not a hair out of place nor a wrinkle in his uniform. His calculated demeanor gave me the impression that his friendliness was a tool he used to measure our responses. Human lie detector, Officer Samir, was here to discover our motives for coming to his little nation.

Samir explained why our arrival was so odd. Three weeks prior, a militant Islamic organization unknown to us at the time, al-Qaeda, blasted a hole in the United States Navy destroyer, the USS *Cole*, with a small boat filled with C4 explosives while the ship refueled in a Yemen harbor. Seventeen American sailors were killed, and 37 others were injured in a suicide bombing, making it the deadliest attack against a U.S. naval vessel. This took place eleven months before the events of September 11, 2001.

Al-Qaeda took responsibility for the deadly act. Comorians and political extremists from several nations were part of the plot. This triggered a string of events that put Comorian's politics and economy into a tailspin. The U.S. and several other Western embassies pulled out of the country as heavy sanctions were imposed against the nation of 200,000 people. When we landed, no fuel or food had reached the island in over two weeks. Mass protests had erupted in the streets. We saw the red glow of huge bonfires three miles away from our hotel as they burned in the capital city of Moroni.

Keith shared how he loved carrying the cross during political crises when people were looking for hope and peace. Samir was fascinated with Keith's calling to carry the cross. He reached out and shook Keith's hand like a brother.

"Finally," he declared, "a Christian bold enough to stand for what he believes."

After an hour of questioning, Samir shared his story. The son of a fisherman, Samir, during his late teens, wanted more for his life. Samir needed a quality education. His family was poor. The sons of fishermen stayed fishermen. Samir made a desperate decision and obtained a sponsorship to a top university in Cairo. Al-Qaeda fully funded his education. But there was a price.

After completing university at the top of his class, Samir was assigned to train under Osama Bin Laden in Libya. Samir's intelligence and charm helped him move through the ranks until he was reassigned as one of four police commissioners in the Comoros Islands. As he recalled his time in Libya, the grief in his eyes gave us chills.

Sensing he had shared too much, Samir changed the topic. He told us that we could visit the island as long as we were chaperoned by his brother, Ismael, and another young man. Samir's story made me believe that this powder keg of an island contained a strong possibility of danger for us. Secretly, I hoped we might be put right back on the airplane. Instead, one of the highest-ranking military officials in the Comoros Islands arranged our excursion into chaos.

Ismael and his friend, Mohammed, picked us up for a day of exploration. We started in Moroni's capital city, a ghost town. Our first stop was the U.S. Embassy, a freshly burnt-out shell with epitaphs of hate scrawled in French on its crumbling walls. Ismael noticed our confused faces.

"You're Americans. We thought you might like to see this."

We did not.

Thrilled to leave the city, we rambled up into burnt brown hills that mutated into volcanic fields of charred stone. The Comorians were accustomed to the whims and fits of their volcanic home. The road ran through bantam villages with a handful of families scraping out meager gardens from the rigid earth. One of these villages demanded a stop at the memorial home of Amir Mbaye Trambrue, the last Sultan of the Comoros Islands. His home, built in the 1700s, is considered sacred ground, untouched from the moment of his burial 300 years ago. After he died, he was too fat to be removed from his bedroom, so they buried him under the floor.

As we moved up the volcanic mountains, we saw swaths of destruction that had swallowed entire villages in the 1980s. We snaked our way up a shadowed road to an ancient battlefield of historical significance. The acreage was magnificent. Hundred-foot cliffs created a semi-circle around one end of the field. Goats chomped the tall grass, oblivious to our intrusion. Walking into the middle of the pasture, listening to the story of a legendary battle, we heard a metallic clinking under our feet. Bullet shells were scattered throughout the tall grass. As I leaned down to pick one up, a shepherd ran to the field gate, flailing his arms and yelling, "ARRET." His cry was so alarming we froze. We had stumbled onto the edge of a military installation. He pointed at us to look up. Two snipers aimed at us at the top of the cliff face. We backed away, looking as unconcerned as one can when one has nearly wet himself.

By this point, my mind was wading into a swampland of irrationality. I was convinced that we were being set up as hostages. Somewhere down the road, al-Qaeda insurgents were waiting, blockading the way. We'd be detained and held captive for a hefty ransom paid out by the U.S. government for our safe return. Sometime during the kidnapping, Keith would preach about Jesus, and we'd die a martyr's death. Our bodies would never be found, leaving our families to ponder our fate. I wondered how slow the car would have to drive for me to jump out, roll into the jungle, and run at top speed while dodging bullets. To say my faith was shaky was underselling my paranoia.

The island we were visiting has 780 mosques. Arriving at the doorstep of a famous mosque, we were given a great honor: permission to climb to the top of the five-story tower where the call to prayer faithfully occurred five times a day. As I climbed, I hugged the wall. There was no protective railing and a seventy-foot drop. The view was remarkable, but I had a ridiculous thought. Had we been led to the tower to be hurled from the top as infidels? This reluctant pilgrim stood trembling, not recognizing the esteem I had been given, but obsessing over my prejudice-provoked fears. From the pinnacle, Keith spotted a place on the beach where he wanted to begin his cross-walk. His excitement was building while my stomach was performing summersaults.

Mohammed drove us to the shore. My reluctance escalated as Keith assembled the cross on the lonely beach. His two-mile walk from the beach into the nearest town passed a sizeable religious school specializing in educating Muslim clerics. I knew a lot could happen in that short span of time: stoning, beating, beheading. I wanted to be anywhere else except next to that large cross.

We had barely walked off the sand when Keith turned to me.

"Why don't you and Ismael go ahead with the car to meet us on the outskirts of the town? If Mohammed and I walk, it will be easier to interact with people."

Reluctant Pilgrim

Although his words caused me to jump for joy, I maintained an outward look of sincere concern.

"Are you sure? I can stay if you need me to."

"No. You guys go ahead. We'll meet you in an hour."

At that moment, I decided I'd faithfully record Keith's martyrdom. *"A world wandering cross-bearer stoned to death for his faith on a tiny island off the east coast of Africa."* I'd be a witness to his last days, his courage, his humanity, and his faith. As long as I was the one who told the tale and not the one being pelted by rocks or tortured for my faith, all was well.

Ismael and I drove a couple of miles up the road and parked on the outskirts of a village. A day full of tension had squeezed me so tight I needed to relieve my aching bladder. I took a short hike into the jungle as a peaceful breeze tickled the canopy of leaves overhead, helping to alleviate my fears. A few minutes later, I heard a muffled commotion around the car as I walked out of the forest. Ismael was agitated. He was hopping up and down, waving his arms like a sideshow caller to attract the villagers' attention.

He shouted in French, "The man with the cross is coming! The man with the cross is coming!"

Confused by his erratic actions, I joined the tiny crowd. My sizeable white physique, emerging from the jungle, drew inquisitive stares and chuckles. I stared at Ismael, trying to understand why he had become so agitated when the hairs on the back of my neck stood on end. I turned my head. Not twelve inches from my nose stood a wild man panting in my face. He was half my size, his lean frame revealing a person of little means and significant bouts of hunger. I was almost knocked over by the putrid breath that moved through his stained teeth. His tousled hair, matted with mud, looked artificial.

Covered in shabby rags, he was a man, I later discovered, who had slept on the jungle floor for years. His fearsome, piercing, yellowed eyes carried the vacant stare of the living dead. Neither fear, consciousness, nor humanness filtered through the windows of his soul. Paralyzed by the man's gaze, I understood what had happened.

Ismael had been casually leaning against the car when the wild man emerged from the jungle, frightening him. His cries to gather locals were his desperate act to draw a crowd around for safety. The villagers mockingly referred to the yellow-eyed man as Chief. A decade ago, he had shattered his mind through profuse drug abuse. From the viewpoint of this strict Islamic culture, the loss of Chief's mind triggered the loss of his soul. He was an outcast. Forced to reside in the jungles on the outskirts of the village, Chief survived by sneaking scraps of food from rubbish bins at night. He was a creature teased and attacked by rock-throwing kids. Unworthy of consideration, this village pariah bore my soul with empty eyes. I did not doubt that, if provoked, this man could do me a fair amount of physical damage.

Like an angry tiger at the zoo, Chief suddenly turned and began to pace around the car and crowd. A guttural growl gurgled from his throat like an animal assessing his prey. After an entire circuit, he stopped again, an arm's length away from my face, and soundlessly stared at me. He repeated this a few times to the growing amusement of a crowd now laughing at my uneasy countenance. I felt trapped, unaware of how to react. All of my biting fears about Comoros were manifesting in this crazy man. When I saw Keith's growing figure down the road, I sighed in relief. Suddenly the cross I had been avoiding all day became my saving grace.

Keith was surprised to see this circle of Comorians excited by his arrival. He greeted the people. Ismael was also relieved and started translating for Keith as he answered questions fired at him in rapid succession. I knew this was my chance to break away from the menacing eyes of Chief.

Coming to the cross, now leaning on the car, I bent out of view to remove the wheel. Two feet appeared in my line of sight. Crouching down with palms to the earth, Chief looked into my eyes, curious at my feverish ratcheting.

Avoiding Chief's eyes, I stared at what used to be shoes. The toes of the shoes were ripped open, revealing greasy green socks that peeked through like a pair of sickly iguanas. The shoes were glued to Chief's feet by sweat and soot. He wore this form of footwear for no other reason than to maintain a bit of humanity. I looked at my feet shod with slick black Nikes, newly broken in by the hot roads of five African island nations. A thought too quick to call my own burst out of my mouth before I had sense enough to stop it.

Calling Ishmael over, I asked him to translate what I was about to say to the crowd. Keith looked at me, wondering what was about to happen.

"I would like to make an exchange of friendship. I want Chief to have my shoes."

In rapid-fire French, Ismael translated my declaration. I removed my shoes. The mood of the crowd turned jubilant. Chief immediately removed his shoes with a sound like a boot being removed from the miry muck of a mud hole. After peeling off his greasy green socks and throwing them in the bushes, he grabbed my ebony Nikes and placed them on his feet. I stopped him and gave him my clean white socks. The shoes fit so ideally that Cinderella would have been jealous. Though he showed no emotion in his eyes, Chief concentrated as he tied the shoes. Slowly walking in place, he carefully evaluated the shoe's feel, weight, and quality.

He then abruptly stopped and stared at me.

The crowd hushed.

Turning to Ishmael, I said, "What's everyone waiting for?"

Ishmael, in a serious tone, replied, "You told everyone you would make an exchange of friendship. According to our customs, you must fulfill your vow and wear Chief's shoes."

I was aghast. Recalling the sound of those bacteria sponges coming off Chief's feet made me ill. Without socks, I had no protection. I looked at the crowd, then Chief, and I discerned putting on the tattered shoes was better than offending the villagers. When I slipped them on, it felt like I was dipping my naked foot into a waste bin of lukewarm wet noodles. The crowd broke out in a festive cheer.

Wanting to capture the absurdity of the moment, I asked Keith to snap a quick photo of Chief and me. Chief removed his shirt to display his tattoo-covered torso when he saw the camera. He stood facing the lens with his hands extended out in front of

Into the Wonder

him, hands upturned as a gesture of emptiness. Keith decided to uptick the fun as I turned to face the camera.

"You know what that means, Shawn. You have to take off your shirt!"

Before I could stop his insane advice, Ishmael had translated Keith's words to the crowd. Affirming cheers erupted. I removed my multicolored button-down shirt, standing in all my pasty pudgy glory, mimicking Chief's stance. Next to him, my 270-pound frame made it look as if I had consumed three small Comorian children for lunch. Boisterous laughter swiftly replaced the cheering. After the picture was captured, realizing I could not be humiliated much more, I offered my shirt to Chief. He put it on with the reverence of a priestly vestment. Chief noticed the Celtic cross tattoo on my upper left arm. He was mystified as he traced the cross repeatedly with his fingers. Something about the artistic symbol captivated him.

Now shirtless, I turned to Ishmael and asked if, by chance, he had anything in his car to cover my nakedness. He dug through various piles of stuff in his trunk. With a victorious "oui!" he handed me a wadded-up t-shirt with the Guinness Harp of Ireland emblazoned upon the front. Ireland was home to me. It's where I received the Celtic cross tattoo and learned to love pilgrimage. Receiving this shirt was God saying, "I am watching out for you. Nothing is an accident." At least, it felt that way until I put it on. Do you know what a 270-pound man looks like in a small-size t-shirt? Imagine Santa Claus in a sports bra, and you'll start to get the idea. I wore it in stride.

As Chief stood in his new shirt, white socks, and black shoes, the crowd began to chant: "CHIEF! CHIEF! CHIEF! CHIEF! CHIEF!" Possibly, for the first time, Chief was receiving shouts of affirmation and praise. The crowd's response invited this jungle outcast back into the clan of humanity. It echoed the truth that Chief was human, worthy of respect, affirmation, and life.

I walked around to the car's front door and was about to get in when I realized Chief was on my heels. Grabbing his hand, I traced the cross on my arm, then I pointed to the stars, hoping somewhere in the back of his mind that his Muslim upbringing would trigger a sense of God. Once again, I took his hand, traced the Celtic cross on my arm, and touched his shirt. Again, after tracing the cross, I pointed to his new shoes. Lastly, I traced the cross and put his hand on my heart. It's impossible to describe the intimacy of that moment. Most likely, Chief had not experienced human touch in years. Because the image is seared into my memory, I can say that those dead eyes became alive with tears. Chief grabbed my wrists and squeezed them. Chief didn't break sight in the rearview mirror for as long as we were in view.

The weight of my encounter with Chief didn't hit me until I was on my way home. Looking back on my African journey, I had been a reluctant pilgrim, a coward for the faith, and a shaker of biblical boots. I did not feel particularly inspired. As a sort of penance, I picked up my Bible, desperate for resolve. I turned to the words of Paul. "Think of yourselves the way Christ Jesus thought of himself. He had equal status with God but didn't think so much of himself that he had to cling to the advantages of that status no matter what. Not at all. When the time came, he set aside the privileges of deity and took on the status of a slave, became human! Having become human, he stayed human. It was an incredibly humbling process. He didn't claim special privileges. Instead, he lived a selfless, obedient life and then died a selfless, obedient death—and the worst kind of death at that—a crucifixion" (Philippians 2:5–8 MSG).

I closed the pages and looked out the window at the shrinking waters of the Indian Ocean down on beaches strewn with blackened pumice on the island's edges. I was struck with an epiphany. As Chief put on my shoes, he did not simply gain protection for his feet. He was gifted with a long-denied dignity. A village that regarded him as little more than a wild beast had acknowledged him with joy-filled affirmations as a valuable human. A friendly touch, a memento of compassion, had brought tears to an outcast's eyes.

Into the Wonder

    Chief gave me the gift of perspective. I remembered a newborn baby in a stable, the image of an unseen God wrapped in tattered cloth. In a moment of wonder, this Chosen One took on the ragged wrecked shoes of humankind and, in turn, gave us His finest sandals. He removed His white woolen garments and placed them on our naked flesh. In taking on the tattered hearts of humanity, He became a touchable God. Chief allowed me to see Christ's exchange in a way now tattooed onto my soul.

I cleaned those ragged shoes, soaking them in bleach water to remove the stench and bacteria deep within the remaining fragments. They sit on a shelf in my office. For years after I placed those shoes on my feet, a persistent fungus called chromoblastomycosis plagued me. The rare skin disease found primarily in the tropics is caused by a fungus in the soil. The islands in the Indian Ocean are a hot spot for chromoblastomycosis.

    Though I only had the shoes on my feet for a few minutes, the disease in the shoe attacked the tops of my feet. For years, my feet looked nasty. The red, blotchy, flaking infection persisted no matter what I did or what medicines doctors prescribed. When people saw my bare feet, they gasped with disgust. Though the rash looked horrid, it neither itched nor caused me any physical discomfort. After a few years, the rash cleared, leaving scars that remind me of my encounter with Chief.

    My 16-hour flight back to Dallas allowed me to contemplate the first 30 years of my life. From my earliest memories, the Spirit of God had enticed me with wonder, like points on a treasure map, leading me ever closer to the love of Christ. In extreme moments of sublime awe or through dark valleys of despair, wonder shone out from the most unusual sources. Though once hunted by the monster of aloneness after the loss of my parent's marriage or my high school years where I engaged in an agnostic treasure hunt for the truth, God was with me in my friends, my hunger for discovery, and my questions. In extreme moments of sublime awe or through the darkest valleys of despair, wonder shone out from the most unlikely sources. My story was ongoing. Every bit of our search for God is an encounter *with* God.

From the moment I encountered the presence of God in that little church in New Jersey, I had a strong sense I was part of an ongoing adventure. Cheryl was God's gift of wonder in a life partner, but God had provided others like Mike Yengo, Mama Val, and Keith Wheeler, mentor pilgrims, to move me forward. At times, especially after several devastating car wrecks and two failed churches, I wandered an existential desert wondering if there was a God. After years of searching and seeking my weird pastoral decade, my love for travel, everything that happened to me, good and horrible, was redeemed by the Storymaker into a larger tale.

My life, this ongoing pilgrimage, challenged me to give up all to seek the One I cannot live without. I love the way John Eldredge writes about our journeys. "God has been wooing us all our lives, calling us up out of our small stories. As Simone Weil said, he sends to us beauty and affliction, he haunts us with a memory of Eden, and he speaks through every story we've ever loved, calling to our hearts: 'Do you trust me? Will you let me come for you?'"[37]

God whispers into our spirit, "There is a story I have created for you. Will you join me on this journey?"

I've often been a reluctant pilgrim, but I am still a pilgrim, moving forward into mystery. This movement into the unknown, whether with boldness or apprehension, will bring about scars. These scars occur when I walk with the downtrodden or face injustice, when I battle my hypocrisy or experience the cost of sacrificial love, and when I dare to dirty my hands by serving the needs of others. Scars are inevitable if we decide to join God's story of wonder. It's comforting to know Jesus carries the scars on His hands, back, and side. They are the visual sign of His unfathomable love. Today, I look at the scars upon my feet fondly, for they represent one precious life on a small island in the Indian Ocean. Chief and I are not so different. We are wandering

---

37 John Eldredge, *Epic: The Story God is Telling* (Nashville: Thomas Nelson, 2004), 71.

souls looking for love, looking for friends, longing for a moment of wonder to draw us into a transforming love.

By the end of my African voyage, I knew a life of leading pilgrimages, a doorkeeper inviting others into wonder, is a call worthy of any sacrifice. Wonder changes everything.

Epilogue

Into the Wonder

Pembrokeshire, Wales - July 2001

I trembled as I fell to my face and hugged the cold granite, the literal peak of the mountain, with white fingertips. A nearly imperceptible voice whispered into my ear. Neither height nor the elements posed any threat to my physical person. I shook because I was dumbstruck by an unexpected Presence. Unable to stand on Holy Ground, I lay still, holding my breath, in a liminal space between our world and the *otherworld* as I processed the fiery words consuming my spirit.

Throughout my brief life, I have experienced countless moments of wonder where the unexpectedly revealed presence of Christ obliterated my fears, aloneness, and tormenting doubts. My nagging questions flew off the mountaintop like dried chaff in a hurricane. I was awed with love. Wonder was my call. Wonder was my purpose. Wonder was the gift I'd give my life to give to others.

We were well into Wonder Voyage's second summer in Ireland. The previous year had been financially slim and emotionally taxing. Still, the thrill of establishing something new in the world, something truly one-of-a-kind, kept us going.

Our family had rented a sheep farm on the edge of the Esker Monastery in Athenry, County Galway, where we based our summer operations. While our teams of American pilgrims enjoyed the monastic guest house and forested grounds, we kept a semblance of familial normalcy on the farm. Learning from past mistakes, we found a rhythm for our visiting teams. With the help of fantastic volunteer staff, Cheryl hosted the teams while I led

Into the Wonder

them on excursions throughout West Ireland. Spiritual direction, cultural exploration, storytelling, and a safe place to explore their faith brought Wonder Voyage into its own.

Midway through the summer, we took advantage of a two-week gap between teams. Emotionally drained, physically exhausted, and ready to explore a new location for inspiration, we took the ferry across the Irish Sea to Wales for a short adventure. Landing on the glorious Pembrokeshire coastline, we had no specific plans. A journey over the Preseli Mountains brought us to the isolated Cwm Gwaun Valley.

The Cwm Gwaun, Pembrokeshire's hidden treasure, is a place out of time. Surrounded by the largest concentration of megalithic and Celtic Christian sites in Wales, the Cwm Gwaun is overshadowed by bleak and bare mountains, which eventually tumble into mid-mountain farmlands. The valley's single road meanders through a steep wooded vale thick with crawling vegetation, ancient oaks, and summer flowers. Fewer than 100 residents live along the six-mile mountain vale, sliced through the middle 10,000 years ago by jagged, unforgiving glaciers. The locals keep the seasons by the pre-1752 Julian calendar, preserving its timelessness. These folks are purposeful in their preservation of the past. Most are families that have owned their ancestral lands for dozens of generations.

In the sixth century, the Irish monk St. Brynach arrived on his wonder voyage in this valley, rumored to be ruled by demonic forces. Over time, Brynach's evangelistic fervor cleansed the valley of its darkness. As it became his base of operations, it transformed into a haven for the light of Christ.

As we snaked through the vale, we drove past the picturesque church built on the site of Brynach's original mission. We came to the base of Carli Angli, the Mount of Angels, where the saint often climbed for a panoramic view of the countryside. From his viewpoint, Brynach prayed for the light of Christ to illuminate the Welsh.

Turning through an iron gate wrapped in ivy, we ascended sloping hills, surrounded by verdant uncut fields of grass speckled with grazing sheep, trickling streams reflecting the sunlight off dancing wildflowers. We were passing through an impressionist painting. Fflad-y-Brenin (Sheepfold of the King) was a farm converted into a Celtic-style retreat center in the 1980s. Hovering above the thick woodlands of the valley floor, Ffald-y-Brenin was a wonder to behold. Hand-cut stone buildings punctuated the property, each with a gray slate roof. The architecture flows like water with no straight edges within its white cinder interior. There is theology to the architecture of Ffald-y-Brenin that evokes availability, serenity, and the weaving of the eternal into the temporal.

At the center of the property is the conical roofed chapel. When the builders went to clear the grounds, they discovered a problem. One mountain peak protruded where the floor was designed to go. Dynamiting the rock meant endangering all the surrounding buildings, so a compromise was made. The structure was constructed around the stone, which, in turn, became the chapel's altar. It lies at the heart of Ffald-y-Brenin.

The following day, I slipped into the chapel as the sun still slept, my morning breath visible in my small puffs of prayer. Sitting on the stone bench outlining the inner walls of the rounded chapel, I soaked in the stillness. Unloading the leadership burdens of a newborn organization, I methodically released cares into the arms of the Father: marriage, family, finances, the vast details wrapped up in our pilgrimages, and our volunteer staff. My prayers continued until I emptied my mind of my anxieties.

I picked up a Bible lying on the bench and opened it to the book of Jeremiah. There was a particular verse in Jeremiah 33 that came alive. "Thus says the LORD who made it, the LORD who formed it to establish it (the LORD is his name): 'Call to Me, and I will answer you, and show you great and mighty things, which you do not know.'" I stood before the mountain altar and spoke a prayer I'd prayed every day since Wonder Voyage's inception on New Year's Day of 2000. A seed of doubt still plagued my psyche. The doubt caused me to start my daily prayers with this line: "If Wonder Voyage is not Your will, and You want me to let this go, I will. Just give me the word."

A wave of consuming love overtook me as I stood before the mountaintop altar, like the first moment I experienced God's presence when I was 17. It started like the wisp of smoke after extinguishing a candle flame. But that wisp, instead of dissipating, grew until the roof was filled with a thick blanket of fog. I fell to my face, hugging the rock, not wanting to look up. His presence filled the chapel. A question, like a disembodied voice, echoed through my spirit.

"Who is the author of Wonder Voyage? Who is the author of your story?"

Another verse came to my mind from Proverbs 3:5–6. "Trust in the Lord with all your heart; do not lean on your own understanding. In all of your ways, acknowledge Him, and he will make your paths straight."

I lay there and acknowledged that the Spirit of Jesus was the one who started my wonder voyage and this new venture. He, and He alone, held my ever-evolving story in His hands. The Creator granted this gift to draw others to God's unfathomable love. Wonder Voyage was not mine to own and control. I partnered with the Creator to engage in this adventure of a lifetime.

As I departed the chapel, I vowed never to ask my doubtful query again.

My voyage into the wonder had only just begun.

Gratitude

My story is the amalgamation of the people who've crossed in and out of my life. We tell our stories from our limited perspective. Others who weave in and out of my tales may have a different view of what happened. I can only tell the story from my memories. My perspectives are captured in 35 years of journaling preserved on my bookshelves. Every story I've written starts with my journal entries. Minor embellishments flesh out the tales I've told, but each story is true to the words I wrote down in real time as events unfolded.

This is my attempt to thank others for their part in my story.

To those who inspired my imagination.

My 3rd grade teacher Mrs. Simmons for showing me the power of exchange, and my 12th grade English teacher, Mrs. Simpkins, who encouraged me, in all my laziness, to share my stories through the hard work of proper grammar and syntax. George Lucas and Steven Spielberg for giving me a hero when I needed him the most. Some of the writers who have intellectually formed me: Thomas Cahill, Viktor Frankl, Abraham Joshua Heschel, JM Barrie, and Brennan Manning. I am a steadfast disciple of CS Lewis. (He would have hated that sentiment.)

To those who touched this book.

My publisher, Larry Luby, has singlehandedly brought many of my books into the world. Jeff Johnson for years of travel with my favorite bard and your beautiful introduction to the book. For my sister Georgia who designed the small WV icon in between stories. My brilliant editors, Coeli Lawhead, whose patient guidance brings out the best in my work, Lori Janke, who makes me look way more intelligent than I am, and Ryan Sanders who somehow made it through the first draft without going crazy. My best friend

Cheryl who came up with the title in five minutes after I wrestled with it for five years.

To those in this book.

The unknown ER doctors and EMTs who kept my family alive. Neely, Liz, Spencer, Cyndy, Joe, and my YWAV friends for introducing me to a faith community. Keith Wheeler, who models the life of a true pilgrim. Anthony Does, who walked through my darkest valleys by my side. The Colony Crew (Darin, Walter, Scott, and Don), brothers to this day. Stephen Lawhead, not only my favorite author but my friend and father to my son-in-law. Darren Bruce and Mike Yengo challenged me to dive into new worlds.

To those who I cannot live without.

Mama Val showered our family with abundant love and fried chicken. When I ponder the word 'home,' I think about my grandparents, Marie and Leonard Lindgren. My parents, Bonnie and Dick West model unconditional love and endless curiosity, and Larry and Mariette Small introduced me to a liveable and vibrant faith. My siblings, all of whom I adore (Shane & Georgia, Audra & Darryl, Christopher (I miss you!), Jared & Megan, Jordan, Lisa & Eric (I miss you!)) My Wonder Voyage Board (Ken Janke, Michael Fleming, Brent & Jamie Richardson, and Michael Damiano) who have walked into the wonder with me for 25 years.

God's most precious gift, my family.

My grandchildren: Theo, you make me swoon when you whisper "papa." Gwendolyn is the most brilliant human in the family. Kit is the fastest comedian on the planet. Jane was the first little one to carry my heart around in her soul. My children: Antonio and Anida, the bonus children I never expected. Hunter, whose tender heart and longing for justice will one day collide into something the world needs. Kayla and Mason for a love well beyond its years. Coeli and Ross, an imagination supernova waiting for the world to discover. My bride of 35 years at the publishing of this book, Cheryl. Without you, none of my words matter. You are my muse who brings color to my world, music to my ears, feeling to my fingertips, and who remains the closest representation of God's love I've known. Always and forever.

We shall not cease from exploration
And at the end of all our exploring
Will be to arrive where we started
And know the place for the first time.
—*Little Gidding, T.S. Eliot*

About the Author

Shawn Small is the founder and Executive Director of Wonder Voyage, a unique non-profit organization dedicated to leading seekers on the ancient sacrament of pilgrimage. He is an award-winning writer of books, including *The Via Crucis* (2009), *The Via Advent* (2011), *The Chronicles of C.S. Lewis* (2015), and *An Tobar Nua* (2017). His first children's book, *I Dream of Water* (2021), won the prestigious "Outstanding Book Award for The Book Most Likely to Save the Planet" in the Independent Publisher Book Awards. A proud member of the Explorer's Club, Shawn has traveled to over 100 countries. Husband to one, father to four, and grandfather to four, Shawn considers his family his greatest accomplishment. For more, visit ShawnSmallStories.com.